Tangled Webs of History

DIANNE NEWELL

Tangled Webs of History:
Indians and the Law in Canada's Pacific Coast Fisheries

UNIVERSITY OF TORONTO PRESS

Toronto Buffalo London

© University of Toronto Press Incorporated 1993
Toronto Buffalo London
Printed in Canada

Reprinted 1997, 1999

ISBN 0-8020-0547-0 (cloth)
ISBN 0-8020-7746-3 (paper)

Printed on acid-free paper

Canadian Cataloguing in Publication Data

Newell, Dianne, 1943–
    Tangled webs of history : Indians and the law
    in Canada's Pacific Coast fisheries

    Includes bibliographical references and index.
    ISBN 0-8020-0547-0 (bound)   ISBN 0-8020-7746-3 (pbk.)

    1. Fisheries – British Columbia – History.
    2. Fisheries – Licenses – British Columbia.
    3. Salmon fisheries – British Columbia. 4. Salmon
    canning industry – British Columbia. 5. Indians
    of North America – British Columbia – Legal status,
    laws, etc. I. Title.

    KEB529.5.H8N49 1993   343.711'07692   C93-094387-2
    KF8210.H85N49 1993

This book has been published with the help of a grant from the
Social Science Federation of Canada, using funds provided by the
Social Sciences and Humanities Research Council of Canada.

FOR SKIP

CONTENTS

Illustrations following page 146

FIGURES AND TABLES

FIGURES

TABLES

PREFACE

There must always be certain things that drop out of history. Only the broadest movements and themes can be recorded. All the multifarious choppings and changings, all the individual hazards and venturesomeness, and failures, cannot be recorded. History is full of mysteries, even as family histories are full of gaps and embellishments.
V.S. Naipaul, *A Turn in the South* (New York: Alfred Knopf, 1989), 86.

The patterns that I explore in this book began to emerge for me a decade ago when, as a historian of technology, I started studying 'choppings and changings' in Canada's Pacific Coast fishing industry. My particular interests were then, as now, the impact of technological change on the regional network of labour, resource management, and patterns of production. However, my recent experience as a courtroom observer in trials and appeals concerning BC Native land claims, and as an expert witness in a Native commercial fisheries trial, convinced me to focus my fisheries research specifically on the crucial contemporary issue of Indians and the law. Beyond that, I decided that, as a scholar, I could contribute to the debate by publishing my research – informing public opinion – rather than by simply attempting to inform the court. Without doubt, the courtroom is an inadequate, even hostile, environment for exploring the tangled webs of history.

I am grateful for having received a Writer's Award from the Association for Canadian Studies and a UBC Isaac Killam Memorial Research Fellowship from the University of British Columbia (UBC). The latter made it possible to spend my 1990–91 sabbatical year abroad and use the rich international collections of the British Library in London. A major research grant, 1984–86, for historical archaeology from the British Columbia Heritage Trust made to Arthur Roberts of the Department of Geography, Simon Fraser University, and me established much of the data base for the current book. Other grants from UBC and the Social Sciences and Humanities Research Council of Canada supported aspects of my ongoing fisheries research.

My appreciation goes to the staffs at the British Columbia Archives and Records Service (especially Brian Young), Victoria; Henry E. Huntington Library and Art Gallery, San Marino, California; National Archives of Canada and the National Library of Canada, Ottawa; Graphic Collections, Pacific Press Limited (notably Kate Abbott), Vancouver; Vancouver Public Library; UBC Library; Manuscript Library, University of Washington, Seattle; libraries of the Vancouver offices of the federal departments of Fisheries and Oceans and of Indian and Northern Affairs; and the Native Brotherhood of British Columbia, Vancouver and Prince Rupert offices.

Questions and advice from women and men at a number of conferences and seminars are also appreciated. These included meetings of the American Ethnohistory Association; American Historical Association (Pacific Branch); Canadian Historical Association; Indigenous Land Rights Workshop, sponsored by the Nagi Tahu Maori Trust Board, Commonwealth Geographical Bureau, and University of Canterbury, New Zealand; Social Science History Association; Southern Economic Association; and Triangle Workshop in Economic History (North Carolina).

Cecil Hill of the Kitkatla Band and his crew on the seiner *Western Spirit* – Cliff, Dan, Karen, Matthew, and Teddy – could not have been more unsparing or helpful during my April 1992 field work on the north coast fishing grounds. The same is true of Robert Hill, executive director of the Tsimshian Tribal Council and business agent for the Native Brotherhood of BC, Prince Rupert. My thanks to Ingrid Hill and Anna Allman for their practical suggestions, to Everett Pierce for sharing with me his experience in the processing sector, to Colleen Hemphill for interviewing her relatives and family friends who used to fish or work for coastal canneries, and to Jocelyn Smith for carefully transcribing those marvellous interviews.

William Allman provided library and editorial assistance on fisheries regulations and case law and made helpful suggestions on a preliminary draft of this book, David Dmitrasinovic helped with library searches in Vancouver, and Stuart Daniels generated the sort of maps and graphs that many scholars have come to expect from this excellent cartographer. The keen eyes and tactful proddings of UBC graduate students who read the manuscript – Laura Cameron, Robert McGeachy, Wayne Melvin, Susan Neylan, Van Nguyen, Joanne Poon, and Pam Brown – are treasured. The unnamed readers for the publisher and the Social Science Federation of Canada made thoughtful and helpful comments on the manuscript, and Laura Macleod and John Parry have proven to be superb editors.

Over the years I have learned so much from conversations with people who are old hands in the various areas that form the subject of my book. They include Julie Cruikshank, David Flaherty, Ursula Franklin, Robert Galois, Tipene O'Regan, Arthur Pape, Keith Ralston, Stuart Rush, Douglas Sanders, and several Gitksan, Wet'suwet'en, and Heiltsuk people. Arthur J. Ray, Philip Resnick, and Frank Tough commented on the entire manuscript, and Peter Usher reviewed several chapters. I am grateful for the sharpness with which these four scholars bring into focus certain analytical approaches to the study of the state, the politics of resource management, and Indian economic and political strategies. Encouragement, advice, and criticisms from Arthur Ray have been essential throughout the research and writing of what I found to be a daunting project. No scholar could ever ask for more support than I have always received from this wonderfully generous, highly original thinker.

Having acknowledged these special debts, I must add that responsibility for the content and interpretations in this book is mine, and mine alone.

NOTE TO THE SECOND PRINTING – 1997

I have taken this opportunity to make a few minor editorial changes to the text, notes, and index. No changes affecting the substance or interpretation of the original book have been made. However, two important matters that were pending when the manuscript first went to press deserve updating here.

First, although in its landmark decision *R. v. Sparrow* ([1990], 1 *SCR* 1075), the Supreme Court of Canada gave priority to aboriginal fishing rights in BC, subsequent judicial decisions in BC and elsewhere in Canada over the next six years denied commercial rights. However, the August 1996 decisions by the Supreme Court of Canada on three BC appeals related to aboriginal rights to sell fish, *R. v. Gladstone*

([1996] 137 *DLR*, [4th] 648), *R. v. Van der Peet* ([1996] 137 *DLR* [4th] 289), and *R. v. N.T.C. Smokehouse Ltd.* ([1996] 137 *DLR* [4th] 528), may have changed the situation. In these decisions, the Supreme Court of Canada addressed the issue left unresolved by its 1990 judgment in *Sparrow*: do the aboriginal rights, recognized and affirmed by section 35(1) of the Constitution Act, 1982, include a right to a commercial fishery?

Van der Peet was a salmon-fishing case that dealt with whether the Sto:lo Nation, of which the appellant was a member, possessed an aboriginal right to the commercial use of fish. Chief Justice Lamar, writing for the majority, held that claims to aboriginal rights must be adjudicated on a specific rather than general basis, and that for a practice, tradition, or custom to constitute an aboriginal right it must be of independent significance to the aboriginal culture in which it exists. In *Van der Peet* the court found that the appellant failed to demonstrate that the exchange of fish for money or other goods was an integral, central, or defining part of the distinctive Sto:lo society which existed prior to contact, thus the appellant failed to demonstrate that the commercial use of salmon by the Sto:lo is an aboriginal right meriting constitutional protection. The appeal was dismissed, as it was on similar grounds in *N.T.C. Smokehouse*.

In *Gladstone*, however, which involved members of the Heiltsuk Band charged with selling herring spawn-on-kelp caught without a commercial licence, the appeal was allowed. The Court explicitly recognized a commercial right to fish that is protected under section 35(1) of the Constitution Act, 1982. The Court's analysis is as follows: a right exists; it has not been extinguished; it has been infringed by the 'J' (spawn-on-kelp) licensing scheme; is the infringement justified? The Court referred the critical question concerning infringement back to the trial court.

Second, the Nisga'a Tribal Council's treaty negotiations with the governments of Canada and BC finally resulted in the Nisga'a Agreement-in-Principle in February 1996, the first modern-day treaty in BC. In it the Nisga'a exchanged existing, constitutionally guaranteed but undefined aboriginal rights to harvest fish for annual treaty entitlements of salmon – specific, clearly-defined fixed allocations that are considerably higher per capita than in the recent past – an allocation of non-salmon species for domestic purposes, and funds for a fisheries-management trust fund. It is, however, questionable whether this agreement-in-principle could ever serve as a model for settling other land claims in BC. Indeed, many close observers doubt that the Nisga'a arrangement will survive long in its present form.

Tangled Webs of History

1 Introduction: The Politics of Resource Regulation

Thomas Berger, former justice of the British Columbia Supreme Court, tells us that aboriginal rights constitute both the oldest question of human rights in Canada and the most recent.[1] Only lately has it entered 'our' political consciousness. Pacific Coast Indian men and women have always claimed aboriginal title, or rights, to their fisheries. They understood that they could not survive as 'distinct societies' without a great deal of control over their economic destinies. The fisheries were and still are, I argue, a key to those destinies.

The fact that most BC Indian societies never signed treaties has raised questions about extinguishment of aboriginal rights. At the heart of the argument is the fact that aboriginal people were here first and have a special relationship with the land and living resources. Their claims to fish rest on their aboriginal rights. For thousands of years before Europeans arrived, Indian economies on the Pacific slope centred on marine resources; the sea and coastal rivers were at least as important as the land. There were regular, prolific salmon migrations into the fresh-water areas of every aboriginal society on the coastal rim. From northern California to Alaska-Yukon, aboriginal peoples harvested prodigious quantities of local resources, especially salmon, which they processed and used for personal consumption, trade, and ceremony. Such well-managed enterprises allowed them to support a pre-epidemic population numbering in the hundreds of thousands without destroying the fishery resources.

The pattern of undifferentiated mixed use of fish continued for decades after Europeans arrived on the Northwest Coast in the late eighteenth century. It persisted during the first few decades of the development of a state-managed fishery and a salmon-canning industry in the 1870s and 1880s. BC Indians incorporated fishing and cannery work into the existing web of familial and seasonal activities. They participated in the industry on a grand scale, despite growing competition from European and Asian in-migrants. Although they never surrendered their rights to the fisheries and repeatedly sought protection for their fishing customs and hereditary fishing territories, they eventually became marginalized within one branch of the fishery after the other.

The state and its administrative agencies and courts, backed by private industry and non-Indian fishers, characterized Pacific Coast Indian fishing traditions as destructive and demonized Indian food fishers as predators. The historical record of fishery regulations for British Columbia reflects this thinking. In the 1970s, armed police raids on Indian fishing camps, confiscation of gear, cars, and fish, and imposition of fines and criminal charges for contraventions of the Fisheries Act became routine for many BC Indian communities. No evidence was ever uncovered to support the strong and persistent rumours of massive overfishing and large illegal sales of Indian-caught food fish. This harassment continues. Meanwhile, as a legacy of the fisheries policy introduced in the late 1960s, only a tiny portion of the commercial licences remains in the hands of Indians, and the old network of coastal fish plants that always depended on the labour of Indian families is gone.

In British Columbia (as in the older colonies in earlier times), the crown – i.e. the federal government, since 1871 – has always interpreted the traditional Indian fishery as a strictly subsistence activity, one to be continued as a privilege, not a right.[2] The crown and the courts have also always denied the existence of an aboriginal right to fish commercially. If Indians had ever had such a right, or in the limited cases on Vancouver Island where aboriginal fishing and use rights were guaranteed by the Douglas Treaties (1850–54) before British Columbia joined Canada, such rights would have been *extinguished*, the argument goes, by more than a century's worth of federal enactments and regulations imposed benevolently to conserve resources (while ignoring those aboriginal rights and interests).[3]

The basis of the crown's argument for denying an aboriginal right to fish commercially is this. 'Aboriginal rights' reflect pre-contact aboriginal systems and values. Because pre-contact Indian peoples did not use a market-based system to organize production or exchange in their own or inter-national economies, the reasoning goes, Indians could not have an 'aboriginal right' to participate in a fishery based on such a system. Therefore, the crown claims, Indians, when participating in the modern market-based industrial fishery, are in the same *legal* position as all other Canadians and so may exercise only the *privileges* granted under government policy.

With the recent decision by the Supreme Court of Canada in *Regina v. Sparrow* (1990), which recognized an unextinguished aboriginal right of the Musqueam Band in British Columbia to fish for food and for social and ceremonial purposes and which rejected the crown's standard argument about extinguishment, it looked as though Pacific Coast Indians would gain a greater role in managing fisheries, a larger share of the catch, and, possibly, recognition of the right to use their 'food fish' catch commercially.[4] In June 1992, the federal fisheries department actually negotiated experimental agreements with three Indian bands on the lower Fraser River to allow sale of their food fish and promised that agreements with other bands would follow. Yet the Fisheries Act itself is unchanged, and Indian claims to aboriginal fishing rights remain a bitter contemporary issue of economics, property, and race. Most bands refused to negotiate fishing agreements. And fishing cases involving BC Indians continue to pile up in the trial and appeal courts. Why?

The major Canadian inquiry into the Pacific fisheries in 1981, the Pearse Commission, had more to say about the rights, history, and future of Indians in the Pacific Coast fisheries than any of the two dozen such inquiries that preceded it. Pearse reported (*Turning the Tide*, 1982) that the current sorry situation for Indians in the fisheries was the legacy of a century of state policy development: 'Throughout, the basic issue has been that of reconciling the conflict between Indian traditions of fishing and hereditary fishing areas, on the one hand, and the early British colonial policy, federal-provincial constitutional responsibilities over Indians and fisheries, and the need to conserve fish stocks on the other.'[5] These are reasonable sentiments, of course. But they only reinforce the image that governments promote of themselves – that of benevolent referees: there are rules, there are conflicts, and there are balances to be struck. The government merely mediates. Is this perception realistic? The Supreme Court of Canada in *Sparrow* did not think so, commenting: 'Our history has shown, unfortunately all too well, that Canada's aboriginal peoples are justified in worrying about government objectives that may be superficially neutral but which constitute *de facto* threats to the existence of aboriginal rights and interests.'[6]

DISPELLING THE MYTHS

Social scientists tell us that a host of myths exists about public regulation of economic activity in industrial societies. These include the ideas that regulations are forced on unwilling producers, or are created simply to increase economic efficiency, and that they are developed by 'arm's length' experts, or mainly involve technical questions that are of little interest and relevance to the public.[7] In practice, government policies and regulations usually are responses to pressure from industry to reduce competition and frequently are not in the best interests of the other user groups, although the process by which this one-sidedness occurs may be gradual.[8] Ultimately, writes Michael Trebilock, 'most major regulatory decisions ... involve matters of immense political and social importance, e.g., highways *versus* public transportation, energy resources *versus* the environment, foreign investment *versus* broadcasting or publishing freedom.'[9] The tremendous conflict created by proposed federal changes to drug patent legislation in Canada in the 1990s is a new example of the old pattern: foreign investment versus Canada's universal health care system. By contrast, the contemporary legal and regulatory issue of Indians versus conservation can be traced back to the nineteenth century.

Canada's Pacific Coast industrial fisheries have been and still are among the most regulated in the world. The public justification now, as in the past, for most such federal regulations and policies is conservation of fish stocks. But protection for whom, and at whose expense? Whose interests are served? Legal arguments historically affirm that fish in the ocean, unlike most other natural resources, are not private property but rather commonly owned until caught. European-based conventional wisdom holds that people who fish have no incentive to conserve fish stocks; on the contrary. So preservation of this commonly owned resource required government intervention. Policy-makers assumed that they had no choice when it came to ocean fish. But 'common property' is a European concept without parallel in Canadian aboriginal systems. As is well known and of great current interest, pre-industrial societies around the world developed an array of systems with which to manage their natural resources for millennia on a sustained basis. It is largely thanks to those systems that there are any resources left to speak of today.

The usual argument about a technological imperative – that technical advances in fishing automatically accelerate the need for strict government control of all types of fishing – is compelling but misleading. There is no denying that the nature of industrialized fisheries – the ecological, biological, and technological facts – affected the development of a specialized regulatory structure for managing them.[10] Fish stocks sustain themselves by breeding enough new adults to balance losses from year to year. In theory, the technical ability to 'overfish' develops (through increased net capacity, for example), and, with it, regulations emerge to ensure that enough fish reach the breeding grounds (by limiting numbers of people or boats fishing and/or restricting nets and fishing times and areas). These events in turn trigger technological advances along other lines (more mobile vessels, electronic fish-finding apparatus, and multipurpose gear), which give rise to yet more regulations (such as restricted entry and catch quotas).

This pattern is evident in the history of Canada's Pacific Coast fisheries, where, as will be seen, technology and regulatory structure evolved in tandem and in sequence. At no time, however, is use of new technology an independent, unstoppable force. Lewis Mumford cautions: 'Technics and civilization as a whole are the result of human choices and aptitudes and strivings, deliberate as well as unconscious, often irrational when apparently they are the most objective and scientific.'[11] State regulations routinely limit or even prohibit use of specific techniques and equipment. The impact of technological advances in industrial fisheries, I argue, depends largely on policies adopted, on political will.

Realistically, then, although pressing conservation issues arise for modern fisheries, conservation is only one of the problems that governments must consider in planning strategies to manage fisheries and assist in economic development generally. Making the actual choices of strategies for managing the fishery – such as controlling use of specific fishing techniques; allocating catch among gear, users, species, and regions; choosing to prevent overfishing rather than improving fish habitats or operating fish hatcheries; and promoting certain products, markets, and types of racial composition for workforces over others – involves political, social, and economic decisions. Despite government publicity to the contrary, the choices are often not about conservation per se.

State management policies – whether aimed at conservation, economic development, or some other goal – had differential impact on various groups of fishers and plant workers. Because the Pacific fisheries are complex, even piecemeal or temporary changes to rules could be felt throughout the industry. Over the years, distinct racial and ethnic groups became associated with different types of gear, different varieties and species of fish, different regions, different processing methods, and different labour organizations in British Columbia. Indians and Japanese specialized in sockeye salmon gillnetting for the canneries, whites and Japanese, in purse-seining for herring for the canneries, salteries, and reduction plants. Whites and Indian communities on the outer islands specialized in trolling for the fresh- and frozen-fish trade. Whites monopolized longlining for halibut. Until the Second World War, Chinese males under labour contracts, and Indian, and to a lesser extent Japanese, women and their families, held most of the jobs in the salmon canneries, while Japanese males did most of the work in herring salteries. So in the Pacific Coast fisheries, any law, regulation, or special program enacted to favour one type of gear, processing method, region, or user group benefited some people at the expense of others.

Although the federal fisheries department has traditionally treated Indians as only one of a number of 'user groups,' Indians have a special claim. Simply put, what sets Indian 'interests' apart from the larger pool of interests in the fisheries are both the aboriginal rights that they claim and the crown's general fiduciary obligations to protect aboriginal peoples and their lands. Winning recognition of aboriginal rights in Canada, however, has involved a long-standing, monumental political and legal struggle.

Brian Slattery, in the *Canadian Bar Review* in 1987, likens the subject of aboriginal rights to 'an overgrown and poorly excavated archeological site.'[12] Visitors to the site may be fascinated with the landscape before them, but the meaning of the fragments and tangle remains unclear. Indians have sought legal recognition of aboriginal rights in the three direct sources of law recognized in the English legal system – the royal prerogative (as in the Royal Proclamation of 1763 – sometimes called the 'Indian Bill of Rights'), common law (decisions of the courts case by case, or 'judge-made' law), and statute law and subordinate legislation ('parliament-made' law).[13] Collective rights that may exist have to pass through the courts, with their deep British-law (and since 1982, Charter of Rights and Freedoms) tradition of balancing interests and respecting individual concerns. The greatest problem for aboriginal values in the British-law system, however, is probably its systemic protection of proprietary interests granted or recognized by that system.

Some legal scholars argue that the doctrine of aboriginal rights has formed part of the basic constitutional structure of Canada since early colonial days.[14] But as late as the 1960s, aboriginal claims to lands were not even recognized by the Canadian government as having legal status.[15] That changed in the early 1970s with the famous *Calder* case. The Nishga Tribal Council put forward its long-standing claim that aboriginal title to the Nass River Valley in British Columbia had never been extinguished in *Calder et al. v. Attorney-General of BC* (Supreme Court of British Columbia, 1969; Supreme Court of Canada, 1973). The claim failed technically at trial and in the Supreme Court of Canada but established the possibility that unextinguished aboriginal rights existed in Canada.[16] This possibility led to revision of federal policy on claims and a promise to negotiate with Indians.[17]

Since 1974, officials of the Department of Indian Affairs and Indian representatives have attempted to negotiate major modern treaties, called comprehensive claims agreements, which refer to claims based on traditional use and occupancy of the land if Indian interest has not been 'extinguished by treaty' or 'superseded by law.' By and large, the modern Canadian claims process has been remarkably ineffective south of the 60th parallel.[18]

Recently existing treaty and aboriginal rights of aboriginal peoples, defined as Indians, Metis, and Inuit, have been constitutionally recognized and affirmed – entrenched, not created – in the Constitution Act, 1982, section 35(1). This section, which aboriginal groups fought to have included, became a key element in Indian fishing disputes and litigation, for lack of definitional limits on aboriginal rights in the constitution leaves an unlimited range of native interests open to constitutional protection.[19] *Sparrow* (1990) is the first case that has reached the Supreme Court of Canada concerning section 35(1). It dealt with the nature of the constitutional protection created by that section in the context of non-treaty fishing rights. This landmark decision addressed the state's responsibility to act in a fiduciary capacity with respect to aboriginal peoples, agreeing with recent

judicial decisions that emphasized that the historic relationship between the federal government and aboriginals is trust-like, rather
than adversarial.

GOVERNING FISH

The fisheries present an intriguing arena for understanding issues of
aboriginal peoples and the law. Not only were fisheries, including
freshwater fisheries for inland peoples, important to most aboriginal
economies, but fish is one of the few types of natural resources or
commercial wildlife *not* to be regulated mainly by the provinces.
Under section 91(12) of the British North America Act, 1867 (later
renamed the Constitution Act, 1867), the government of Canada was
given exclusive legislative authority over 'sea coast and inland fisheries.'[20] Canada administers and regulates the marine fisheries under
the Fisheries Act, which did not come into force in British Columbia
until 1877, and through a fisheries department.[21] There are separate
federal fisheries regulations for each province. The federal British
Columbia Fishery Regulations determine the time, place, and conditions under which commercial, sports, and Indian (food) fisheries
may be conducted and include measures to protect the freshwater
spawning beds of the anadromous species such as salmon.

As the Pearse Report (*Turning the Tide*) noted, however, the
division of constitutional responsibilities for fisheries and management of fish habitat is 'both tangled and subtle.'[22] For one thing, the
province can grant proprietary interests – such as leases – in a fishery, where it owns the bed of rivers. It also, as owner of most of the
coastal foreshore, grants proprietary interests to mariculture fisheries
such as oysters and clams in the intertidal zone and, more recently,
ocean (salmon) ranching, under federal-provincial agreements. Although Ottawa has exclusive power to regulate for conservation, the
province exercises administrative powers of this sort pursuant to
federal-provincial arrangements, under delegated federal powers.

Although Canada originally exercised exclusive authority over
the Pacific salmon fisheries, 'from sea to shelf,' that control quickly
produced a two-sided dispute – three-sided, if we include Indian
claims. British Columbia created its own, limited fisheries bureaucracy in 1901, developed its own parallel force of fisheries overseers,
and collected fees from fishers and cannery operators.[23] The fight
between Ottawa and British Columbia over legislative jurisdiction

concerning fisheries was settled in 1929, when the Judicial Committee of the Privy Council in London ruled that cannery licensing lay
outside federal authority and actually trod upon provincial jurisdiction.[24] So British Columbia has a long history of regulating the shore-
based processing plants and issuing licences for non-tidal sport-fishing.
Additionally, the province has always regulated sale of fish within its
boundaries, but the federal government, by virtue of its jurisdiction
over interprovincal and international trade, has been responsible for
inspecting fish that are to be shipped out of the province, which has
always amounted to most of the commercial catch. Both Victoria and
Ottawa claim jurisdiction over marine plants.

Overlap in Victoria in the areas of agriculture, forestry, hydro,
mining, and urban development affected Ottawa's ability to protect
fish habitats for the varieties of fish under its complete jurisdiction.
In all cases of jurisdictional overlap and dispute in fisheries matters,
intergovernmental agreements have been difficult to arrange.

The Pacific Coast fisheries are vast. The BC coast occupies the
whole of the sea front between the 49th and 55th parallels of north
latitude (see Figure 1). This part of the coast is adjacent to fully two-
thirds of the 518,000 km² section of the continental shelf that consti-
tutes an extraordinarily rich fishing ground of shallow banks and
island chains stretching south from southern Alaska to northern Washington state. Prodigious peaks rise straight out of inlet waters. The
picturesque inside passages, channels, fjords, and broad river estuaries, laced with sloughs and channels, provide both exceptionally well-
sheltered waters for marine fishing and interspersed beaches and
quiet lagoons for operating shore plants to process the catch.

Pacific salmon are easily found and fished, and overfished, on
their spawning runs.[25] Salmon is an anadromous fish – it spends
most of its adult existence in the ocean and returns to the gravels of
its native freshwater creek or stream to spawn. Unlike Atlantic salmon
(genus *Salmo*), Pacific salmon (genus *Orcorhynchus*) is semelparous,
dies after spawning once, and so can be harvested only while as-
cending. Moreover, salmon migrates from a deep sea home base to
its native coastal spawning districts and grounds in definite seasons
and in cycles of from two to six years, depending on species and
area. Timing of the cycles varies among areas and occasionally the
peak (or trough) years for several species of salmon in a single area
coincide.

Species also differ greatly in size, quality, and abundance. The

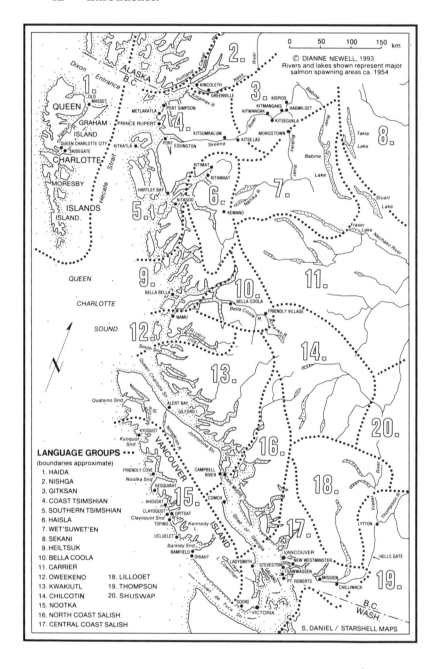

© DIANNE NEWELL, 1993
Rivers and lakes shown represent major
salmon spawning areas ca. 1954

LANGUAGE GROUPS • • •
(boundaries approximate)
 1. HAIDA
 2. NISHGA
 3. GITKSAN
 4. COAST TSIMSHIAN
 5. SOUTHERN TSIMSHIAN
 6. HAISLA
 7. WET'SUWET'EN
 8. SEKANI
 9. HEILTSUK
10. BELLA COOLA
11. CARRIER
12. OWEEKENO   18. LILLOOET
13. KWAKIUTL   19. THOMPSON
14. CHILCOTIN   20. SHUSWAP
15. NOOTKA
16. NORTH COAST SALISH
17. CENTRAL COAST SALISH

S. DANIEL / STARSHELL MAPS

largest is spring (also known as chinook, king, quinnat, and tyee – *Orcorhynchus tschawytscha*) salmon, weighing up to 45 kg. It begins its inshore spawning runs in the spring and still may be caught into the fall months, but historically it is the least abundant of the BC salmon species. The best and most valuable species for canning, sockeye (or red, O. *nerka*), enters the rivers between midsummer and late August, in four-to-five–year cycles, and characteristically travels the greatest distances inland to spawn. Pink salmon (or humpback – O. *gorbuscha*), the next to appear, from July through early September, is the smallest (averaging 1.0–2.5 kg) and has a fixed, two-year life cycle. The pink tends to spawn closer to the sea than any other species, although there are many important spawning areas in the Fraser and Skeena rivers located far inland. Following it, cohoe (or silver – O. *kisutch*), which matures in its sixth year, and chum (or dog, keta – O. *keta*) salmon run in the fall. As far as we can tell, chum has always been the most plentiful BC species, although for marketing reasons it has been the cheapest grade for canning.

Inshore invasions of spawning runs tend to be progressively later from north to south. Also, duration of runs and timing of cycles of abundance vary by species, stock, and area. Sockeye runs, for example, last three times longer in the lower Fraser, where time of spawning for different stocks varies greatly, than in the lower Skeena. Runs of pink salmon occur to southern British Columbia only in odd-numbered years, and to the Queen Charlotte Islands and Skeena River, mainly in even-numbered ones. Wind, tide, and fluctuations in stream temperatures affect the timing and the intensity of upstream migration of certain species.

Figure 1 Indians of BC Pacific slope: language groups and place names. *Sources*: Based on Wayne Suttles, ed., *Northwest Coast* (1990), volume 7 of the Smithsonian Institution's *Handbook on North American Indians*, and the University of British Columbia's Museum of Anthropology, First Nations Language Groups in British Columbia, working map, under review 10 July 1992.

This figure is a guide to this book; like the maps on which it is based, it is not an authoritative depiction of territories. Simplified ranges shown are a generalization of the situation in the early to mid-nineteenth century. The current (1992) First Nations spellings for the historic names of particular language groups are as follows: Nuxalk (Bella Coola), Kwakwaka'wakw (Kwakiutl), Nuu-chah-nulth (Nootka), and Hlaka'pamux (Thompson). *Note*: The Wet'suwet'en are a sub-group of the Carrier.

Cyclical, seasonal, and regional variations added to the uncertainties and risks for harvesters. They also produced the potential complementary basis for trade and, with the coming of an industrial fishery, created incentives for fish-packing companies to set up regional networks of shore operations and camps. And they generated a regulatory challenge for bureaucrats and politicians.

When the first Europeans arrived on the coast, freshwater spawning areas could be found from northern California north to Alaska, along the Arctic coast as far east as the Mackenzie River, and also along the Aleutian chain. Salmon of some species ran in nearly every stream and creek emptying into the sea, but only in the long rivers with large drainages extending beyond the Coast Range, such as the Fraser and Skeena, did salmon run in the millions and in most varieties. The Indian salmon fishery took place mainly inland, at specific sites along the creeks, rivers, and river canyons, where salmon were more concentrated, so more easily caught, rather than in saltwater locations. The industrial salmon fishery was a different story. Once under way in the 1870s, industrial salmon fishing would be legally restricted to tidal areas, at the start of the harvesting chain, with seasonal processing camps sited on sheltered beaches in river estuaries, sounds, and inlets and on the coastal littoral (see Figures 2–6).

Historically, over half of the salmon caught in BC waters came from the extensive Fraser and Skeena river systems, where all five species native to the North American coast are found. Together, these two life-supporting drainages encompass most of the province's land area. The Nass, Bella Coola–Atnarko, and Nimpkish rivers, and Rivers and Smith inlets (with a system of ten productive rivers in the vicinity), were next in importance. The 1,600-km Fraser River, which drains much of the rugged BC interior, historically has supported huge salmon runs of between two and twenty million individuals each year; the Skeena was second, with runs of one to four million.[26] The majority of Fraser River stocks channel through Juan de Fuca Strait, location of the BC-Washington marine boundary, and thence into the US territorial waters of Puget Sound on their migration route back to their native spawning streams in British Columbia.

Spatially, then, the continuing 'Indian fishery' occupied the politically vulnerable middle ground between the locales of commercial catches and those of spawning areas, in the massive, one-way drive of salmon to their home streams. It became the business of governments and the courts to decide just how and why the various interests would be accommodated.

Salmon was not the only saltwater fish to thrive on the Pacific North Coast. The other harvests, from seals and whales to halibut and herring, to codfish and shellfish, could be conducted only in the open sea and in the inshore, nearshore, and intertidal zones. For these prolific varieties of sea mammals, fishes, and marine invertebrates, traditional Indian fisheries and newer industrial operations had to compete in the same locations.

GOVERNING INDIAN FISHING

Whether through Indian legislation or through fisheries legislation, the federal government deals with Indian fishing. The Constitution Act, 1867, assigned Ottawa exclusive responsibility for 'Indians, and lands reserved for Indians.' The administration of Indians is the responsibility of the federal Department of Indian Affairs, as delegated in British Columbia originally to local officials organized under the federal commissioner of Indian Affairs into local agencies.[27] The Indian Act of Canada, first passed by parliament in 1876 and amended frequently thereafter, gave Ottawa various powers – to administer the affairs of Indians through its provisions on land-holding and land transfer, taxation, local government, education, Indian band membership, and so on; to intervene in Indian social and cultural practices; and to help Indians to participate in economic activities.[28] The provisions of the Indian Act apply to status, or registered, Indians. Special federal status, however, whatever its advantages, made Indians politically subservient in a way that neither the general population nor any other racial-cultural minority has ever been.[29]

The changing demographic characteristics of Canada's aboriginal societies have strongly influenced state policies towards Indian societies and economies. Generally speaking, before the 1930s it appeared that North American Indians were a dying race. This was so even for the Pacific Coast, where so many Indians resided.

The aboriginal people of British Columbia were distributed among two dozen 'territorial cultural' groupings, each speaking a mutually unintelligible language.[30] Most of the people lived in the coastal portion (see Table 1). To the best of our knowledge, the Indian

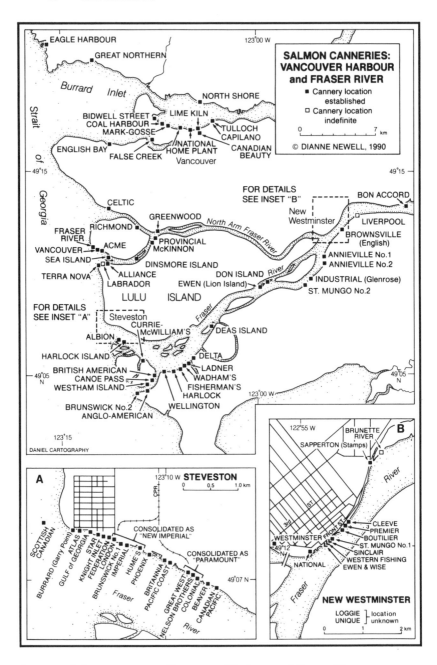

Figure 2 Salmon canneries: Vancouver Harbour and Fraser River.
Source for Figures 2–6: Author's research files.

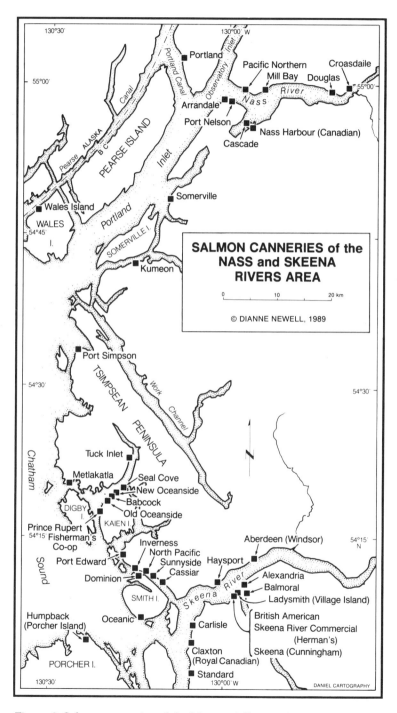

Figure 3 Salmon canneries of the Nass and Skeena rivers area.

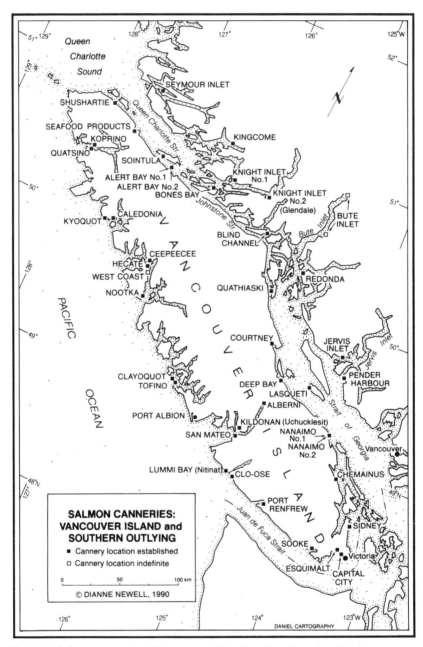

Figure 4 Salmon canneries: Vancouver Island and southern outlying.

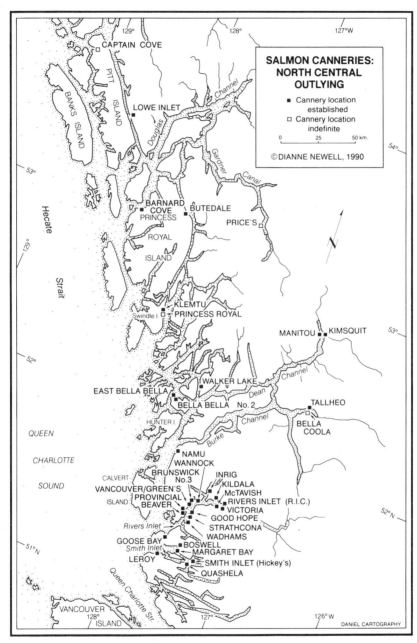

Figure 5 Salmon canneries: north central outlying. Included are Rivers and Smith inlets.

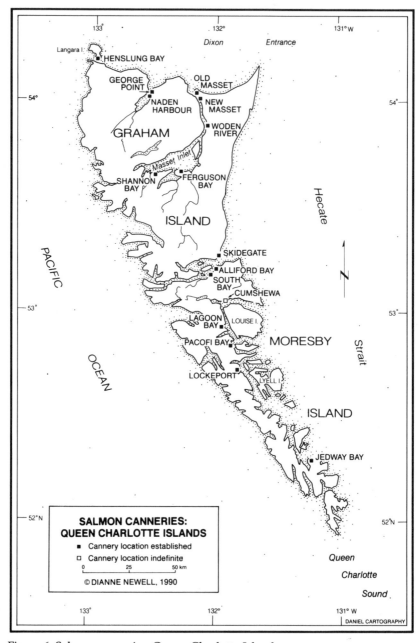

Figure 6 Salmon canneries: Queen Charlotte Islands.

TABLE 1
Population of BC coastal tribes,* 1885–1984

Year	Haida	Tsim-shian	Bella Bella, Haihais, Haisla, Kwakiutl, Oowekeeno	Nootka and Nitinaht	Bella Coola	Coast Salish	Totals
1885	(800)	(4,550)	(3,000)	(3,500)	(450)	(5,525)	(17,825)
1895	(663)	(3,550)	2,401	(2,834)	(340)	4,737	(14,525)
1905	599	3,565	2,052	2,264	288	4,377	13,145
1915	588	3,618	1,917	1,835	253	4,120	12,331
1929	691	3,626	1,854	1,626	249	4,320	12,366
1939	790	3,779	2,148	1,605	259	4,722	13,303
1949	895	4,290	2,817	1,815	334	5,738	15,889
1959	1,062	5,691	3,853	2,501	460	7,686	21,253
1969	1,363	7,545	4,879	3,267	596	10,047	27,697
1979	1,560	9,452	5,768	4,240	745	11,786	33,551
1984	1,701	10,503	6,167	4,720	830	13,044	36,965

Source: J.E. Michael Kew, 'History of Coastal British Columbia since 1846,' in Wayne Suttles, ed., *Northwest Coast*, vol. 7 of *Handbook of North American Indians* (Washington, DC: Smithsonian Institution Press, 1990), 165. Bracketed figures are estimates.
* The term 'tribe' is difficult to employ without ambiguity in a work of history and so I have avoided it in this study. An exception is made, as here, when I am citing a specific source.

population in the province plummeted by 80 per cent between 1774 and 1874, mostly because of exotic European diseases.[31] The trend continued until the total for the coast reached its historic low point in 1915 (1920s for the province as a whole), after which it gradually rebounded both there and in the rest of Canada. After the Second World War, Indians would be identified as the fastest-growing people in the country.

Although Ottawa has been responsible for *administering* Indian policy, the provinces have *controlled* the land and most of the resources needed to fulfil federal responsibilities to Indians. Until the 1980s, only about half of Canada's legal-status Indians had treaties with the crown; in immense portions of the country, aboriginal title was never officially extinguished and aboriginal peoples continue to press their claims. In the 1990s, most of British Columbia still has Indian reserves but no Indian treaties.

Fisheries are a prominent issue in most of the comprehensive claims submitted since 1974 for negotiation in British Columbia. However, the BC government, alone among provinces and territories, has steadfastly refused either to acknowledge aboriginal land rights, which would form the basis of negotiating, or to negotiate.[32] In 1990, the province's Social Credit government established a claims task force. Leaders of the province's New Democratic Party (NDP) while in opposition promised, if elected, to recognize aboriginal rights and negotiate with the Indian claimants. The NDP achieved power in October 1991. In 1993, it formed the British Columbia Treaty Commission, but it remains to be seen what the promises or the treaty commission will amount to.

The federal Indian Act empowers Ottawa to help Indians, with treaties or without them, to participate in economic activities. However, although Indian Affairs has traditionally encouraged the economic self-sufficiency of its 'wards,' it simultaneously supported efforts to undermine Native culture, in keeping with the state's agenda of assimilation. The economic activities originally envisioned related mostly to agriculture. Nevertheless, the department has from time to time obtained special fishing privileges, or compensation for loss of them, for reserve communities. (The Indian Act gave its officials power to supervise fishing on reserves.) More recently, the department has financed various fishery-related programs and projects – such as establishing an aquaculture task force (1982) to develop Indian pilot projects and provide management training – and approved Indian band by-laws that permit members to manage aspects of their local fisheries.[33] Officials from Indian Affairs have also worked with other provincial and federal agencies, such as those involved in fisheries, wildlife, and regional economic expansion, as well as with industrial users of resources, such as the fish-processing industry. These cooperative efforts promote, defend, or control the economic activities of Indians.

Normally it is reasonable, when studying Indian history in Canada, to focus on the role of one department – Indian Affairs. But in the Pacific Coast fisheries, because of the traditional importance of fishing and fish processing for the Indians of the Pacific slope, the federal fisheries department probably has played an equally major role. Certain regulations under the Fisheries Act made special allowances for Indian fishing, as provided for as early as the Fisheries Act of 1868 and even earlier in the older colonies.[34] Section 88 of the Indian Act makes all provincial laws of general application applicable to Indians. Treaties usually protect Indians with treaties from provincial legislation that interferes with their rights, although this is a complex legal question. But in treaty and non-treaty areas alike, fishing rights have been overridden by general federal legislation in the form of the Fisheries Act, just as occurred with Indian hunting rights under the federal Migratory Birds Convention Act, 1916. Peter Usher suggests that in fish and wildlife management, a strong case can be made that government policies and regulations 'have been used as a means of social control and engineering of aboriginal people, with no less disruptive effect than Indian administration itself.'[35]

DEFINITIONS

In this study, an 'Indian Band' is the effective social and political unit above the family officially recognized by the Indian Act. The act also recognizes 'Indian Band Council' (local elected government), 'Indian Reserve' (land set aside for Indians of a specific band), 'Indian Agency' (regional administrative unit encompassing many bands and reserves), 'Indian Agent' (government agent who dealt directly with the Indians of an agency, a position recently abolished), and 'Indian Commissioner' (or 'Superintendent'), who was the government official responsible for the agencies in British Columbia. Most major tribal villages became bands under the Indian Act in the late nineteenth century. In 1992, there were nearly 600 bands in Canada, one-third of them in British Columbia. Tribal councils such as the Nishga Tribal Council mentioned earlier – post–Second World War creations – are regional political alliances of Indian bands that lobby and negotiate on behalf of bands.

   The spelling of the names of Indian language, cultural, and political groups, of Indian communities, and of geographical features is tricky, for there is no consensus on these matters. It was usual in times past to render Indian words into English by approximate phonetic spellings. As a result there are widely varying forms in the published literature. Also, the contemporary Indian cultural resurgence has led to revival of ancient pronunciations and terms, and hence spellings, such as 'Nisga'a' for 'Nishga,' which had itself replaced 'Niska.' The 'Bella Coola,' 'Kwakiutl,' and 'Nootka' peoples want to be recognized as 'Nuxalk,' 'Kwakwaka'wakw,' and 'Nuu-chah-nulth,' respectively. Unless quoting directly from a published source or referring to the official title of an organization, I have for the sake of consistency used as my authorities *Subarctic* (1981), edited by June Helm as volume 6, and *Northwest Coast* (1990), edited by Wayne Suttles as volume 7, both in the Smithsonian Institution's *Handbook on North American Indians*.

I refer throughout to the 'Department of Fisheries' and the 'fisheries department,' always meaning the federal department responsible for fisheries, even though its name has varied over time (from 'Marine and Fisheries' through 'Naval Service' and 'Fisheries' to, most recently, 'Fisheries and Oceans').[36] Similarly, I use the term 'Indian Affairs,' although frequent organizational changes in government varied the name of the Canadian department responsible for Indians (originally 'Interior,' then 'Indian Affairs,' 'Mines and Resources,' 'Citizenship and Immigration,' 'Northern Affairs and National Resources,' and, most recently, 'Indian Affairs and Northern Development').

Following ordinary legal usage in Canada, I use the term 'Indian' (for the post-Confederation period) to refer to status Indians, even if people have mixed ancestry.[37] Statistical data on Indian participation exclude the non-status Indian population; little is known about its role in the fishery. I use the word 'industrial' rather than 'commercial' for the commercial fisheries established and controlled by non-Indians in the late nineteenth and twentieth centuries. Indian people have always used fish commercially – that is, as an exchange commodity – both before and since the government of Canada's regulations and policies in 1888 defined Indian fishing in British Columbia as a strictly subsistence activity.

HISTORIOGRAPHICAL CONTEXT

This book approaches a momentous subject, Indians and resource politics in the evolving Pacific Coast fisheries, from aboriginal times to the present, and it offers the first Canadian coast-wide analysis of it. It includes an examination of the remarkable *Sparrow* decision set fully in its historical and ongoing political context. My study would not have been possible without the existence of an exceptionally rich and diverse literature on specific aspects of Pacific Coast fishing, fish-processing, and Indian fishing societies, and the hundreds of articles, books, government-sponsored reports, and unpublished graduate studies in anthropology, economics, history, law, and other fields that reflect the contemporary global interest in both aboriginal rights and the environment. Since the late 1960s there has been a remarkable outpouring of academic and popular literature on Indian rights to land and Indian history in Canada, and scholarly works are increasingly relied on in litigating aboriginal rights issues. The writings of legal academics such as Douglas Sanders and Brian Slattery have been especially influential in recent court decisions that are breaking new ground and changing the law on Indian fishing.

Though polemical and hastily produced, Rolf Knight's 1978 ethnohistorical study, *Indians at Work: An Informal History of Native Indian Labour in British Columbia, 1858–1930*, deserves special mention, for it exposed Indian participation in the early industrial economy to re-examination in ways that continue to stimulate Canadian scholarship in the 1990s.[38] Knight challenged the old assumptions and conclusions of previous ethnographies and works of history that treated Indians as simply part of the pre-European past. He objected particularly, and quite rightly, to a contemporary, award-winning Indian history by Robin Fisher, *Contact and Conflict: Indian-European Relations in British Columbia, 1774–1890* (1977), for alleging that after the end of the age of BC fur enterprise, about 1858, Indians were reduced to irrelevance in the industrial economy established by white settlers.[39] Fisher continues in the new, 1992 edition of *Contact and Conflict* to defend his conclusion and declares that no others have successfully challenged it.

Knight's *Indians at Work* established that wage work in the major industries of British Columbia has been an intimate feature of Indian life for over a century. In *Aboriginal Peoples and Politics: The Indian Land Question in British Columbia, 1849–1989* (1990), Paul Tennant drives home parallel points raised in Knight's book and in an earlier, sociological study by Forrest LaViolette, *The Struggle for Survival: Indian Cultures and the Protestant Ethic in British Columbia* (1961, reprinted 1973): that the Indian land question is older than the province itself, that Indian peoples have constantly sought peaceful resolution, and that 'their efforts to do so are at the heart of their modern political history.'[40] Although no Canadian histories investigate the struggle for recognition of Indian fishing rights in British Columbia, two excellent American-based studies, Fay Cohen's *Treaties on Trial: The Continuing Controversy over Northwest Indian Fishing Rights* (1986) and Daniel Boxberger's *To Fish in Common: The*

Ethnohistory of Lummi Indian Salmon Fishing (1989), both on the salmon fisheries of western Washington state, examine the issue in the US legal context.[41]

Recent scholarship that seeks the origins of the post-1945 crisis in the Pacific Coast fisheries, with some references to contemporary Indian fishing issues, includes Arthur McEvoy's influential legal history, *The Fisherman's Problem: Ecology and Law in the California Fisheries, 1850–1980* (1986), and a collection of essays by Patricia Marchak and her colleagues with the 'Fish and Ships' sociological project at UBC, *Uncommon Property: The Fishing and Fish-Processing Industries in British Columbia* (1987).[42] These works, and a popular history by a labour journalist, Geoff Meggs, *Salmon: The Decline of the British Columbia Fishery* (1991), while quite different from each other, forcefully challenge the popular 'tragedy of the commons' myth.[43]

The idea behind the myth of the tragedy of the commons is that the open nature of fishing inevitably causes those who fish to overfish and that overfishing is responsible for the economic and social crisis facing ocean fisheries today. In the debunking of that myth, fingers point in many directions, but I agree with McEvoy's observation that 'the fisherman's problem consists as much of people stealing from each other as it does of people stealing collectively from nature.'[44] And I disagree with Meggs's passionate but misleading characterization of the history of the salmon-fishing industry as a war between two groups – commercial fishers, who were and still are solidly united and more conservation-minded than profit-oriented, and fish processors, who were and still are solidly united, crass profiteers, with no interest in conservation. In Meggs's scenario, government officials were and are simply toadies of the processing companies. I am concerned specifically about the Indians, who claim aboriginal rights to fish regardless of end use, and about the crucial role and responsibilities of the state in such matters.

WHAT FOLLOWS

Although Indians traditionally harvested all types of aquatic resources, this study is mostly about salmon-fishing and -processing. It must be. Salmon has been the most important marine resource for all BC Indians, both aboriginally and historically. Salmon-fishing was responsible for the earliest and greatest number of fishery regulations.

And the salmon-canning companies have generally controlled most commercial fishing and fish-processing in the province, with their coastal cannery camps serving as the heart and hub of activities.

The discussion begins with the salmon fishery and the management and use systems of aboriginal British Columbia (chapter 2) and then moves on to the industrial era. In chapters 3–7, I explore technological and business changes in the salmon industry, evolving regulatory policy for salmon, and the implications of all these developments and the common law for Indians through five historical periods, to the present. (Not discussed is steelhead [*Salmo gairdneri*], a sea-run trout reclassified in the 1980s as a Pacific salmon [*Oncorhynchus mykiss*].) Before concluding, I turn in chapter 8 to the history of the other Pacific fisheries – mainly halibut (*Hippoglossus stenolepis*) and herring (*Clupea harengus*) – in which, until recently, Indians managed to stay at least marginally involved. Introduction of the industrial herring-roe fishery in the 1970s and resuscitation of the traditional and tiny but lucrative herring roe–on-kelp harvest have kept a few Indian individuals and bands in today's fisheries. The herring roe–on-kelp harvest is the only fishery for which Indians and Indian bands hold most of the licences.

Regardless of the type of fishery or the region involved, Pacific Coast Indian women and men have always insisted that their involvement in industrial and subsistence fishing and fish-processing is culturally as well as economically motivated: 'Without fish,' testified the Native Brotherhood of BC to the Pearse Commission in 1981, 'we have no culture and with no culture we are not a people ... To us, the marine resources of BC are part of our struggle to survive and grow.'[45] This is no idle rhetoric. Pacific Coast Indian fishing societies have generated some of the most influential aboriginal causes, aboriginal case law, and aboriginal leaders in twentieth-century Canada.

2 The Aboriginal Salmon Fishery and Its Management

For Pacific Coast Indians before contact with Europeans, adaptation to the Pacific inshore, intertidal, and riverine environment was as crucial as adaptation to the land. For thousands of years, Indians harvested all types of aquatic resources, preserving most of the harvest and using it for subsistence, trade, and ceremonial purposes. These people were accomplished traders, and fish was a major trade item in aboriginal British Columbia. Many types of fish, shellfish, and sea mammals were available to coastal peoples, but the staple of diet and trade was the anadromous Pacific salmon. Indians harvested tremendous amounts of salmon in the centuries before the industrial fishery. Their choice of fishing sites and harvesting and processing technologies typically took advantage of micro-environmental conditions and diversified marine resources. Variations in supply and differential distribution helped to link families in a web of production, co-use of sites, and exchanges of goods.

Freshwater, rather than tidewater, locations were the most productive for salmon-fishing in aboriginal British Columbia, and these could be found right into the mountain elevations. Harpoons and traps were the most widely used techniques, but there were dozens of specialized variants of these and all the other technologies in use. Some methods of capture were capable of preventing any fish from reaching the spawning grounds. And yet the presence of tremendous stocks of salmon and other high-quality marine resources noticed by the early European explorers and traders attests to the determination and ability of the large, 'pre-epidemic' Indian population to manage the resource and maintain their dynamic fish-based societies and economies.

THE IMPORTANCE OF SALMON

The peoples of the Northwest Coast were fishers much more than hunters.[1] The rich, maritime, temperate-zone habitat provided by the presence of the continental shelf and the upswelling of colder water offshore created ideal conditions for sea life. But control and use of coastal food resources were complex. Indians could find, on a single occasion, tons of food; but as the anthropologist Wayne Suttles warns, the significance of the phrase 'on a single occasion' has usually been overlooked. The food supply here, as in any food-producing region, was anything but constant. As expressed by Suttles, 'abundance [on the Northwest Coast] consisted only of certain things at certain places at certain times and always with some possibility of failure.'[2] Differences in abundance ranged from the mixture of types of food, through local changes in occurrence of those types, to seasonal variation and fluctuation in supply from year to year caused by the cyclical nature of food resources, hydrographical features, and weather. Aboriginal people developed strategies for coping with gluts, scarcities, minor fluctuations, and local failures. These methods included establishing systems of resource exploitation, co-use of harvesting sites among groups, food preservation, and patterns of specialization and inter-village exchange. Northwest Coast Indians could thus live at a level and population density well above the average of the world's non-agricultural societies.

In aboriginal British Columbia, preserved salmon was the principal food for Indians who occupied the coastal areas and the salmon rivers draining the Pacific slope; for many it was the main source of both protein and calories.[3] As an English businessman who operated out of Alberni in the 1860s, Gilbert Sproat, observed, this rich and abundant food was to Pacific Coast Indians what the corn crop was to the English, or the potato crop to the Irish.[4] And, we could add, what the buffalo hunt was to the people of the North American plains.

The salmon harvests were enormous, although we can only estimate the numbers. In the century before colonial settlement, an estimated 200,000 Indians inhabited the Northwest Coast culture area (from northern California to the Gulf of Alaska); about 60,000 occupied the BC portion.[5] A crude estimate of annual salmon consumption per person, based on nutritional requirements and the range of food available, was about 220 kg of fresh salmon (edible flesh) each year for the entire Northwest Coast cultural area.[6] There are late-nineteenth-century harvest estimates of 1,000 salmon per family, or 450 kg (fresh) annual per-capita harvest, for the headwaters of the Skeena River around Babine Lake, which quantity was probably greater than that for most areas (other than the lower Fraser) in the BC portion.[7] We do not know if this figure was higher or lower than the average harvests in the pre-contact, pre-epidemic period. (However, the Hudson's Bay Co.'s daily provision allowance for boat-brigade crews in the fur trade era was 4 kg of fresh meat a day.) We do know that this salmon harvest was used for both local consumption and inter-group trade, so how much salmon was traded or potlatched out of or into individual tribal territories and villages each year, and hence even rough levels of local consumption, are unknown.

Extensive trade was essential to the economy of aboriginal British Columbia.[8] And in both the well-developed internal pattern of exchange, within and between local villages, and the external trade networks that extended to other cultural groups, salmon was paramount. In inter-group trade, a salmon also served as a unit of exchange. Written accounts left by the earlist fur traders and missionaries are clear on this point. William Brown, a Hudson's Bay Co. trader and the first non-Indian to travel into the Upper Skeena, arrived in 1822 at Babine Lake, where he established Fort Kilmaurs. Much to his amazement, the Babine villagers (Wet'suwet'en, Carrier people) would not accept the trading prices that he offered them for their large salmon, which Brown thought to be double the value of small salmon. The assembled Indians were seasoned traders, he wrote, who declared that in their territory they were accustomed to dictating the terms of trade to outsiders. Brown's later journal entries show that the Babine traded at the rate of one large salmon to five or six of the small size. His difficulties in reaching price agreements with the local people over salmon (and also, not surprising, over fish nets) caused him to complain that Carrier men and women were inveterate 'fishmongers.'[9] Gilbert Sproat remarked similarly that the Nootka people were 'rather too sharp at bargaining'; the 'Aht' villagers, for example, were 'fond of a long conversation in selling, but seldom reduced their price.'[10] In other words, like the Babine people, they were confident traders who operated in what we might call today a seller's market. When foreigners arrived, Indians routinely used fresh salmon as an article of exchange with them. A Hudson's Bay Co. trader, Peter Skene Odgen, noted a few years after 1800 that in Carrier country the company valued 90 salmon as equivalent to one 'made beaver.'[11] Federal fisheries officers in the early 20th century claimed that salmon formed a 'sort of legal tender' for Indians in the frontier areas of the province, with ten of the fish being equivalent to a dollar.[12]

Without question, need compelled much of the trade by coastal peoples. Gilbert Sproat mentioned that coastal villages exhibited specialization in scarce commodities or distinctive products and traded for the other things that they needed. There were years in Barkley Sound in which 'some of the tribes devote a season to whale-fishing, or to the capture of the dog-fish [*Squalus acanthias*], and supply themselves with salmon by barter with other tribes.'[13] Besides, some groups would have had fewer productive fishing sites than their needs required.

Other factors, however, also fuelled the trade in salmon or other Pacific Coast food products. Perceptive European observers of the eighteenth and nineteenth centuries, such as Sproat, Captain John Jewitt, and the explorer Alexander Mackenzie, suggested other reasons, such as local specialization in producing commodities for trade and a taste for variety. According to Sproat,

> Individuals, as a rule, keep to the arts for which the tribe has some repute, and do not care to acquire those arts in which other tribes excel. There seems to be among all the tribes in [Vancouver] island a sort of recognized tribal monopoly in certain articles produced, or that have been long manufactured in their own district. For instance, a tribe that does not grow potatoes, or make a particular kind of mat, will go a long way, year after year, to barter for those articles, which, if they liked, they themselves could easily produce or manufacture.[14]

The Nootka of Barkley Sound bartered for salmon and fish roes even though local supplies were available.

There are many other examples of this phenomenon. Captain John Jewitt wrote about elaborate exchanges among the Nootka villages of Kyuquot Sound and between the Kyuquot peoples and their neighbours elsewhere on Vancouver Island in the 1790s: 'tribes of savages from various parts of the coast continued coming [to Nootka] for several days, bringing with them blubber, oil, herring spawn, dried fish and clams, for which they received in return presents of cloth, etc., after which they in general immediately returned home.'[15] The Kyuquot peoples had access to local supplies of herring spawn and many of the other items for which they traded. Alexander Mackenzie, recording the trade in fish eggs in the Bella Coola territory in the 1790s, described the wide selection of flavours and textures in the fish-egg products that changed hands. Variety resulted from methods of harvesting and preserving and from berries, plants, or other ingredients used. Coastal Indians, it would seem, were epicures.

HARVESTING AND PRESERVING

Fishing

Salmon of one or more species was easily caught in the major rivers, secondary rivers, and independent coastal streams over a few weeks during the peak of the spawning runs at any one place. An ideal way to think of the aboriginal fisheries is suggested by Patricia Berringer's graduate research: 'During migration anadromous salmon pass through a number of time and space segments where they can be intercepted by fishermen.'[16] A coincidence of appropriate ecological and cultural elements would define a fishery site, and the interaction of all these factors would provide a range of harvesting strategies to be used. The river systems that supported several spawning grounds and had runs of more than one species of salmon would have had longer fishing seasons than the shorter rivers and independent streams, which would have had fewer runs and usually only one principal species. The fisheries of small, short drainage systems were also more susceptible to failure than the large, long drainages.

People who lived in the lower portion of major rivers could intercept the full range of mixed-stock runs headed for tributaries at higher levels, 'thereby tapping the abundance of the entire watershed system' and catching the fish in fresher, sea-run condition.[17] For coastal people to do this, however, often meant moving upriver to fish in narrower channels where harvesting was safer and more efficient. The salmon fisheries at the upper reaches of long drainages would have special problems, too.[18] Because of the sheer distance that the fish had to travel, salmon runs closer to spawning grounds and the headwaters were fewer and subject to more obstacles – natural and human – to fish reaching the spawning grounds. Hence, at headwaters of long river systems, salmon were scarcer, contained less variety, and were in poorer condition than lower on the main river. To the extent that quantity or difference in quality was important, salmon-fishing (or -trading) might move downstream. In short, fishing at either end of the major salmon-river systems was by no means secure, despite the overall abundance of salmon entering the system.

All groups in the Pacific slope of aboriginal British Columbia had access to one or more types of salmon ground for their principal production, and some also had access to saltwater areas. Obviously, groups with access to several streams and many sites could reduce the risk of failures in the salmon runs in ways that those restricted to a single stream or only a few sites could not. In all cases, the regularity of the one-way, seasonal migrations of salmon and their concentration in specific sections of the coast and in the waterways provided a high return for a *somewhat* low level of effort by Indian fishers.

The aboriginal methods of capturing salmon were unbelievably varied, highly adapted to specific ecological conditions, and often quite dangerous to apply. The design, fittings, and scale of salmon-fishing gear and accessories differed a lot. Choices depended mainly on species being harvested and prevailing hydrological conditions at the time of year and location of harvesting. The small amount of salmon-fishing that took place in tidal waters – in the calm inshore channels and estuaries, bays, and inlets where salmon congregated before heading for the spawning beds – involved tidal traps, harpoons, and reef nets and trolling from canoes with hook and line. Indians used traps and weirs, nets, harpoons, spears, and gaff hooks once the salmon ascended freshwater rivers and streams.[19]

Harpooning and spearing salmon required different gear and strategies in deep-river pools than in wide, rapidly flowing rivers or in raging river canyons and rapids, and water clarity was the essential variable for daylight fishing with this type of equipment.[20] The capturing of salmon in deep, still water required long spears and often took place at night, using canoes and flares. Spears were used for catching smaller species of salmon, such as sockeye, at a trap or dam, and in canyons.[21] As a rule, Indians crafted salmon spears of pine, rounded, smoothed, and straightened, with a fixed spear point at the end of the shaft. Harpoons, used by all groups to harvest salmon, were heavy-duty versions of spears for catching the larger species of salmon and other large fish, with detachable heads made of slate or bone, glazed with resin. The heads of these toggled instruments separated from the shaft when it struck the salmon, but both spearhead and fish remained fastened to the line.

Trolling with baited hooks and lines from canoes occurred for only two species of salmon – cohoe and spring, which rise to bait – and for other varieties of fish, such as halibut.[22] The centre of the aboriginal troll fishery for salmon was the Juan de Fuca Strait–Strait of Georgia area. Trolling also took place along the west coast of Vancouver Island. Hooks ranged greatly in size, shape, and material of manufacture, as did the lines. John Jewitt's diary account of salmon-trolling in Friendly Cove, Nootka Sound, at the beginning of the nineteenth century describes extremely skilful use of a small canoe and a barbed hook baited with a tiny, fresh, shiny fish. The hook was fastened to a line of whale sinew tied to the handle of the paddle. The jerking motion of the hook animated the bait, which attracted the salmon. By trolling in this manner, one canoe took as many as eight or ten large salmon in a morning, and 20 to 30 canoes fished at a time.[23]

More productive than spears and hook and line were nets. Nets made of spun nettle fibres, bark, or the fibres of hemp were used alone or with traps or weirs. They came in a wide assortment of sizes, forms, and mesh designs – everything from full-sized beach seines (operating on the 'surround and enclose' principle), reef nets (stationary, tidal), and gillnets (ensnaring), all of which called for specially constructed sinkers and weights, through drag nets (or 'trawl' nets, secured to poles or slung between two canoes) and bag nets (cones of netting attached to frames, sometimes triggered to close or 'purse'), to small, hand-held bag nets, dip nets, and scoops, for removing fish from traps. Indians traditionally changed the webbing in their nets according to what was being caught, and where.

Long nets of the seine, reef, and gillnet type were of limited distribution in aboriginal British Columbia.[24] A few incidences of beach seining are recorded for Indians in the Strait of Georgia region, including the Gulf islands and environs, but the main use was outside aboriginal British Columbia, in the lower Columbia River.[25] Reef nets were confined to a few areas on the coast, in the sockeye and pink salmon fishery at the saltwater shallows of the southern shores of Vancouver Island and around Point Roberts. Deep-river areas with moderate, steady flows and abundant salmon, such as in the mouths of major rivers or the lower courses of large, important salmon streams, provided suitable locations for trawl and dip-net fishing from canoes. Trawling with large bag nets (between 4 and 8 m long) was common in the lower Fraser and its tributaries (for sockeye and pink) and in the Bella Coola–Atnarko system.[26] Mackenzie saw the Bella Coola people fishing the broad lower reaches of the Bella Coola River with a trawl net suspended between two canoes and forced to the bottom with poles.[27] Rigging poles and the forward motion of the canoes against the current of the river or the force of the incoming tide held the mouth of the net open. Gillnetting, a passive netting method, usually with one end staked to the shore, was appropriate in many saltwater and river locations where salmon came inshore to feed and the spawning runs were heavy, but nowhere on the coast were gillnets extensively used.[28] Large, passive nets had to be obscured by silt, sediment, turbidity, dye, or darkness for effective use.

Dip netting as a fishing technique in its own right was practised intensively from stagings built on natural promontories at the canyons and upstream narrows of all major salmon rivers on the coast. At special custom-built dip-net stations or stagings that overhung the eddies and backwaters where salmon rested and gathered their strength, the larger nets were steadied into position and braced against the current to keep the net open and the fish confined, while the smaller nets were actively plunged or swept through the water.[29] Method depended on the variety being fished and the river features at each site. The highly productive summer dip-net fishery of the local people in the Fraser Canyon extended over an 11-km stretch of the river and involved both braced and active nets. On the upper Skeena, most Gitksan families had access to a dip-net site.

The most productive and widely used fishing technology in aboriginal British Columbia consisted of weirs and traps. These devices could be employed under various conditions and allowed Indians to take hundreds of salmon in a matter of minutes at the peak of the spawning runs. Design, construction, and operation often required remarkable feats of engineering.

Weirs were essentially fence-like, openwork barricades with strong permanent foundations to support the superstructure against the current of a river or stream. In most parts of the coast, these were associated with summer and fall runs of salmon. Indians built them from shore to shore in shallow, narrow, slow-moving portions of rivers and streams, to guide the congregating salmon either into traps or towards fishers with other harvesting equipment. Some weirs were large enough to allow construction of catwalks from which fishing could be done.[30] Operators removed screening panels when not fishing.

This technology was practised at hundreds of sites throughout the coast. Some groups – the Haida, for example – built simple weirs across dozens of short streams to produce the bulk of their salmon supply. Large, communal, weirs on the Cowichan River, Vancouver Island, were more complex; they had narrow impounding pens (spearing corrals) connected to the upstream side of the weir. On the mainland, the Fraser and Skeena rivers were too deep for weirs, but local groups installed weirs on the tributaries, such as the Stuart, Allouette, and Chilliwack rivers (Fraser system) and the Babine River (Skeena system).

Traps were the main and probably most productive freshwater method of salmon-harvesting in aboriginal British Columbia. Anthropologists have collected information on dozens of distinct types.[31] It was easier to adapt traps and their arrangements to local site conditions than was true of any other harvesting technology. Fishers could build stationary devices with any of three materials: stones (stone pounds, for use in intertidal zones, and dams and floundering basins, built on small rivers and streams), logs, and wicker-work (shields or grids). These traps either detained fish or funnelled them towards the mouth of other traps that stranded or imprisoned them. There were also basketry traps, which ranged in size and configuration from small, box-like devices to long tubes or cones the size of a large shed. These could be arranged in different ways and in conjunction with other technologies, depending on species of salmon and local environment.

In tidal waters, at the mouths of rivers and sloughs, traps usually relied on intertidal drift. Other types, such as the ones that Mackenzie saw on the Bella Coola River, took advantage of natural rapids and falls in coastal rivers.[32] The Haisla of Douglas Channel and Gardner Canal took salmon on the coast in stone tidal pounds, whereas in rivers they used basket traps and weirs, harpoons, dip nets, and trawl nets.[33] In channels near the mouth of the Fraser, the Musqueam and Tsawwassen made tidal ponds of stakes driven into the river bottom: these were owned by kin groups and their descendants.[34]

Gilbert Sproat observed the basket traps operated by Nootka people of Barkley Sound in the early 1860s.[35] A wing dam of stones and small stakes surrounded large traps to lead the salmon into them. The traps, 3 to 6 m long, and a metre or so wide, consisted of a line of circular baskets of uniform diameter, made of cedar strips ('splinters') tied together, with a few centimetres of space between each. Inside, a series of smaller baskets tapered to about the size of a single salmon. The operators left open the downstream end of the trap for salmon to enter. When a fish reached the upstream end, it could not turn around, and thus was imprisoned.

A single large, cylindrical basket trap could be staked in the stream bed at special sites, such as rapids. Captain John Jewitt's narrative (1803-05) describes a large Nootka conical basketry trap, which he calls a 'pot' or 'waer,' and the method for catching winter supplies of salmon by villagers at 'Tashels.' The village stood at the extreme point of navigation on the river; above the village, wrote Jewitt, 'the river becomes shallow and is broken into falls and rapids':

> A pot of twenty feet [6m] in length, and from four to five feet [1.2 to 1.5 m] in diameter at the mouth, is formed of a great number of pine [sic] splinters, which are strongly secured, an inch and a half [4 cm] from each other, by means of hoops made of flexible twigs, and placed about eight inches [20 cm] apart. At the end it tapers almost to a point, near which is a small wicker door for the purpose of taking out the fish. This pot or waer is placed at the foot of a fall or rapid, where the water is not very deep, and the fish, driven from above with long poles, are intercepted and caught in the waer, from whence they are taken into the canoes.[36]

Jewitt saw over 700 salmon being caught there in a period of 15 minutes.

Trap-based salmon-fishing in northern waters employed impressive, highly specialized technology suitable to conditions on large, productive salmon rivers.[37] On the upper portion of the Bella Coola River, Alexander Mackenzie observed with fascination the harvesting of salmon with what he termed 'weirs,' traps ('machines'), and dip nets, at the peak of summer salmon runs in the 1790s. But as Berringer recently concluded, the Bella Coola 'weir' was actually a trap, because it impeded the flow of the river: 'By building a barrier to obstruct the flow of water, Bella Coola resource users created a multi-purpose fishing facility where salmon could be taken with at least two different trapping strategies and by other means suitable at a "falls," dip netting in particular.'[38] Mackenzie described the scene: 'Salmon is so abundant in this river, that these people have a constant and plentiful supply of that excellent fish. To take them with more facility, they had, with great labour, formed an embankment or weir across the river for the purpose of placing their fishing machines, which they disposed both above and below it ... The river is about fifty yards [46 m] in breadth, and by observing a man fish with a dipping net, I judged it to be about ten feet [3 m] deep at the foot of the fall.'[39] And he went on to say,

> The weir is a work of great labour, and contrived with considerable ingenuity. It was near four foot [1.2 m] above the bank on which I stood to examine it. The stream is stopped nearly two thirds by it. It is constructed by fixing small trees in the bed of the river in a slanting position (which could be practicable only when the water is much lower than I saw it) with the thick part downwards; over these is laid a bed of gravel on which is placed a range of lesser trees, and so on alternately till the work is brought to its proper height. Beneath it the machines are placed, into which the salmon fall when they attempt to leap over. On either side there is a large frame of timber-work six feet [2 m] above the level of the upper water, in which passages are left for the salmon leading directly into the machines, which are taken up at pleasure. At the foot of the fall dipping nets are also successfully employed.[40]

The next day, travelling downstream, where the river was wider and swifter, he found no weirs. Here, the people fished with 'drag-nets between two canoes.'[41] Sizeable traps were set up along the banks.

A large, Skeena River-canyon form of basket trap was used in the sockeye fishery on the Bulkley River at Hagwilget Canyon. It consisted of three parts: a vertical barrier, a long, movable chute or trough supported by ropes from the superstructure of the trap to act as a flume, and a large fish basket at the rear.[42] According to Philip Drucker, other northern-style large-river traps were employed by the Oowekeeno, Bella Coola, Kitamaat, Hartley Bay, and Masset and Skedans Haida people on the productive rivers at the heads of inlets in their tribal territories.[43]

Clearly, the range and quality of gear and its tailoring for specific sites testified to aboriginal technical ingenuity and knowledge of the resource and the environment.

Preserving

Preserving fish and other foods allowed Indians to take advantage of fluctuations in food supplies. Writes Wayne Suttles, 'Limits in the

exploitation of times of abundance may have been set less by people's capacity to *get* food than by their capacity to *store* it.'[44] William
Pierce's autobiography gives us a dramatic but common enough example of the food-supply problem about which Suttles is talking.
Pierce was a Northwest Coast missionary (Methodist) of Indian ancestry working among the Tsimshian in the Nass and Skeena rivers
areas in the late nineteenth century. He heard stories that had been
handed down over the centuries about winters when food became
very scarce and starvation was a serious possibility. Each family
hoarded a few dried salmon for such emergencies. 'This article of
food was then so precious,' relates Pierce, 'that small pieces, a few
inches square, were cut and one piece handed out to each child.'[45]

Coastal Indians developed fish preservation to a fine art. They
devised ways to preserve every edible part of the salmon, including
heads, bones, eggs, and oil. Species, quality of flesh, and prevailing
weather conditions determined method of handling. Sockeye, when
taken in saltwater, is the fattest and most flavourful, but it does not
keep as long as the leaner ones, such as chum, caught later in the
season. Generally speaking, 'there were almost as many ways of
butchering and preserving fish as there were of catching them,' and
each required considerable skill.[46]

Indians processed freshly caught salmon at summer fish camps
on the coast, or on the banks of the rivers and streams penetrated by
salmon on their great annual spawning runs, or at their winter villages. They processed salmon by drying it in sun and wind, or by
smoking it in smokehouses and ordinary plank-house dwellings.
Dried or smoked salmon was stored in baskets or bentwood boxes,
which often were buried in small holes in the ground ('cache pits') or
in cabins ('caches') raised off the ground. So, besides technical skill,
the organization and quantity of labour, fuel, and equipment, and
special food storage arrangements, also shaped food production.

The sheer quantities of fish and the need to process it while
fresh led to development of a tremendous industry during the peak
of the runs. Alexander Mackenzie noted in his 1790s journal how the
women at a village on the Bella Coola River preserved salmon. There
were four piles of salmon, each containing 300 to 400 freshly caught
fish, heaped in front of the chief's house. It required 16 women to
clean and preserve them. The women first separated the head from
the body. The head they boiled, the body they filleted and gutted.
They roasted the bones and, in a more elaborate way, the flesh. They
placed troughs under the roasting carcasses to retrieve the fish oil.

Salmon roes were preserved as a separate enterprise. Mackenzie mentions dishes prepared from dried roe, such as at Friendly
Village (Burnt Bridge), on the upper Bella Coola River. There, he and
his men received not one but two different roe-based dishes: 'We
had not been long seated around [the fire] when we received a large
dish of salmon roes, pounded fine and beat up with water so as to
have the appearance of a cream. Nor was it without some kind of
seasoning that gave a bitter taste. Another dish soon followed, the
principal article of which was also salmon-roes, with a large proportion of gooseberries, and an herb that appeared to be sorrel.'[47] The
women also preserved salmon roes as small cakes. 'From the quantity of this kind of provision, it must be a principal article of food,
and probably of traffic,' wrote Mackenzie.[48] The village contained
many portable cedar chests for packing and transporting roe cakes
and dried or roasted salmon.

MANAGING THE RESOURCE

Northwest Coast social and economic organization developed around
salmon fishing and preserving. Such organization was an essential
ingredient of what were in effect aboriginal systems of salmon management. Strategies differed from group to group, but, as has been
persuasively argued by authorities such as Peter Usher, all systems
of resource management in aboriginal Canada relied on communal property arrangements, 'in which the local harvesting group was responsible
for management by consensus ... [and] management and production
were not separate functions.'[49] Likewise, specific property arrangements
differed but shared certain basic common principles: 'They resemble
neither the individualized private property systems, nor common property (i.e. open access, state management) systems,' that characterized
the settler states of British origin that Canada eventually became.[50]
    Indian societies on the Pacific slope were strongly hierarchical.
Each group occupied specific territories, and there were formal property rights (ownership and control) to particular hunting territories
and to fishing, berry-picking, egg-gathering, and other kinds of harvesting sites based on lineage and descent. Groups on the coast operated under different principles of resource-site ownership. These
ranged from the rather loose system of the Salish to strict individual
ownership among the Nootka and tight kinship-village control among
the main Kwakiutl and Tsimshian peoples. Some groups, such as the

Haisla, apparently had systems that displayed a little of each type.[51] The Hudson's Bay Co. trader William Brown called the 42 House heads of the Babine Lake and Bulkley Valley groups 'men of property,' although they were of course not private property owners in the European sense.[52] 'Houses' were both residential and kin units.

Formal individual or group rights and accompanying obligations to control fishing territories and equipment were an important feature of Northwest Coast societies. Unlike Europeans, however, aboriginal peoples did not consider wildlife or land itself something that could become an exclusive private possession or be alienated. In salmon-fishing, individuals might own and control access to equipment; individual families, dip-net stages and drying stations; and extended lineages, fishing weirs and traps, even entire salmon streams. Whole villages usually owned and managed the most productive technologies. Access to fishing sites often was restricted by property rights.[53] Suttles says of the Coast Salish that typically whole communities built weirs and traps for salmon, perhaps under the direction of the head of an extended family, but individuals or extended families owned smokehouses at weir sites.[54] Likewise, large communal weirs, such as those on the Cowichan River, were built by fishers of the community close to the riverine village at sites that were community-owned; villagers could gaff salmon blocked by the weir, but platforms and traps (which were the productive fishing stations) on the weir belonged to specific families.[55]

Use rights could be acquired from fishing-site owners. Owners of traps and weirs often leased out fishing rights for a specific period, perhaps to downriver groups (especially kin) that had no access to suitable sites in their own territory. This happened in the case of the Fraser Canyon fishery. Fishing sites and stagings in canyons using elaborate traps and/or dip-netting technology were rare and valuable resource sites; they were owned by lineage groups with recognized rites of priority access to the fishery. At the very least, permission to fish at such sites was required from the owners. Owners of sites usually received rewards for their largess. Philip Drucker found that salmon streams were the premier 'economic properties of the Nootka chiefs,' who routinely permitted setting of salmon traps by certain kin and others but claimed the entire first catch of the traps made in their rivers.[56] The four large piles of salmon that Mackenzie saw in front of a chief's house in the Bella Coola village may have been placed there to fulfil a similar obligation.

It seems that for every group, traditional laws governed use and application of fishing technology, forming a strategic aspect of aboriginal fishery management. For instance, because weirs and dams could prevent any fish from escaping to the spawning grounds, Indians developed elaborate systems for using them. The general idea was to operate them for maximum efficiency, which usually meant for short periods during the peak of runs. Sections customarily were removed during the fishing season itself, and the barricades often spanned only a portion of the river. The operators removed all but the framework, or pilings, at the end of the fishing season. Leaving the pilings in place would have both saved labour and marked a claim to the site for others to see. Because upstream groups needed to take their shares of the run, timing of dismantlement at any one site was important. Sometimes groups sought to exert economic or political pressure on upriver neighbours by keeping fish barricades completely closed, thus monopolizing the supply of salmon.

Typically, the system of land ownership hinged on the feasting system, known popularly as 'potlatching.' Feasts were the core institutions of Northwest Coast societies. Through these public gatherings, oral traditions were recounted, basic traditions and values reinforced, rites of passage witnessed and celebrated, economic rights addressed, and disputes settled. Of particular importance to the aboriginal fishery, feasts provided the arena for publicly witnessing transfers of lineage property titles, such as for salmon creeks or individual fishing stations, from one generation to the next and for resolution of any conflicts that arose over territory and access to the key resources therein. Inheritance of fishing rights to specific sections of the Bella Coola dams and weirs, for example, was transmitted, along with a chiefly name that had to be publicly validated.[57] Potlatching also was a system of redistribution and as such was used to deal with periodic shortages of fish and other resources. In the Babine Lake villages, Indians frequently held feasts or gambled to overcome famine.[58] Managing production and distribution (and redistribution) of salmon and other food resources helped reduce the risk of simultaneous failures in the salmon runs.

Characteristically, groups used fishing and fish-preservation sites and technologies within the context of annual seasonal rounds of resource-gathering and trade that lasted from early spring until late fall. The fishing economies in aboriginal British Columbia were highly adapted to a diversity of salmon populations spawning at many times and places. Indian families occupying the coast, who lived almost exclusively from the sea, rivers, and streams, regularly moved encampments several times during the year 'so as to be near good fishing and root and fruit grounds, and to follow the salmon up the rivers to summer encampments,' and then returned to their home village for the winter.[59] Winter was a time for resting and feasting; it was the major sacred season. Because many groups occupied their harvesting sites only during the periods of the year when owners exploited local resources, these sites were physically empty for much of the time. Within their seasonal movements, Indians responded to tidal cycles and reproductive cycles of fish and other sea life in their territories.

Groups of Coast Tsimshian had winter villages on the lower Skeena River as far inland as Kitselas Canyon. Many of them eventually moved westwards to the coast to found new winter villages where the weather was milder but continued to return inland to their Skeena River territories and village sites in summer and autumn to fish for salmon as part of the annual round.[60] The Kitselas and Kitsumkalum, however, did not move to the coast; they kept their winter villages on the lower Skeena, at Kitselas Canyon and near the confluence of Kitsumkalum River, respectively.

The kinship groups that wintered in coastal villages in Prince Rupert Harbour migrated to the Nass River for late winter and spring (February to April). There, they traded and fished for eulachon (*Thaleichthys pacificus*) and manufactured eulachon grease.[61] Anthropologists tell us that the Nass River was the greatest aboriginal trading centre on the northern Northwest Coast during the spring eulachon fishery.[62] This fishery was so much cherished by the Nishga people of that region that a major fishing ground, which Europeans named 'Fishery Bay,' was called 'the heart of the people' in the people language. In May, some went to the outer islands for sea-mammal hunting, deep-sea fishing for halibut, and shellfish-gathering in intertidal areas. May and June were for gathering seaweed and processing it at special camps, and also for harvesting herring spawn on kelp (kelp being a special kind of seaweed) and birds' eggs. Abalone-gathering (*Haliotis Kamtschatkana*) occurred at the lowest tides during summer. The people moved next to villages and campsites on the Lower Skeena, as mentioned, to fish summer and fall runs of salmon and gather and preserve a succession of berries at sites in their Skeena River territories. The traditional fishing sites were under the control of Houses, in this case corporate matrilineages, managed by the House chiefs; each House controlled several fishing stations.[63] After they returned to their winter villages, they occasionally gathered shellfish and hunted sea mammals. Archaeological excavations have identified 48 village sites in Prince Rupert Harbour, some of which were occupied continuously for at least 5,000 years.

Southern Kwakiutl groups undertook seasonal migrations to a series of fishing settlements during spring, summer, and fall. Seasonal settlements could contain several families or sometimes, as at Knight Inlet, members from different Kwakiutl groups living together.[64] Among the Nootka peoples of Kyuquot Sound, informal sharing of the same summer village sites by several local groups who maintained distinct winter and fishing-stream settlements was an old tradition.[65] Many ancient winters of severe hardship on the outer coast had led them to form alliances with groups that had salmon streams.[66] The Nootka built massive house frames at all their principal fishing stations and salmon streams and simply moved wall and roof planks from place to place as needed.[67] The Friendly Cove site is believed to be the oldest dated archaeological site on the outer coast of Vancouver Island: it has been occupied by ancestors of the Mowachaht-Muchalat Band for over 4,000 years.[68]

The Gitksan and Wet'suwet'en of the upriver Skeena and Babine Lake regions were riverine groups of the interior mainland and had more mixed (hunting and fishing) economies than the Coast Tsimshian tribes. They accordingly located their semi-permanent villages beside the choicest salmon-fishing sites in their territories and then exploited other resources, such as game and berries, in adjacent and more distant territories, which they reached by river and overland trail systems.[69] Most of the invaluable Skeena River salmon stocks migrated by way of the Babine River to the rich spawning grounds of Babine Lake, the largest body of fresh water in British Columbia. Each of the Gitksan groups occupied a single winter village, usually along a short stretch of the Skeena at the mouths of tributaries: Kitwanga (Kitwancool River), Kitsegukla (Kitsegukla River), Kitanmaks (Bulkley River, at what today is called 'Hazelton'), and Kispiox (Kispiox River). On the Bulkley River, a single Wet'suwet'en village was strategically placed for salmon-fishing at Hagwilget, at the lower end of Bulkley Canyon. The Babine had four villages on the shores of Babine Lake at the time of trader Brown's first visit. For such inland groups, salmon-fishing spatially anchored their entire economy.

We know that Indian harvests were at least comparable to those of the pioneer industrial fishery that followed and that aboriginal cultures were very knowledgeable about the salmon resource. Resident experts could accurately predict timing and abundance of local salmon runs and potential effects of weather and hydrographical conditions on harvesting sites. Aboriginal groups developed highly successful fishing and fish-preservation technologies and regionally based systems of resource management and distribution. There is no reason to believe that Indians on the Pacific Coast were perfect conservationists. And because of the tremendous amount of salmon caught for subsistence, trade, and ceremony before contact with Europeans, we can safely assume that the aboriginal salmon fishery, with its highly productive technology, was so large that it may have significantly taxed the resource. But parallel to the conclusions of Arthur McEvoy about the salmon fishery of aboriginal northern California, the salmon fishery of aboriginal British Columbia sustained yields for several thousand years.[70] What is striking is the net effect of this system. It assured everyone adequate stocks of fish over the long term. The same cannot be said for the state-regulated industrial fishery that replaced it in the late nineteenth century.

3 Indian Fishery Invented, 1871–1888

In the colonial era, the BC fisheries were not regulated to any extent. Indians continued to catch and to process fish for trade, subsistence, and ceremony. Newcomers encouraged Indians to continue fishing for their own needs and for the food and commercial requirements of the colonial population of fur traders, gold prospectors, and settlers. They considered fish to be an inexhaustible resource. The BC Indians themselves seemed threatened, however; as indicated earlier, disease had slashed their population by about 80 per cent between 1774 and 1874. A new era for Pacific Coast fishing began in 1871, when the British Columbia Terms of Union made the colony a province of Canada and the first salmon-canning factory began to operate on its shores. Each cannery, requiring its quota of fishers and cannery workers, comprised a village during its operating season.

With salmon-canning, a single species – sockeye – and a single technique – gillnetting – dominated the early industrial fishery. The first regulations for the province under the Fisheries Act of Canada 1868, were not promulgated until 1878, and, with respect to the commercial fishery, they applied only to some aspects of salmon-fishing. By that year, a dozen canneries packed salmon on the Fraser and a handful packed in the prime sockeye areas of the north, where missionaries and gold prospectors also operated.

Regulations were minimal so as to allow growth of salmon-canning. The state clearly took into account the critical role that Indians played in servicing the industrial fishing and fish-processing sectors. The regulations indicated in particular that Indians had the right to carry on their traditional fisheries. Indian men and women operated the gillnet fleets, and Indian women and children did most of the handling of raw fish. The Indian fisheries and the boom in salmon-canning influenced even the size and location of Indian reserves.

From the earliest years of salmon-canning, however, cannery operators saw the traditional fishing practices and requirements of Indians as a major obstacle to profits for the industrial sector. By 1888, federal fisheries officers would introduce new regulations to license the industrial fishery and give Indians the freedom to catch salmon to feed themselves; but officially, Indians had to compete on an equal footing with others when salmon-fishing for commercial purposes.

REGULATING THE PIONEER SALMON-CANNING INDUSTRY

Pre-Industrial Beginnings

In the first half of the nineteenth century, the Hudson's Bay Co.'s fur-trade operation in the interior mainland (New Caledonia) depended on the huge supplies of salmon provided by Indians. Trader Peter Odgen noted that in the New Caledonia district the company needed to secure a stock of 30,000 preserved salmon from the Babine each fall, and 20,000 from Fraser Lake, as a hedge against failure in the Babine Lake fisheries.[1] Even for decades before that, Indians routinely sold large amounts of fresh salmon to the American maritime fur traders who came to the coast to bargain for pelts and provisions.[2] From 1835 to the 1850s, the company sought external markets for salmon, experimenting with a small salt-salmon trade with the Sandwich (Hawaiian) Islands and Asia. Indians furnished the fish, but this was a fairly small operation. In general, salmon seemed so abundant and the commercial fishery so unimportant to non-Indians that competition with Europeans was virtually unheard of.[3]

This initial lack of conflict and dispute partly accounts for inclusion of guarantees for traditional Indian fishing practices in the Victoria (or 'Douglas') Treaties – the only treaties negotiated with Canada's Pacific Coast Indians. In these agreements – arranged in the years 1850–54 between the Hudson's Bay Co. and 14 Indian 'tribes' on Vancouver Island through the colonial governor and experienced fur trader (Sir) James Douglas – these peoples, surrendered their lands for ever. Each agreement stated that Indians would be 'at liberty to hunt over the unoccupied lands, and to carry on [their] fisheries as formerly.'[4] To the detriment of Indians, over time 12 of the described areas became 'occupied.' And no other treaties were negotiated elsewhere in the coastal area to protect Indian fisheries.

Reluctant to Interfere

At Union (1871), and for a few years afterwards, there were no immediate plans to extend the Fisheries Act to British Columbia. The Department of Fisheries expressly did not want to throttle an embryonic Pacific Coast industrial fishery, nor to interfere with Indian fishing.[5] As with much early legislation in the new dominion, the Fisheries Act of 1868 owed its jurisdictional framework and main policy directions to the former Province of Canada.[6] Drastic declines in eastern Canada's lake, river, and estuary fisheries, primarily of Atlantic salmon, led to concern for biological conservation of stocks, which became a principle of Canadian fisheries management even before anyone talked about 'maximum sustained yield.' Conservation principles and regulations to control access to fish – through closed seasons and times, bans on certain types of nets and fishing practices, and licensing and leasing of fishing rights – had become a fact of life in the older colonies before Confederation.[7]

Federal regulations were applied to the Pacific Coast fisheries in 1874 as a matter of general federal policy, not because of any particular events in British Columbia. The government of Canada simply made provisions for extension of the Fisheries Act to each of the newly acquired provinces, British Columbia, Manitoba, and Prince Edward Island.[8] The Fisheries Act was not proclaimed to extend to British Columbia until order in council in 1876; it went into force there on 1 July 1877 and resulted in regulations for the BC fishery from 1878.[9] Another decade would lapse before fishing licences would be required.

The supply of fish was no obstacle to expansion in the first few years of the salmon-canning industry.[10] Only the most productive areas and a single species were being exploited: the industry wanted sockeye salmon exclusively. During the year in which the Fisheries Act came into force in British Columbia, 1877, half a dozen canneries were operating on the Fraser and the first one in the north, on the Skeena, had just opened.

Lack of markets for salmon species other than sockeye and

plants' restricted capacity limited spread of the industry. It was unprofitable for cannery operators to equip themselves with enough people, supplies, and machinery to take full advantage of the short-term availability of salmon.[11] Seasonal, cyclical salmon runs made it economically impractical to build plants large enough to handle periodic, unpredictable gluts of fish. Besides, dependence on a single species resulted in an extremely short active season – about six weeks – for the industrial salmon fishery. So, like the aboriginal fishing camps, cannery camps were deserted most of the year and frequently even in the 'off' seasons for local supplies of salmon. In the years and on the days in which there were gluts of salmon, canners found themselves so short of processing capacity that they had to refuse fish; worse, they even ordered their fishers to dump fish. They coped with periodic abundance by wasting fish.

Seasonal demand for cheap labour, especially in the early days and in isolated spots with few or no local workers, led cannery operators to rely on migrant Indians and on labour contractors who supplied the entire Pacific west with many of the people needed for all types of seasonal and short-term work. Operators negotiated with Chinese labour agents to put up the canned-salmon pack at each plant. 'Pack' is the standard term to describe salmon cannery output, with the unit of measurement being a 48-lb (22-kg) case of canned salmon, regardless of the size or shape of the tins. The labour agreement for the BC canneries, termed a 'Chinese Contract,' ensured supply and coordination of short-term skilled and semi-skilled workers required by an operator. These contracts detailed tasks, price per case, and payment schedule. The contractor supplied Chinese workers and bosses and provided their transportation, food, clothing, bedding, and other necessities. The Chinese bosses also oversaw and tallied the efforts of Indian and, later, Japanese plant workers who laboured mostly for piece rates.

Licensing Fishing

The Canadian government's first fishery regulations for the province in 1878 demonstrate the extent to which Ottawa was reluctant to interfere with the pioneer industrial fishery. The regulations were minimal and applied only to salmon.[12] They confined drifting with salmon nets to tidal waters and banned salmon nets of any kind from fresh water. Nets for salmon were not to obstruct more than one-third of the width of the river, and there was to be a weekly 'close time' for salmon-fishing. All this was standard wording, right out of existing federal regulations.

An order in council of 11 June 1879 gave the Department of Fisheries the right to grant licences and leases for fishing for salmon in Canada, although not until 1888 would licences actually be required to fish in British Columbia. The original Fisheries Act had contemplated a system of granting titles for fishing privileges as a basis of administering this common-property resource. The federal commissioner of fisheries, W.F. Whitcher, reported in 1873 that 'certain of its provisions are predicated on the supposition that leasing and licensing would become general, providing always for necessary exceptions as to legal titles, prior occupancy and preferential claims.'[13] Evidently the government regarded 'occupation under licensing' as a means to preserve and increase estuary and river fisheries and provide stability and permanence in a fishery. Whitcher made no specific mention of prior occupancy or of preferential claims on the part of Indians. Officially, the licensing regulations were intended to help the department to 'improve and protect' fisheries, but also to define and defend the respective fishing places used by fishers where 'confusion and intrusion might otherwise occur.'[14]

As predicted, 1883's sockeye runs were outstanding. The canned-salmon pack was based overwhelmingly on the Fraser River estuary, where another ten canneries had opened. That year, industrial fishing, sealing, and salmon-canning in the province employed about 14,000 people, most of them Indians. There was little to celebrate, however, because everyone knew that the pack ought to have been even larger. Day after day, anxious crowds gathered on the banks of the Fraser estuary to watch boat loads of unprocessed salmon being chucked overboard after the canneries had reached their physical limits. Much fish was wasted in the canning process, too. There was time to can only the thickest part of the fish; the rest of the carcass joined the entrails and the floating, rotting mass of rejected salmon already in the river.

Regulating Fishing Technology

Following the pattern of regulations everywhere for industrial fisheries, early regulations for Canada's Pacific Coast took three forms in succession, with limits first on gear, next on times, and finally on locations. Mobile gear was the norm in the BC industrial fishery. Unlike in American coastal waters, the massive, highly productive salmon fish wheels and traps were essentially banned from the beginning in British Columbia.

Net fishing included gillnetting and seining. Gillnetting is the oldest form of industrial salmon-fishing on the Pacific Coast. In British Columbia, it was used almost exclusively for catching sockeye. A small boat spins out a wall of net, weighted at the bottom and floated at the top, in which salmon are trapped by the gills when they attempt to swim through it. Gillnets are used principally in or around the mouths of the larger rivers and inlets. They are most effectively fished in murky waters, at the mouth of the Fraser, for example, and at night, when the mesh is not visible to the fish. Until the first decade of the twentieth century, gillnet boats were powered relatively inexpensively by oar or sail and usually required two persons: a fisher to handle the net and a 'boat puller' to handle the oars.

Seining includes purse seining, in which an encircling type of net concentrates schools of pelagic fish, and drag or beach seining. In purse seining, the top of a long net is set in position and then floated to the surface and drawn in a circle around the school of fish. The bottom is drawn together (pursed), and the fish are scooped up. The early purse seiners were flat, scow-like vessels powered by either sail or oars, or both. It took a crew of about nine to haul the net and operate the oars. Purse seines became used more widely after 1900, following introduction of the power boat. Application of motor power greatly increased the efficiency and effectiveness of handling the net.

Drag seines were nets weighted at the bottom and floated at the top, which were hurled from a vessel to enclose an area of water between the vessel and the shore and then drawn ashore. The government occasionally granted exclusive, long-term privileges of operating drag-seine licences. These leases amounted to fishing monopolies that encouraged prospecting for good seining grounds. Industrial drag-seining grounds were established quickly at the mouth of the Nimpkish River (near Alert Bay), and on salmon rivers flowing into Smith Inlet and Clayoquot Sound, for example. One person received seining licences for over 320 km of the coast.[15] Another got one for Smith Inlet in 1884, and it was not cancelled until 1919, after resentful First World War veterans attacked and destroyed the nets. Such monopolies were officially issued only to cannery owners.

In the pioneer period, it was generally recognized that some spawning adults must be allowed to pass through the fishery and reach the spawning grounds; but fisheries officials were not particularly concerned about what constituted a sufficient amount. They knew little about the biology and migratory habits of Pacific salmon. They and the processors hoped that fish hatcheries would guarantee abundant supplies of fish for canning. As early as 1874, government officials suggested the need for a program of artificial propagation, which they believed would increase total supply and reduce the extraordinary cyclical variation in the fabulous Fraser River runs of salmon. A number of privately and government-owned salmon hatcheries were built. (The fisheries department also 'improved' access to a number of rivers and streams by blasting, in the hopes of creating new, natural spawning grounds.) Eventually these artificial hatcheries were found to be uneconomical and inefficient; they did not begin to solve the problem for the industrial salmon fishery.

IMPLICATIONS FOR INDIANS

The Industrial Fishery: Helpers, Not Competitors

Exercise of control over traditional Indian fisheries was ad hoc during the colonial period and for the first few decades after British Columbia joined Confederation. The fisheries department did not interfere with traditional fishing activities and technologies in the 1870s. Indeed, fisheries inspectors in the province were reluctant to do so. The department's annual reports show that even the traditional methods for catching salmon (such as weirs, dip nets, and spears) continued in both the Indian fishery and the incipient industrial fishery.[16] Indians used their own dug-out canoes for travel and to fish well into the twentieth century, adopting them to the early industrial fishery and pelagic seal hunts. Haida and Nootka were major suppliers of the large sea canoes. According to a government observer in 1884, 'Masset is the shipyard of the Hydas [sic], the best canoe makers on the continent, who supply them to the other coast tribes ... Here may be seen all stages of construction of these canoes, which, when completed, are such perfect models for service and of beauty.'[17] Indians were seen as the natural harvesters and processors of fish. Despite decreasing population, they outnumbered non-Indians in the province by roughly three to one and remained virtually the sole occupants of the vast areas outside southern Vancouver Island and the lower mainland. Newcomers wanted the fishing in-

dustry to prosper, and everyone concerned knew that the cooperation of Indians was key.[18] But they wanted Indians as helpers, not as
full participants or competitors.

With the general shortage of labour in the province, rivalry for
Indian workers was so stiff that fisheries officials asked Indian agents
to encourage Indians to work for the salmon canneries.[19] Some agents
did; others warned Indians, especially women, against abandoning
their gardening and other economic activities on the reserves.

Participation in the industrial fishery required major adaptations by Indians, particularly given the many changes in technology,
policies, and regulations. Even though BC Indians had always been
fishers and fish processors and had employed an impressive variety
of techniques, the gear, methods, knowledge, and context of industrial fishing and processing were largely novel for them.[20] For one
thing, when essentially no salmon other than sockeye was canned,
harvesting with oar- or sail-powered gillnets in river estuaries and
inlets was the vogue. The regulations prohibited commercial salmon-
fishing and use of nets, except by Indians, in non-tidal waters. For
another, Indian industrial fishers were not harvesting in their traditional fishing grounds. Before the early twentieth century (and again
after the Second World War), canneries were relatively few and concentrated in specific regions. Because of the long distances travelled
to catch salmon for the canneries, Rolf Knight concluded that 'many
Indian fishers (possibly the majority) came to novel fishing grounds
and had to learn the peculiarities and secrets of local tides, runs,
glory holes, and snags as much as any newcomer.'[21] Besides this, the
variety and cost of regulation salmon-fishing gear and methods increased over time, which was an additional burden to Indians, who
had little access to cash.

Similarly, Indian women, girls, and old people who received
wages or piece rates in the fish plants – for scraping and cleaning whole
salmon in tubs of cold water; filling cans with salmon; lacquering, weighing, and labelling cans; pickling salmon; making or mending fish nets;
and so on – worked in supervised, racially segregated factory settings
unlike anything in their aboriginal processing routines. Until the 1940s,
Chinese bosses coordinated the efforts of Indian plant workers. Cannery records usually identify Indian women as 'Kloochmen' and Indian
plant work in general as 'China labour' or 'China crew.' This set-up
differs strikingly from the scenes of salmon-processing witnessed by
Alexander Mackenzie in the 1790s.

There is no question that Indians were the labour backbone of the salmon-canning industry during its chaotic rise in the late-nineteenth century or that most Pacific Coast groups, including upriver villagers, participated on a tremendous scale. The published annual reports of Indian agents for British Columbia chart yearly village migrations to the cannery camps. Because these agents had to keep track of the economic situation of the bands under their supervision, and because it was in their interest to be as optimistic as possible about the economic 'progress' being made, we can hardly consider these people neutral observers. But their detailed annual reports in these early years at least indicate trends.

Indian villages in the southern part of the Cowichan Agency were almost entirely deserted; villagers worked at the salmon canneries on the Fraser, and Indians from Kincolith, Alert Bay, and villages in the Fraser River Agency, at local canneries.[22] The Bella Bella Indians, 'who subsist largely on fish and game, both of which are plentiful,' got jobs at the Rivers Inlet canneries when there was demand,[23] while those from Kitasoo (or 'Klemtu'), who 'subsist mainly on fish, halibut, salmon, and herring,' earned small sums at neighbouring canneries.[24] The Kitkatla found 'ready' employment during summer at canneries on the Skeena River.[25] Fraser River canneries drew at least 1,700 Indians from throughout the coast and as far away as the Upper Skeena.[26]

Cannery operators provided powerful economic and social incentives for Indian individuals and families – men, women, boys, girls, and old people – to participate in fishing and shore work over the short industrial sockeye-fishing and -processing season, during July and August. Such labour meshed well with Indians' traditional seasonal round. Whole households migrated to the cannery camps where they lived – rent-free – and worked during the sockeye-fishing season. Men and women of rank could control who went, and even to which plant.[27] Indian leaders recruited the Indians for cannery labour. Chinese labour bosses usually kept account of the plant work of Indian women.

Seine licences were not granted to Indians before the 1920s, as a matter of departmental policy. Nevertheless, fisheries department officials often attached stipulations requiring cannery operators to employ local Indians in drag-seining and plant work and to conserve salmon in the area by operating a fish hatchery, and Indian chiefs directed the industrial drag-seining operations.[28] The involvement of high-ranking Indians in recruiting Indian fishers and plant labour, and directing drag-seining operations, represents continuing aspects of traditional fisheries practice but also creation of 'ethnic straw bosses' for the fishing and fish-processing industry.

Individuals' seasonal earnings were marginal in relation to plant owners' profits but were never meant to constitute an entire year's income. Credit for supplies and equipment was readily available to Indians at the cannery store. So were the cash advances that guaranteed that Indian fishers and plant employees would return the next season. Many Indian bands came to depend on working for the salmon canneries for their supplies during winter. Goods and equipment from the cannery store went for direct consumption, subsistence and commercial activities, and traditional exchange, including potlatching. The rates of exchange set in cannery stores on the Skeena determined the exchange rates at Hudson's Bay Co. posts in the interior.[29]

Indian harvesting technology and labour were critical. But disputes over rights to salmon increased with the growth and geographical spread of the industry. Although collectively Indians earned substantial sums in the industrial fishery and seal hunt, they clearly were unwilling to hand over their fishing territories.[30] A recurrent point in today's debates on aboriginal rights is that Indians traditionally have been willing to share their resources, but not to alienate their rights to them and thereby lose control over resource management and use.

Indian Fisheries and the Land Question

Remarkably, scholars have virtually ignored the role that the early conflict between the Indian fisheries and the expanding salmon-canning industry played in pressing governments to settle Indian fishing and other rights in British Columbia. When one is studying aboriginal rights in Canada, it is tempting to focus on land. But the main issue is maintenance or regaining of aboriginal control of resources in traditional areas of occupation. The highly productive Indian fisheries influenced crucial late-nineteenth- and early-twentieth-century decisions about the size and number of Indian reserves in the coastal and inland river areas.

When British Columbia joined Canada in 1871, everyone anticipated that treaties would be signed with the Indians who occupied the territory. The Royal Proclamation of 1763, often thought of as the 'Indian Bill of Rights,' required officials of the crown to purchase

Indian lands in public ceremonies as the crown extended its jurisdiction in British North America.[31] Apart from the Douglas Treaties of 1850–54, however, no new treaties or surrenders of land have ever been negotiated with the Indians of Canada's Pacific slope.

In the 1870s, it also was assumed that Indian issues, including land and fishing rights, would be settled through creation of reserves, as dictated by article 13 of the British Columbia Terms of Union Agreement of 1871.[32] The article required the province to convey to Canada, for the use and benefit of Indians, 'tracts of land' of such extent 'as it has hitherto been the practice' of the colonial government. Generally speaking, all public lands became vested in the province, which agreed to furnish adequate lands for Indian reserves. The provincial government controlled all other land and thus could limit the size and location of future reserves and, as it turned out, 'frustrate the more liberal policy urged by federal representatives' of the day.[33]

Although provincial officials established Indian reserves after 1876, reserves were not determined quickly or adequately enough to keep pace with non-Indian movement into Indian territories. These movements threatened Indian sea- and land-based economies and killed off Indian people through disease. Some groups, most notably the Nishga of the Nass River territory, resisted accepting reserves until aboriginal title had been settled. Nearly 100 years would pass before the Nishga would achieve even partial victory, in the Supreme Court of Canada's decision in *Calder* (1973).

In the BC coastal region, the provincial government awarded reserves under the assumption that Indians would have access to their productive fisheries and therefore required nothing more than a postage-stamp–sized land base, averaging about 5 ha per Indian; over time, politicians even whittled this amount down. This approach stands in marked contrast to awards of land, averaging 65 to 260 ha per Indian family, for the indigenous hunters and trappers in Canada's western interior. In 1874, Indian Affairs officials urged that the province get on with the granting of Indian reserves, keeping in mind Indian fishing needs: 'Great care should be taken that the Indians, especially those inhabiting the Coast, should not be disturbed in the enjoyment of their customary fishing grounds, which should be reserved for them previous to white settlement in the immediate vicinity of such localities.'[34]

BC Attorney General George Walkem recommended that – because of the Indians' 'habits and pursuits' and the province's physical structure – BC Indians, especially those who inhabited the coast and engaged in fishing, did not need very large reserves. BC Indians, he suggested, fell into three classes: fishers and hunters, small-scale stock-breeders and farmers, and labourers. The first category made up a large proportion of the Indian population, including 'about 30,000 "Coast Indians," who live on the seaboard, besides two or three thousand Indians who live in the Interior and in the Southern parts of the Province.'[35] Walkem said that granting large tracts of land to Indians would simply divert them from more lucrative economic activities, such as fishing, which in turn would inflict 'a serious injury upon them and the Province.'[36] These people could be 'provided for in other ways, by reserving their fishing stations, fur-trading posts and settlements.'[37] Ottawa ultimately accepted a version of these recommendations – a major retreat from established policy.

Walkem seems to have been following the advice of the Rev. William Duncan to the federal minister of the interior, David Laird, who was in charge of Indians. Duncan was the Church Missionary Society (Anglican) missionary who founded and led the Coast Tsimshian Christian industrial village in Prince Rupert Harbour, Metlakatla, established in 1861. He became a controversial and legendary character on the North Coast. A portion of Duncan's letter appeared in the BC *Report on Indian Reserves* (1875): 'In addition to the reserve for each tongue, I would earnestly beg the Government to hold in trust for the benefit of each tribe its respective fishing station, though it may not come on the reserve and be only occupied (of course) [sic] part of the year. To allow whites to pre-empt or occupy *such clearings* would not only be a great injustice, but would, I am sure, be a fruitful source of trouble to the Province.'[38]

Duncan's suggestions did not end there: he suggested that Indians were on the verge of getting into the cannery business and other industries themselves.[39] This goal, of course, was exactly what Duncan was trying to accomplish at Metlakatla. Included among the industries at Metlakatla would be an Indian cooperatively owned salmon cannery, which was built in 1881 and operated for several seasons. Duncan moved the village, including the cannery, north to Alaska in 1887.

Duncan proposed that the government adopt a flexible policy: the size of Indian reserves must be determined according to the number and pursuits of Indians in specific localities, and each 'nation' of Indians should be dealt with separately on its claims.[40] Duncan may have been unorthodox in his missionary work, but, like the Hudson's Bay Co. traders before him, he also was a keen observer of Indian economic behaviour.

Three factors – clashes between the province and the federal government over Indian reserves (already by 1875 considered a 'long-pending controversy'), the unresolved issue of land title, and realistic fears of Indian uprisings against whites – finally brought results. A joint federal-provincial Commission for the Settlement of Indian Reserves was set up in 1876.[41] Village sites, cemeteries, and many fishing stations were reserved, but as specific, separate small plots of land rather than inclusial territories. Away from the coast, in the middle and Upper Skeena, for instance, some village sites at traditional locations of salmon-fishing were reserved. Examples are Hagwilget and Kitanmaks.[42] However, tribal territories and many land resources were not given the protection of reserve status, and over time the province cut back (reduced through 'cut offs') existing reserves.

The rivalry between the Indian fisheries and the new and rapidly expanding salmon-canning industry was not far from the minds of the northern Indians or the second Indian reserves commissioner, Peter O'Reilly (1880–98), who replaced Gilbert Sproat (1877–80). O'Reilly admitted that he went into the Nass and Skeena rivers country in 1881–82 to set apart reserves mainly in accordance with the Indian fisheries there. 'Unless immediate action was taken,' Duncan had warned him, 'the Indians would be great sufferers, and much discontent would be the result ... There was great demand that season for land on which to establish canneries.'[43] He also set aside small reserves in the Queen Charlotte Islands, largely on the basis of what he learned about the Haida's current harvesting and preserving of different types of fish (salmon, dogfish, important for its oil, and halibut), sealing, and cultivating of root vegetables.[44] On some Queen Charlotte reserves with productive salmon streams, O'Reilly included the right of fishing for a specified distance above tidal water or upstream of the reserve. This was the case at Lan-as (Reserve No. 4, on Ya-Koun or Yakoun River) and Ja-Lun (No. 14, on Ja-Lun River), claimed by the Masset Band, or Dee-na (No. 3), on Skidegate Inlet, claimed by the Skidegate Band. Masset Reserve No. 2, Hi-ellen, on the north coast of Graham Island, included 'the fishing traps in the river, about 400 yards from its mouth.'[45] It is no coincidence that in Skidegate Inlet, the largest reserves were associated with the Skidegate (dogfish) Oil Works, the only Indian-run industrial fish-processing operation on the Queen Charlottes. Similarly, in requesting their reserves, the Ohiaht of Vancouver Island argued that five of the sites that they sought were associated with their dogfish-oil and sealing stations.[46]

The original reserves proved unsatisfactory to coastal Indians, mostly because of fisheries. By the late 1880s, inadequacies in number and location of fishing sites and further spread of salmon-canning in the north made it difficult for northern Indians to control or conduct their traditional fisheries. Fighting and quarrelling among Indian communities and between Indians and non-Indians helped inspire appointment of a three-person commission to inquire into the state and conditions of the Indians of the Northwest Coast in 1887.

The commissioners visited representatives of the Nishga at Nass Harbour and Kincolith and of the Coast Tsimshian at Port Simpson and Metlakatla. They found that opinions diverged among villagers on such issues as Indian title and the authority of Indian agents. Yet all groups asked for extension of existing Indian reserves, reservation of numerous fishing stations (for the two most important local types of fish, salmon and eulachon), the setting aside of extensive tracts for hunting.[47]

The Port Simpson people (descendants of the inhabitants of the ancient winter villages in Prince Rupert Harbour) wanted the whole of the Tsimshian Peninsula, all the salmon streams on the Skeena, and extension of the commonage of the eulachon fishing reserves.[48] The Kincolith and Greenville villagers of the Lower Nass wanted reserves, rivers, and streams on Observatory Inlet and Portland Canal, and also on the Nass River itself. The commissioners appear to have understood the message. As far as they were concerned, 'doubtless' most of the hunting and fishing places on the different canals, inlets, and rivers asked for were used regularly by the Indians demanding them and were required 'as giving a *"pied a terre"* to either some salmon fishing privilege or to some extensive range of hunting ground in the vicinity.'[49]

At the Kincolith meeting, Frederick Allen, a Nishga school teacher there, spoke of the chiefs' discontent with reserve allocations to date. There were far too few reserves. Many were located in the wrong place, while others were too small originally or had been reduced in size by the government's policy of cutting off land from existing reserves. Chiefs complained of having been improperly informed and consulted by the Indian reserve commissioner. Some Indians, for example, said that they had asked for a reserve on Portland Inlet, but the commissioner chose an inappropriate site at the mouth of the Kin-na-max River (Kinnamax Reserve, No. 15). This site offered little to the Indians, as it did not give them access to their fisheries: 'We want the whole of the Kin-na-max River. We want from the mouth of Observatory Inlet right up to where we have our little houses for a salmon drying station, right at the head of the Inlet.' Not unreasonably, they sought more than one salmon river for fishing: 'We do not want the whole of [Portland Canal], only some places. We have good reasons for wanting these places secured to us. Sometimes the salmon is scarce in one stream, then we go to another. All the Naas [sic] Indians when the salmon is scarce up the river go to these inlets. We ask for the reserves on Observatory Inlet and Portland Canal and at Kin-na-max for the whole of the Naas tribes, not for the Tsimpseans [sic] or any other tribes.'[50] In response, the government in 1888 set aside Talahat Reserve, No. 16, occupying both banks of the river, 4 km from the mouth, as an exclusive fishery for the Nass River people.[51]

The initial spread of salmon-canning to Nass and Skeena sites had already created problems. Take the case of Croasdaile's ('Nass River') cannery. In 1878, the provincial government granted a 4-ha piece of land on the Stoney Point Reserve, which a Mr Croasdaile subsequently purchased for a salmon cannery and sawmill, which he built in 1881. Besides the impropriety of the province's action, operation of the cannery led to fights between the Kincolith and Greenville people over which of these Nishga groups would occupy the reserve.[52] The villages had been established in 1867 and 1872, respectively. Although Kincolith people claimed the right to Stoney Point (including the vital eulachon-fishing grounds at Fishery Bay), 10 or 12 families belonging to the Greenville village lived at Croasdaile's cannery for about one month during the fishing season and had potato patches there. On this basis, the Greenville people asserted a claim to the reserve. The government's solution had been to divide the reserve between the two groups. But in 1884 the cannery closed, the machinery was taken away, and the Greenville Indians left. As far as the Kincolith people were concerned, the Greenvilles could no longer claim part of the reserve.[53] This situation led to friction between the villages – even though the culprit, so to speak, Croasdaile's cannery, no longer operated.

At Port Simpson, the commissioners took testimony from Coast Tsimshian. They learned that 'land grabbers' – mainly cannery owners – were selling land that belonged to Indian people; unless the two levels of government changed the law, there would be endless trouble in the north. They heard: 'It is the same with the land everywhere, which the white people have everywhere, from here down to the Skeena, where canneries are – Mr. Williscraft's [sawmill], Mission Point, Inverness, Aberdeen, Essington, and other places.'[54] Traders had set up independent trading posts in the Skeena estuary, at Inverness (Woodcock's Landing) and Port Essington (Spokeshute), in the early 1870s. The first of the Skeena salmon canneries started up at Inverness in 1876, while Port Essington quickly became the major distribution point and salmon-canning headquarters for northern British Columbia.

The Metlakatla people requested that their ancient fishing stations on the Skeena, which were 'very useful' to them, be surveyed:

Q – 'Oh what part of the Skeena are [the fishing stations]?'

A – 'Near the mouth.'

Q – 'Do you know there are reserves at different places there?'

A – 'I know; but we want three more.'

Q – 'Mr. O'Reilly, in his report, says you got all you asked for.'

A – 'We are frightened to say what we want.'

Q – 'Speak out; don't be afraid.'

A – 'There are some white men's fishing camps near there, and we want our own secured for us. Their names are Kshaoom, about three miles [5 km] above Inverness, on the opposite side of the river – there are two little houses there now; Me-an-law, almost opposite Port Essington – there are Metlakatlan [sic] and Tsimpsean houses there; Kishneelt, a little above and opposite Port Essington. I wish to explain about Kshaoom: There is an open passage; we want a little on each side.'[55]

Apparently the commissioners acted on some of these complaints: O'Reilly allotted 'Kashaoom' reserve (2.25 ha) and 'Meanlaw' reserve (3 ha) jointly to the Tsimshian of Port Simpson and the Metlakatla in 1888.[56]

Fears about loss of access to resources such as those expressed by the Tsimshian had been reinforced by Canada's anti-potlatch laws (1884), which also threatened the traditional socioeconomic system of Pacific Coast Indians. Perhaps the award of additional fishing sites to Indians and the limited protection of an Indian food fishery provide for in the 1888 federal fishery regulations for British Columbia were responses to Indian demands for protection of their resource base. To all appearances, Indians were dying out; perhaps Canadian officials thought that food fish provisions were all that was necessary for the Pacific Coast groups.

Inventing the Indian Fishery

The Indian food-fishing regulation equated Indian fisheries strictly with subsistence harvesting: 'Indians shall, at all times, have liberty to fish for the purpose of providing food for themselves but not for sale, barter or traffic, by any means other than with drift nets [floating net that drifts freely with the tide or current], or spearing.'[57] This provision in theory capped production in the aboriginal fisheries in order to reserve supplies for the fishing industry. The idea was not original to British Columbia. As early as 1859, because of increasing pressure on the fish supply from non-Indian commercial fishers, the government of the Province of Canada interpreted Indian fishing rights as domestic-consumption fishing rights.[58] Unlike in the eastern parts of the country, however, Pacific Coast Indians were fish-based societies.

The Indian food-fishery regulation raised two separate but profound issues for Pacific Coast Indian societies. First, it separated Indian harvesting and personal consumption of fish from economic, social, or cultural purposes. As we have seen, the distinction between fishing for food and fishing for any other purpose was foreign to Indian culture and practice. Second, it separated production of resources from management of them, officially transferring all management of this crucial food and commercial resource from Indians to the state. The takeover was unilateral: there were no negotiations. And in the bargain, the state and the industry lost the fisheries expertise of Indian people. This early policy created, among other things, a lasting image of Pacific Coast Indians as simple subsistence people who were quite unlike the commerce-minded Euro-Canadians – a stereotype that, tragically, continues to be accepted in Canadian courts today.

How are these prohibitions against Indian economic activities and social practice to be explained? Creation and regulation of Indian food-fishing in British Columbia can be traced back to the province's pioneer canned-salmon industry. From the beginnings of salmon canning on the Fraser, cannery operators and non-Indian commercial fishers pressed the federal government and its local officers to curtail traditional Indian fishing practices in spawning rivers and creeks. In the early years, fisheries officials were sympathetic to the Indians. The new inspector of fisheries for British Columbia, Alex Anderson, argued against banning the traditional Indian fishery. He repeatedly stated that the Indian modes of fishing were 'simple but efficacious,' and recommended that there be no interference with them.[59] Anderson also advised that any regulations developed for the BC fishery not apply to Indians 'working to supply their wants in their accustomed way.'[60]

When the Fisheries Act came into force in the province in 1877, Anderson stipulated to his officers that, 'where fishing with white men and with modern appliances, the Indians so fishing should be considered as coming in all respects under the general law.'[61] But officers were not to interfere with the Indian population, 'save in cases of obvious abuse, while fishing for their own use in their accustomed way.'[62] Anderson seemed convinced that exercise of aboriginal fishing rights – fishing for other than strictly commercial purposes – could not be legally interfered with. He also feared stirring up trouble between Indians and settlers.

Anderson sought to protect Indian fishing interests until such time as the Indians won a settlement over land. His official reports in the late 1870s show that he expected the government to negotiate treaties, as the law required. When a cannery owner applied to lease the exclusive use of certain 'drifts' for the catching of salmon, Anderson recommended that the matter be put on hold in view of 'complications' connected with 'existing Indian rights,' and for other reasons.[63] He also recommended securing the Indians' hereditary rights in 'such small rivulets along the coast as have heretofore been used by them as fishing-stations, and on which they are largely dependent for subsistence.'[64]

Similar suggestions came from the Indian superintendent for the BC region, I.W. Powell, who wrote to the minister of fisheries that growth of salmon-canning made it essential that the province set aside certain fishing grounds for Indians.[65] Powell's three inspection tours of the North Coast, in 1873, 1879, and 1881, required back-up by a government gunboat to underscore the state's authority: in 1879, Tsimshian chiefs at Kitkatla had exerted their authority by confiscating the nets of a canning company when it trespassed on the village fisheries.[66] The Tsimshian people generally continued for the next century to show aggressive leadership in assertion of aboriginal rights, including joining in fishing disputes and attempts to unionize fishers in the north. They were a power for the state to reckon with.

Anderson drew the department's attention to the government's pamphlet on the Indian land question (1875), which contained copies of the Douglas Treaties. He pointed to the clause in each treaty that stipulated that the Indians in question would be at liberty to carry on their fisheries 'as formerly.' 'Formerly,' of course, Indians fished for subsistence, trade, and ceremonies, not just or even mainly for their own food. He concluded: 'Fourteen tribes, under distinct treaty, have their fishing rights thus indefeasibly [sic] secured to them; and the same right, though unexpressed in writing, has of necessity been understood, as settlement extended, to be secured to all the rest ... I earnestly repeat, therefore, my former recommendation, that the Indians of this Province be formally exempted, by Order in Council, from the application of the general fishery law. In this way their position will be publicly understood.'[67] Anderson knew about the fishery conflicts in northern waters and urged that nothing be done to encourage Indians 'to dispute with their white co-citizens a share in the copious sea riches with which nature has blessed our shores.'[68] In other words, he thought that there were plenty of fish for everyone.

But now, by the late 1880s, salmon canneries and other coastal businesses had spread, the non-Indian population grew, and Indian numbers declined both absolutely and in proportion to the total. Some reserve lands, as explained, had been set aside, but treaties still had not materialized. Nor would they. With completion of the transcontinental railway (1885) and the new mood of federal officials that favoured the interests of white settlers in the west, fisheries officials and cannery operators on the Fraser River soon launched serious attacks on the Indian fisheries. This began in 1886. With over 6,000 commercial fishers on the Fraser that season (double the figure of the previous year) and a dramatic increase in the number of canneries, over-fishing became evident. It was a poor-run year in the sockeye cycle, and Indian fishing in the headwaters was blamed.[69] Two years later, the fisheries department brought in the Indian food-fishing regulations.

The heart of the issue was competition between Indians and non-Indians for salmon. Yet competition was still limited in scope. In the pioneer industry, cannery operators did not yet can chum (or dog) salmon. They put up sockeye and threw back or gave to their Indian and Japanese workers to dry for their use incidentally caught chum. Chum was plentiful almost everywhere on the coast, and most tribes prized it for drying. The Indian reserve commissioner spoke to the 1887 Dominion Commission on North-West Coast Indians:

Q – 'For whom did you reserve Kinnamax, on Naas Straits?'
A – 'For the Naas tribe. There is a good fishery here for dog salmon; a fish in great demand among the Indians but worthless for canning purposes.'[70]

Because the chum fishery was a fall activity, Indians could fish or work for the canneries during summer and then return to their traditional waters. There, the men fished for fall salmon and the women harvested shellfish and berries, which they used as food, articles for winter feasts, trade items, and so on. This pattern would break down after 1900, once processors found markets for chum and the other, cheaper grades of salmon.

For Indians, the pioneer salmon-canning industry represented a new economic opportunity compatible with their traditional economic activities. But fisheries regulations of the late 1880s launched a new era in which management and use of salmon would move from their hands to state control. Thereafter, Indians' role in salmon-canning would decline in one area after another. Cannery operators on the Fraser soon replaced Indian family labour with Japanese. In plants located outside the Fraser River district, Indians would continue to dominate for some time to come. Although many Indian groups of the Pacific slope would seek to maintain their own fish-based economies, the Canadian state, through the fisheries department, would seek increasingly to limit Indian access to and use of fish.

4 Indian Labour Captured, 1889–1918

After 1888, the business of fishing and fish-processing in British Columbia passed through a long period of intense structural change and growth, with production continuing to soar well into the 1920s. Along the way, the province's ocean fishing ground became among the most productive and heavily regulated for its size in the world, and by 1905, the BC fishery ranked first in Canada. Every aspect of the industrial salmon fishery, including the processing sector, came under heavy regulation. The industrial harvest was increased after 1900 by both more intense fishing in areas currently used and the finding of a market for all species of salmon, which permitted exploitation of 'virgin' fishing grounds and expansion to a range of gear types. Logging, mining, and railway construction threatened to inhibit expansion of the industrial fishery. During the First World War, the salmon fishery in the most significant salmon-canning district, the Fraser River, fell into long-term decline when rock slides caused by railway construction at Hell's Gate, a rocky gorge in the Fraser Canyon, destroyed major interior runs of sockeye and pink salmon.

Ottawa and Victoria tried in vain to keep up with all these changes. They convened several fisheries commissions to decide on limiting such factors as the number of fishers, the type and amount of gear and boats, and the number of processors in the industry. The Department of Fisheries undertook 'improvements' of salmon rivers and construction of salmon hatcheries. The Northern and Vancouver Island districts received special treatment. Restrictions and enforcement of them generally became more severe over the period, although the rules were slackened to meet European wartime demand, as well as political concerns of other government departments and agencies in Canada.

By the turn of the twentieth century, Indians made up only a small proportion of the total BC population, about 14 per cent, dropping to only about 5 per cent by 1911.[1] As both the salmon-canning industry and the non-Indian population grew and spread along the coast, Indians ceased to be the sole source of industrial fish supplies. In the Fraser River district, fishers and cannery workers of Japanese origin came to dominate after 1900. Most cannery operators preferred Japanese for fishing; they were supposedly the most dependable and cooperative. As a matter of industry and government policy, and under pressure from Indian communities, Indian agents, and missionaries, Indians stayed heavily involved in the other cannery districts. The majority fished under cannery contracts. New regulations for the industrial fishery tended to protect this type of Indian participation on behalf of the processing sector. Simultaneously, under the prompting of the fishing industry and European settlers, the fisheries department's policy and enforcement shifted from loose interpretation of Indian food-fishing to strict control and curtailment, and Indians' access to traditional fishing sites and technology declined. By the end of the First World War, senior federal officials talked of ending Indian food-fishing privileges altogether. The state had invented the concept of an Indian food fishery in 1888, and the state's definition of what constituted 'subsistence' became ever narrower as the Canadian process of criminalizing aboriginal resource activities evolved.

'PROTECTING THIS VALUABLE INDUSTRY'

Between 1889 and 1914, in a period of world-wide economic boom, cannery operations spread to every corner of the Northwest Coast.[2] As early as 1905, half of the salmon-canning sites ever established in British Columbia had already been developed, although, as can be seen in Table 2, no canneries would be built in one region, the Queen Charlotte Islands, until 1911. With export markets still the focus of production and the United Kingdom the main market for the sockeye pack, salmon-canning expanded into production of the lower-grade (non-sockeye) species, for which foreign customers had to be found.

TABLE 2
Chronology of BC salmon-cannery districts by year of initial site development,
1871–1966

| Location | | Year of cannery construction | | |
District/region	Area	First year	Final year	Total sites
Fraser	Fraser River	1871	1965	74
	Vancouver	1901	1956	14
Skeena	Skeena River	1876	1929	20
	Prince Rupert	1882	1960	9
Naas River		1881	1918	12
Central	Rivers Inlet	1882	1932	14
Coast	Northern outlying	1890	1927	11
	Southern outlying	1890	1928	8
	Smith Inlet	1883	1929	5
Vancouver	East coast	1881	1966	21
Island	West coast	1895	1934	19
Queen Charlotte Islands		1911	1958	16
Total				223

Source: Dianne Newell, 'Dispersal and Concentration: The Slowly Changing Spatial Pattern of the British Columbia Salmon Canning Industry,' *Journal of Historical Geography* 14 no. 1 (1988) 29.
Note: The Port Simpson Cannery, Nass River, 1974, packed salmon only one season, and so has not been included.

By 1911, the combined pack of pink and chum salmon outstripped that of sockeye. This growth is all the more impressive, given government and cannery operators' control of fishing in this period. Limitation of licences started in the 1890s in the original district, the Fraser, where it quickly failed, and in the 1910s in the rising Northern district. (See Figure 7 on the canned-salmon pack from 1903 to 1967.)

Ottawa based its policies and regulations on a biological-conservation argument known as 'maximum sustained yield,' which in government circles remained popular until after the Second World War. The idea was that enough spawners had to escape the fishers each year to replenish stocks; what constituted 'sufficient' would vary by species and habitat.

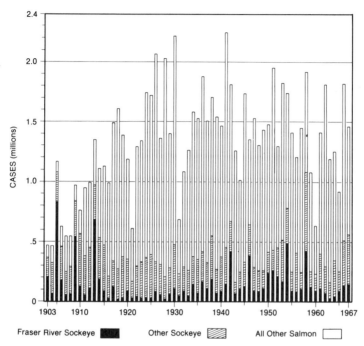

Figure 7 BC canned-salmon pack (sockeye/other), by area (Fraser/other), 1903–67. One case weighs 48 lb., or 22 kg. *Source:* Cicely Lyons, *Salmon: Our Heritage* (1969), 719–20.

The Fraser

The 1888 Fisheries Regulations for British Columbia, which had introduced licensing, had also anticipated the next round of regulations by reserving for the minister the right to decide the number of boats, seines, or nets to be fished annually in the province.[3] In 1889, 'phenomenal runs' and wholesale expansion of canning activities occurred on the Fraser and in the northern sockeye areas. The cannery operators were anxious to keep out competition for salmon – whether from new operations or from the growing numbers of independent fishers, mostly whites, attracted to the industry by the fresh- and frozen-fish trade. The independents created pressures for competitive prices. So, for the first time in the provincial fishery, a specific limit of 500 licences was imposed for the Fraser River district, in

1890; a small number went to independent fishers and fish-freezers, but most went to salmon canners.[4] The climate of crisis, conflict, and expansion that followed forced Ottawa to dispatch Samuel Wilmot, dominion superintendent of fish culture, to resolve the issues.[5]

Cannery owners pleaded with Wilmot to stabilize the regulations: 'From year to year we are in jeopardy – don't know the number of licences we will get, five, ten, or forty. It was varied in '89 – some had forty, some eighteen, and so on according to the previous pack – the number was different. Last year, for instance, we had to order our material in October and the regulations for fishing were adopted in May, and that, I contend, was not giving our industry fair play, and the sooner it is settled the better.'[6] Licence-limitation, as Wilmot would discover, posed a serious political problem. White fishers resented any denial of access to what was, at least within British tradition, a common-access resource.

Wilmot also discovered that licence-limitation did not even guarantee that enough salmon would get to the spawning grounds each year.[7] Rather than reducing the amount of fishing, the policy simply led to a boom in new construction by cannery operators who wanted to get additional fishing licences. The number of canneries on the Fraser rose from 12 to 18, or by 50 per cent, between 1888 and 1891, and that figure would triple over the next decade, even though markets for the product were not secure. So, this first experiment with licence-limitation on the Pacific Coast created a spiral of demand and conflict that quickly forced the government to return to unlimited licensing and canning-company control of the fishing sector.

On the basis of the 1892 recommendations of the Wilmot Commission, the government issued regulations for British Columbia that covered licensing of fishers', type of gear, and areas of and periods for fishing.[8] There would be no limit on the number of licences issued, but in a move to please the white fishers and Indian agents, who objected to competition from Japanese and Americans fishing in BC waters, only British subjects would qualify. Also, canneries now had to submit lists of their 'attached' fishers to fisheries officers, who issued them permits. By 1893, there were 1,174 boats fishing on the Fraser, and cannery operators owned 909 of them. A newly formed union of fishers struck for better prices that season, and the chaos and uncertainty continued.

British Columbia was not the only part of the country having problems with federal fisheries policies and regulations. Licence-limitation failed in the Maritime provinces as well. On both coasts, the goal of developing what officials referred to as an 'acceptable allocation mechanism' proved elusive.[9] By the turn of the century, the dominion commissioner of fisheries, E.E. Prince, would criticize the government's hasty formulation of regulations for the whole of Canada. Overlapping, inconsistencies, and absolute self-contradictions occurred, and no fewer that 309 orders in council embodying new fishery regulations were issued between 1890 and 1901.[10]

Two resource economists, Anthony Scott and Philip Neher, have recently suggested that, after failure of this first experiment with licence-limitation, the state used licensing mainly to identify fishers for statistical purposes in the salmon fishery and other fisheries as they, too, came under licensing; conservation policy rested increasingly on restrictions regarding time, area, size, and gear.[11] But their assessment is not accurate, as will be seen. Licensing would continue to be a way of legally controlling who would get fish – and who would not.

The Staggering Growth of Salmon-Canning

The boom began in 1895, when BC salmon became the most profitable fishery in Canada. Growth of the processing industry proceeded at a reckless pace, with 22.25 million kg of salmon being canned at mid-decade.[12] The Fraser River district set the trend, but its four-year cycle for sockeye runs was the most pronounced on the coast. In the largest 'big-run' years ever recorded for Fraser River sockeye – 1897, 1901, 1905, 1909, and 1913 – the district pack averaged 798,700 (22–kg) cases whereas the average for the smallest-run years in the cycle – 1898, 1902, 1906, 1910, and 1914 – was only 216,240 cases, a fall-off of roughly 75 per cent.[13]

The Fraser's all-time big-run year for sockeye was 1901. By then, 49 cannery camp–villages dotted the river banks from New Westminster, where many of the first plants had been built, to where the south and north arms of the Fraser empty into the Strait of Georgia. The previous year had witnessed a major fishers' strike that ended in armed confrontation and a three-way conflict among Japanese, Indian, and white fishers.[14] In anticipation of the next 'big' year, 1905, nearly half of the BC cannery operations consolidated to form a new monopolistic company, BC Packers Association, and the industry staked out new cannery sites in the untapped outlying areas.[15] Pow-

erful new regional associations of cannery operators and fishers' unions and organizations developed. Through voluntary limits on the
number of boats to be fished ('boat rating') in each region, cannery
operators attempted self-regulation of competition for supplies. The
voluntary arrangements collapsed during the mad scramble in the
'big-run' year, 1905.

Until about 1905, overseas markets for canned salmon were
strictly for sockeye. Some chum salmon was canned in 1900 (between 90,000 and 100,000 cases), and also pink salmon (7,000 cases)
in the previous year – but simply, the fisheries department admitted,
to make up for 'failure' of the sockeye and cohoe runs.[16] Also, the
Japanese produced and exported salted chum (and herring) to China
and Yukon gold-fields. This involved a small-scale purse-seine fishery and initially took place only in the Fraser River district.[17]

Then a major shift deepened the social, economic, and geographical impact of the salmon-canning industry on Indians. Beginning about 1905, the industry found permanent markets for canned
pink and chum. Demand for a broader range of products led to
longer seasons for canning operations, proliferation of plants in older
areas, and expansion of canning into new regions, such as the Queen
Charlottes, where pink salmon abounded. The abundance of chum
on the west coast of Vancouver Island led to considerable cannery
construction there. The salmon-cannery camps of British Columbia
also became major centres for processing (by freezing, canning, smoking, pickling, drying, and mild curing) other types of ocean fish,
including shellfish, once these also became economically marketable.
More workers were needed for plants than ever before. Mechanization of parts of the salmon-canning process had begun, but hand
work was still important, especially in the Northern and Vancouver
Island districts. BC salmon-canning remained remarkably labour-
intensive until well after the First World War.[18]

Like salmon-canning, salmon-fishing also stayed labour-inten-
sive. As long as canning was the main method of processing the
catch, and sockeye the most valuable species for canning, gillnetting
was standard for industrial salmon-fishing. Gillnetting had been a
localized, two-person operation; it spread once canners began operating powered collecting boats between the fishing fleet and the plants.
Because it is possible to regulate depth and mesh sizes of nets, gillnets
are highly selective between species and among sizes of individual
fish in a given run, and so they are conservationally sound. Indians

and Japanese specialized in gillnetting. By 1903, in response to expansion of the industry into catching a greater variety of salmon and other types of fish, purse seining (for herring and chum salmon) required a licence. Whites controlled this branch of fishing.

Trolling became common toward the end of this period; unlike gillnet fishers, troll fishers usually were independent sellers, not under the control of processors. A boat in motion drags weighted lines with baited hooks and lures. Since they did not suffer ugly net gashes, blackened scales, or softened flesh, troll-caught salmon (spring and cohoe) commanded high prices in the fresh- and frozen-fish and mild-cured trades. Hand-trolling with a single line from row-boats had started on a small scale before 1900, but the rise in cold-storage operations about 1910 led to trolling with larger, powered boats rigged with poles and lines of cotton and linen. Japanese specialized in trolling, in addition to gillnetting. Trolling came under licensing in 1917.[19]

Restricting the Northern District

In 1905, when the Fraser River sockeye pack still set the standard for the entire industry, the canneries had their most successful year to that date. Canning capacity had increased dramatically. Only the relative scarcity of labour and fish slowed things down. The government decided that it was time for major expansion of the scope of BC fisheries regulations. Accordingly, the dominion commissioner, E.E. Prince, headed a commission to look into the state of BC fisheries. Focusing on current licensing and leasing arrangements, the halibut and herring fisheries, and international competition for Fraser River sockeye, the Prince Commission worked from 1905 to 1907.[20] Canada also toyed with the idea of closing the Fraser to fishing, something that independent fishers and operators of small canning businesses successfully fought.

Out of the Prince Commission came a revised code of regulations designed to curtail construction of additional salmon canneries, limit licences on fishing in northern waters, and improve salmon rivers. The first step was the 1908 federal requirement that all salmon canneries and salmon-curing establishments obtain operating licences.[21] Apparently, northern cannery managers regarded restrictions on new canneries as promoting cold-storage operations, which may well have been true.[22] Limiting the number of canneries and

TABLE 3
Drag-seine licences issued in British Columbia, 1915–16

	1915	1916
ABC Packing Co. Ltd	10	10
BC Fisheries Ltd	6	6
BC Packers Assn	21	22
BC Canning Co.	1	1
Canadian Fish & Cold Storage Co.		1
Clayoquot Sound Canning Co.	1	2
M. Des Brisay and Co.	4	0
Draney Fisheries Ltd	6	6
Gosse-Millerd Packing Co.	9	12
Johnston, R.G.	1	0
Metlakatla Indians (c/o C. Perry, Indian Agent)		1
Robertson, Gilbert	1	1
Todd & Sons, J.H.	4	1
Total	64	63

Source: British Columbia Archives and Records Service (BCARS), GR 435, BC Department of Fisheries, box 97, file 957, 1915–16, untitled report; file 958, 1915–16, Drag Seine Tax Receipts, 1915 and 1916.

attaching all vessel licences to cannery operations constituted the only way to restrict fishing in the north. Unlike in the south, cannery operators in the north already controlled the industrial fleet, which was composed mainly of Indians and some Japanese. Independent fishers were rare.[23]

The Dominion–British Columbia Boat-Rating Commission sat in 1910 to consider formal allocation of fishing licences to canneries in the interests of conservation. The result was that no independent salmon-fishing licences would be issued for the north: all fishing licences would be attached to cannery operations. Limits were placed on the numbers of licences for boats and drag and purse seines issued to each cannery and curing plant in the province.[24] The minister ruled that no one could receive a seine licence unless that person built or owned a cannery, a policy that kept seine fishing in the hands of whites; Table 3 lists drag-seine licences for 1915–16.

From the spring of 1911 (effectively until the 1924 season), regulations banned use of 'a motor boat or a boat propelled otherwise than by oars or sails' in salmon-fishing in the Northern district.[25] This was amended in 1912–13 to apply only to gillnet boats.

What appeared on the statute books does not, however, tell the whole story, for the fisheries department itself did not stick to the principles of limited entry. Wartime demand was a factor, to be sure, but even before the war, major exceptions had been made. Federal policy required that the number of fishing licences for each area remain the same each year. This did not happen. Under pressure from major cannery operators, the Department of Fisheries licensed ten new canneries in the period 1910–17 and increased the number of fishing licences accordingly.[26] And in the 1912–13 season, it gave in to pressure from the province to grant 'exceptional privileges' for white settlers in the north by reserving a certain percentage of fishing licences for white fishers who were British subjects owning their own boats and nets.[27] This plan was not particularly successful.[28] During the war, the fisheries department actually tried to abandon its restrictive policy for the northern salmon fishery, but, on the advice of a federal inquiry into the fishery of the Northern district in 1917 (the Evans Commission), stopped this proposal in its tracks for another five years.[29] Ultimately, destruction of the big Fraser River sockeye and pink salmon runs in 1913 and 1914 by railway construction at Hell's Gate (with damage not apparent in the case of sockeye until 1917) permanently increased the canning industry's demand for salmon on the other fishing grounds.

IMPLICATIONS FOR INDIANS

'White People Would Not Do This'

Perhaps at no time were the inconsistencies and shifts in fisheries regulations and their enforcement more noticeable than when Indians were involved. Although officially they were to compete on an equal footing with non-Indians in the industrial fishery, Indians were in such demand in salmon-canning that the government usually created regulations and policies to guarantee their labour in areas and years of high demand. A quite blatant example surfaced in the 1890s. After introduction of fishing licences, most Indian fishers neglected or refused to pay for them.[30] And Indians without licences routinely sold salmon to fishers on licenced vessels, which was, strictly speaking, illegal. The Indians themselves explained why they paid little or no attention to the licence requirements.[31] For one thing, they considered harvesting of salmon their traditional right and so were offended at the idea of having to pay for the privilege. (Similarly, Indians in the BC interior took the view that grazing their cattle on crown range was an inherent right, and some refused to pay the grazing fees involved.)[32] For Indians who lived outside the lower mainland, applying for a fishing licence also was impractical. Licensing officers were located hundreds of kilometres away, at New Westminster. Cannery operators were at first only too willing to apply and pay for fishing licences under Indian fishers' names.[33]

The special arrangements for Indian fishers should be seen within the context of the high value that cannery operators placed on Indian village and family labour as a whole. By their own admission, canners paid the token fee for the Indian licences to persuade enough Indian women, men, and children to work in their plants.[34] Cannery owner Marshall English went right to the point at the Wilmot Commission's hearings in the early 1890s: 'These [Indians] come from all parts of the country and bring all their belongings and fish for five or six weeks and then go home again – white people would not do this.'[35] He meant that white settlers were dependent on local, full-time work – something that cannery operators could not provide until well after the Second World War.

In this context, the new fishery regulations for 1900, which created a special cannery licence for Indian fishers and exempted Indian boat-pullers from the new requirement to hold a licence, make sense. Clauses 3 and 8 pertained to Indians: Clause 3 reads in part: Indians shall be exempt from registration or enrollment, required under clause 1 and this clause. Each firm, company or person engaged in the canning of salmon shall be entitled to ten fishing licences in the said firm's company's or person's name, and each of such licences shall be valid for and used only by a fisherman whose name is duly registered, or shall be valid for and used only by an Indian.' According to clause 8, 'No one except an Indian shall be engaged or employed as a boat puller or boatman on any boat engaged in salmon fishing operations under license, unless he holds a boat-puller's permit.'[36] Many Indian boat-pullers were female relatives of the fishers, although cannery operators discouraged the practice when they could; they preferred to have the women working in the plants.

For many, probably most, Indian fishers the informal arrangement of fishing for the canneries under cannery ('attached') licences for low daily wages with their own vessels or company-owned ones was acceptable.[37] But some Indians in the lower mainland wanted independent licences. Of the over 3,000 Indians fishing on the Fraser in 1892, only 40 individuals had independent licences and could negotiate a price for salmon. The independent licences belonged apparently to members of only few of Indian bands, all from the Fraser River area. This caused a certain amount of inter-village rivalry, especially because the federal fisheries inspector, by his own admission, routinely rejected applications for independent licences from Indians who lived outside the Fraser valley.[38] Through a witness who was an Indian agent, Indian fishers requested that 100 independent licences be set aside for them.[39] When Wilmot commissioners asked Marshall English about the wisdom of this, his answer suggests that cannery operators objected to the economic independence that Indians might gain under such a scheme.[40] The commission's report was silent on the granting or reserving of independent fishing licences for Indians. It was only the first of a long line of commissions that would look at but fail to deal adequately with Indian participation in the fishing industry.

By getting government to issue the bulk of fishing licences to canneries, by making it easier for Indians than for other fishers to fish for them, cannery operators assured Indians' participation in the industry for decades to come. Many Indians owned boats and nets and could have operated under independent licences. Licensing and regulation had thus served to capture Indian labour for the white-owned industry at a time when labour was scarce. But Indians became involved under a scheme that paid them for their labour, not for the sale of their resources, as some government officials would later imply. Corralling Indian labour for the white-owned industry, along with other measures such as banning use of the highly productive Indian fishing technologies, eventually undermined Indians' ability to continue their ancient entrepreneurial traditions on their own terms.

Not surprising, Indians who fished or worked for the fish plants continued to enjoy certain benefits. In 1891, the head of the Williams Lake Indian Agency explained that some of the Nequatqua (Anderson Lake) Band 'proceed every summer to New Westminster to work in the salmon canneries, and earn enough to keep themselves and families in comfort during the winter.'[41] In good years, apparently, Indian fishers earned from $600 to $1,100 in six weeks, at least according to Indian agents.[42] However, unpredictably heavy runs would cause cannery operators to turn away Indian fishers. This happened in

1901 and again in 1905, when insufficient processing capacity forced operators to limit the number of fish that they could accept daily from boats and to reduce the number of contract boats fishing for them.

When salmon runs were poor or markets for canned salmon depressed, many canneries did not operate for a season or more. So fewer Indians found work in those years. This situation could result in major short-term problems for those Indian groups that relied on some income from fishing and fish-processing. Examples are plentiful. When salmon-fishing on Nootka Sound failed in 1897, the new, single cannery there (West Coast Packing) sat idle, never to re-open. This, in combination with a crisis in the community seal hunt, led to suffering within the local Indian community.[43] The Indian agent reported the next year that Indians on the west coast of Vancouver Island had built little for themselves that year, because of 'an unusual lack of money through a partial failure of the salmon catch of last year at Rivers Inlet and Skeena River.'[44] As a result of the scarcity of salmon on the Fraser in the 1904 season (a 'bad-run' year), most of the Indians there 'did not earn more than would pay the advances received by them from the canners, and in fact some went away in debt to the canneries.'[45] The economic recession of 1907, which coincided with a low year in the four-year sockeye cycle for Fraser runs, hurt Indian economies throughout the coastal area.

As usual, Indians were resourceful. To the extent that they could, they spread their risks. Many preferred to fish and work at local canneries when and if they operated, but their choices depended entirely on the Indian group itself and on the local demand. As late as 1900, Indian families still travelled to the Fraser River canneries from all over the coast in magnificent flotillas of great canoes.[46]

Indian recruiters were typically men of high rank, such as Billy Assu, a renowned Indian leader of the Lekwiltok tribe, at the Southern Kwakiutl Indian village of Cape Mudge (the major settlement of the We-Wai-Kai Band).[47] He recruited for the local cannery at Quathiaski Cove, hiring fishers and plant workers, taking care of their living arrangements, and representing their rights in any dispute.

Another Southern Kwakiutl Indian leader, Charles Nowell, recruited for the Rivers Inlet cannery from 1905 to the 1920s. His job may well have been more comprehensive than usual. He lined up fishers and cannery workers before the season, gave notice of prices and contracts, negotiated with the owners for cash advances and other incentives for Indian crews, and even supervised the work of the Indian women fillers whom he had hired. In addition to receiving bonuses for recruiting and wages for supervision, a good recruiter like Nowell could expect a number of perks. In exchange for hiring Indian men and women for the Brunswick cannery (Rivers Inlet), for example, Nowell received the lumber to build his house at Alert Bay from the canning company, BC Packers, and travelled on Canadian Pacific Railway (CPR) boats free of charge.[48] Cannery operators also dealt directly with Indian agents, asking them to rustle up extra fishers or cannery workers at the last minute, to collect debts owed to the canneries by specific Indians, and so forth.[49]

As in earlier years, Indians from a given village did not necessarily work for the same cannery or even for a single company. Three firms operated the dozen or so plants at Rivers Inlet in the 1903 and 1904 seasons (see Table 4).[50] The Kitamaat Indians fished for a single company. Indians from Alert Bay, Bella Bella, and China Hat fished for two of them. The local O-wee-kay-no (or Oowekeeno) Village people fished for all three outfits. Meanwhile, an ancestral group called Kitka'ata, from the new village of Hartley Bay, migrated to three areas during canning season – the Lowe Inlet cannery (built 1890), located nearby; Standard cannery (1890), on the Skeena; and Wadhams cannery (1897), in Rivers Inlet.[51] Apparently the Cape Mudge villagers fished and worked exclusively for the local cannery at Quathiaski Cove, once it opened in about 1903. Yet the crews at this cannery also included other Indians from a wider region, from Campbell River, Comox, Ladysmith, and Salmon River; most were relatives of Cape Mudge people.[52] Most of the Indians from the Kwawkewlth Agency preferred working for the Rivers Inlet canneries, although Indian agents tell us that many were employed by the Fraser River plants and in some years, such as 1899, did much better than those who went to Rivers Inlet.[53] Clearly, no single labour pattern emerges for specific Indian bands, canning areas, or time periods.

The complexities of labour strategies in this industry can even be detected across the life-cycle of individuals. Agnes Alfred ('Axu'), a Kwakiutl woman born in 1889 in the Alert Bay area, spent 50 seasons in coastal salmon canneries. An interview with her in 1984 reveals that she started as a child at the Brunswick cannery, Rivers Inlet, about 1900.[54] She and her family soon had worked at every cannery on that inlet and also at canneries on Lowe and Knight inlets and at Kimsquit. She recalls: 'A lot of people went to Knight's

TABLE 4
Impact of voluntary boat ratings at Rivers Inlet, 1903 and 1904, on fishers, by race

| | No. of boats allotted | |
	Fishers	Company totals
BC Packers Assn		
Alert Bay Indians	70	
China Hat Indians	10	
Kingcome Indians	103	258
O-wee-kay-no [sic] Indians	5	
Whites	70	
BC Canning Co., Ltd		
Alert Bay Indians	12	
Bella Bella Indians	13	
Kitamaat Indians	25	
O-wee-kay-no Indians	12	114
Japanese	30	
Whites	22	
ABC Packing Co., Ltd		
Bella Bella Indians	25	
China Hat Indians	4	
Nox Indians	5	
O-wee-kay-no Indians	3	76
Japanese	6	
Whites	33	

Source: John C. Prichard, 'Economic Development and the Disintegration of Traditional Culture among the Haisla,' PhD dissertation, University of British Columbia, 1977, 85.

Inlet from our people and all other tribes ... The Squamish used to go too.' There were many Bella Bella people with them at Kildala cannery, and Haida and Bella Coola people worked with them at Kimsquit. Local Indians from Kimsquit Village resented these outside groups, although normally, she says, the Indian women looked on canneries as offering a chance to meet Indians from other tribes. She remembers that the companies sent coastal steamers to pick up families in her area and deliver them to the Rivers Inlet canneries. It was an event for the whole community: 'For days at a time our belongings would be piled on the wharf because we never knew when the steamship was going to come in.'

Haida were in great demand as fishers and plant workers. No cannery operated in the Queen Charlottes until 1911, and so in the early years the Haida fished and worked for plants on the Fraser and later for plants on Rivers Inlet, the Nass and Skeena rivers, and in southern Alaska.[55] Florence Davidson tells wonderful stories about her family and the fisheries.[56] In the 1890s, her grandmother, Amy Edenshaw, and step-grandfather, Philip White, were employed at Rivers Inlet, as were most other Masset Haida. A little later, her mother, Isabella Edenshaw, worked at the salteries and canneries at Ketchikan and New Kassan, Alaska, and at Inverness cannery on the Skeena. Her father, Charles Edenshaw, who became famous for his art, usually went along to keep her mother company; he passed his time carving.

It had not at first been easy for Haida to work in the Skeena River area; there, they faced the Tsimshian, with whom the Skeena River cannery operators were better acquainted. As one Haida fisher said, 'In those days the mainland Indians were being assigned all the skiffs and got higher wages as boat pullers.'[57] Skeena cannery operators also recruited from Indian villages up river as far as Kitwanga, Kitsegukla, and Hazelton, and from elsewhere on the North Coast, from Nass River villages, Port Simpson, and Kitamaat.[58] Instrumental in getting cannery jobs for Masset Haida was the local Indian recruiter, Alfred Adams, who later founded the Native Brotherhood of BC. Adams negotiated with some of the Skeena River canneries to set aside boats and housing units for Masset fishers and shoreworkers, thereby breaking the monopoly held by the Tsimshian. He also took Masset to Rivers Inlet canneries, in an attempt to get more money and better conditions for them.[59] The Haida developed preferences among the Skeena plants: the Masset villagers used to go mainly to Carlisle (built 1896) and Oceanic (1903), and the Skidegates to Claxton (1892).[60]

When the first cannery was built on the Queen Charlottes in 1911, at Naden Harbour, Adams arranged for the owners to hire every able-bodied person in Masset 'for a better wage than they had ever been able to command on the mainland.'[61] Even after the opening of this and over a dozen other canneries on the islands, Haida would head for the Skeena during the more lucrative sockeye season there and return to their local plants for the pink season, which began later. In some years, the two fisheries overlapped, leaving Queen Charlotte operations complaining about lack of fishers, and hence of fish to process.

The operators had their Indian labour strategies too. When the Smith Inlet cannery opened in 1902, the owner negotiated a special arrangement with the Indians of Quashela for a dependable supply of local labour. He promised that he would bring in no 'outside Indians.'[62] Henry Doyle, founder and first general manager of BC Packers Association, made a similar deal with local Indians when he contemplated building a cannery on reserve land (belonging to Kincolith people) on Observatory Inlet. Since the bulk of the community fished for another operator, Doyle hoped to secure a steady supply of labour while crippling the competitior's operations.[63]

Few newcomers consulted local Indians when they staked cannery lands or fished in tribal fishing grounds. Of his northern trip in November 1902, Doyle wrote: 'There was an Indian hut on the property [at the end of Way Point, Observatory Inlet], which, while vacant, probably denotes that the place is an Indian reserve, but, being unable to find any posts, we applied for the foreshore and land in the name of A.V. Darling.'[64] Doyle found a nice site on Observatory Inlet, at Salmon Cove. It was an Indian reservation and 'so could not be staked;' another good site nearby was 'probably an Indian reserve, but as no posts could be found we staked it for both land and foreshore in the name of F.M. English.'[65] In this decade, the Pacific Coast was awash with land speculators scouting out potential logging and mining properties, and so Doyle's fairly casual attitude towards Indian lands and resources was probably typical.

Occasional preferential local treatment did not stop Indian fishers and their families from initiating or joining strikes in the chaotic period around the turn of the century. The first fishers' strike, on the Fraser in 1893, included Indians from the north; northern Indian fishers and female cannery workers struck the Skeena in 1894 and the Nass and Skeena rivers in 1896 and 1897 and again in 1904; and Indian fishers joined the massive strike that closed the industry on the Fraser in 1900.[66] The 1904 fishing strikes were the most determined of the northern walkouts to that point; 800 Indian fishers and 200 Indian female cannery workers, unaffiliated with any union, led the strikes on the Skeena just as the sockeye runs began.[67] The Japanese fishers at first joined the strike but eventually gave in to pressure from the cannery operators – much to the disgust of the Indian strikers. On other occasions, the tables would be turned.

Cannery owners attempted to do away with competition for fishers and plant workers, agreeing voluntarily not to 'steal' Indians from other canneries by offering higher wages, better piece rates, and so on. Such agreements were much easier to arrange once the majority of cannery operations came under the control of fewer companies in the twentieth century. Henry Doyle's 1902 letter to Henry Bell-Irving about carving up the Indian work-force indicates that cannery operators viewed Indian labour as simply one more commodity:

> The canneries that in the past two years have had the services of certain tribes are to be left in undisputed possession of such tribes to the same extent that they have enjoyed in the past. That is to say, that in case they have had the exclusive control over any particular tribe, they are to continue to enjoy same. But, where one concern has three-fourths of one tribe, and another the other fourth, the relative proportions should be maintained. Thus, your having the Bella Bella Indians, and messrs. Findlay, Durham & Brodie having the Kitimatts [sic], you would continue to have those, without any attempt on our part to try and induce, or accept, the services of members of those tribes to fish for us; you treating our fishers in the same manner.[68]

Indians resisted such policies, just as they did in the sealing industry, but most of them were already obliged to fish for specific cannery operations because of the cash advances received at the end of the previous fishing season and guarantees of plant jobs for their families. The operators did not hesitate to call on Indian agents to remind delinquent Indians under their jurisdiction of their debts and obligations.

After 1900, however, Indians faced new obstacles in the industrial fishery. With BC Indians still declining in numbers and being swamped by waves of newcomers, Indian fishers had to struggle to maintain their position vis-à-vis Japanese and other fishers, especially on the Fraser River and Vancouver Island. The Japanese originally arrived as sojourners, but in order to remain in the fishery, they took out naturalization papers. They settled as families in new fishing communities such as Steveston, on the Fraser, and at Clayoquot, Tofino, and Ucluelet, on the west coast of Vancouver Island. Because they concentrated on a single enterprise – fishing – the Japanese quickly made inroads in this industry.

As witness after witness testified to Canada's Commission on the Salmon Fishing Industry in British Columbia, 1902, cannery operators obviously preferred Japanese fishers over Indians and whites.

Asked by the commissioners, 'What makes the canner love the Japs so much?,' a white fisher from Vancouver, Theodore Demes, replied, 'They think that the fishers there are the better for them.'[69] 'I suppose the fishers think something should be done about Japs?' was the next question. 'Yes,' was Demes's stony reply. When the same commissioners asked a Skeena River cannery owner, John Wallace, whether he employed 'white-men' to fish with his 74 boats, he answered, 'No, we had to use Japs ... We could not rely [completely] on the Indians and the trouble with the white-men is that they would want to leave at the end of July and go down to the Fraser and so make two seasons.'[70] A rival of Wallace's, Charlie Todd, confirmed the observation that Indians were becoming 'less reliable' and, like others who testified, said that unlike the Japanese, Indians and whites would not travel as far out to sea, or on bad days, or at night (in the case of the Indians). Indians are 'short-sighted and unreasonable,' said Todd: 'Even after their advances have been made they come down late, giving excuses that their hay took their time, or something like that.'[71] Indians would not arrive when there was a strike, he added. For the white fishers, neither Japanese nor Indians were considered reliable allies for strikes. Nor could Indians count on the support of Japanese during the northern fishing strikes led by Indians. There was no big, happy family of BC commercial fishers, then as now.

What developed in the industrial fishery was a racial hierarchy of labour, with Japanese and Indians battling to avoid last place. Gillian Creese's valuable study of class, ethnicity, and conflict in British Columbia posits that the province's ethnically segmented labour market resulted from a combination of factors: intra-class conflict between groups of workers with unequal economic, political, and cultural resources; capitalist employment practices (which find ethnic cleavages useful for controlling workers); and the state's racist immigration policies.[72] She focused on the conflicts among Chinese and Japanese immigrants and 'Euro-Canadians.' In the BC fishing industry, however, the 'ethnic' labour of BC Indians must also be taken into account.

Officials from Indian Affairs actively supported Indians in their struggle against displacement in the industry by the Japanese. Indian agents complained constantly in their annual reports and testimonies before inquiries that Japanese competition made fishing unprofitable for their wards. Officials in both Indian Affairs and the Department of Fisheries agreed that Indians should be given preference over Japanese. For the Canadian government, it was a practical issue of keeping Indians off welfare. Evidence presented by the former dominion commissioner of labour, E.P. Bremner, before the 1902 Commission on the Salmon Fishing Industry, to give but one example, suggested that if Japanese were to replace the 800 to 1,000 licensed Indian fishers, 'in all, including women and children, about 10,000 Indians would be affected ... and if deprived of it would have to be fed from the public purse.'[73] While the figures quoted may have been exaggerated, the racial tension and conflict were not.

Many cannery operators clearly favoured Japanese fishers. Japanese took the greatest risks and came from a maritime fishing tradition and were thus highly productive. And because of their inferior political status in Canada, they were less independent, and so more manoeuvrable, than Indian or white fishers. Federal annual reports on fishing show that the Japanese became the largest single group of fishers on the Fraser and that, unlike Indian people, they tended to make a full-time living out of fishing. In 1883, Indians made up a majority of the 3,000 persons fishing for the canneries. By 1913, Indian fishers were a minority in the Fraser district: of the 2,350 licences issued, 1,088 went to Japanese, 832 to whites, and only 430 to Indians.[74] In the Rivers Inlet salmon-canning area, the overall majority of fishers was Indian, but Japanese came a close second, and there were many whites too.[75] Japanese fishers actually outnumbered Indians and whites at two of the canneries, Kildala and Good Hope.

On the Fraser River, Japanese women were replacing Indian women on the canning lines. One white fisher testified to the 1902 commission that Indian women refused to process salmon except from Indians if ever fishing licences were likely to become limited in number.[76] If true, this might help to explain why salmon-canners wanted to have more Japanese women handling the raw fish.

Operators away from the Fraser were happy to have Indian women. In those districts, securing large work-forces for a growing number of plants was difficult. About two-thirds of fishers outside the Fraser in the early twentieth century were Indians; the others were whites and some Japanese. Whereas in the nineteenth century, northern Indians travelled to the Fraser plants, now south coast Indians who could not find employment in the Fraser district travelled north, thus competing with local groups. In the Vancouver Island and Northern districts, Indian fishers and plant workers prevailed, and they would do so until after 1945.

Securing Indian labour in the Northern district was by no means an automatic process. With the opening up of coastal river estuaries and river valleys to industry and settlement, cannery operators often had to compete with other employers for their Indian labour. This happened during construction of the Grand Trunk Pacific along the Bulkley and Skeena rivers (1907–17), for example. In 1909, the local fishery overseer reported: 'Indians finding a demand for their services nearer home will not come down to the canneries – and that means a loss of not only fishers but of their women whose services in cleaning and packing are even more essential than the fishers, for the latter can be replaced by Japanese.'[77] For cannery operators to value Indian plant workers, mostly women, more than Indian fishers, who could be replaced by Japanese or whites, became more common over time, and many references to this phenomenon can be found in the correspondence files of Indian agencies and in the evidence given before the fisheries commission of 1917, headed by Sanford Evans.

It is popularly, but incorrectly, thought that machines transformed the canneries after 1900. Certainly, aspects of salmon-canning became mechanized before the First World War, but, as I have written elsewhere, adoption of machinery was very slow and geographically uneven in British Columbia, especially in the remote and isolated operations tended by Indian crews.[78] Mechanization eliminated some of the skilled jobs for Chinese contract workers but did not quickly get rid of the work of women and girls and boys, who principally hand-cleaned fish and hand-filled cans for a quality-conscious export market. As (past) Chief Councillor Harry Assu of Cape Mudge recently explained, no machine could replace Indian women: 'Our women selected the slices that had to be put together in one can and wrapped the fish to a tight fit with no gap at the centre.'[79] He was right. Hand-butchering and hand-filling lines persisted, especially for the choicest grade, sockeye, and for the smaller and irregular sizes of tins. When and if BC cannery operators adopted technological innovations in can-making, fish-butchering, filling, and cooking, they usually chose only essential ones that eliminated waste or maintained or improved the quality of the pack.

This aside, BC Indians became far more vulnerable to economic forces beyond their control. Even in northern fishing areas, their position was never secure. This situation led them to organize the Native Fishing Society, with a Tsimshian, Rev. William Pierce, as leader and Port Essington as headquarters. The society, wrote Pierce, 'aimed to unite all the tribes into one body for mutual protection of what they considered their natural native rights.'[80] By 1918, there were 1,800 members and numerous branches among the groups along the coast, from Rivers Inlet to the Skeena and Nass rivers and in the Queen Charlotte Islands. Pierce credited the society with keeping Indian fishers in the northern salmon-canning district, but heavy war-time demand for salmon, the need for Indian women in shorework, and the federal prohibition of gas boats for gillnetting in the Northern district had probably been decisive.[81]

Indian Fishery and Indian Lands

The changes in Indian involvement in the industrial fishery coincided with the province's decision around 1910 to make no further allotments of lands to Indians. Eventually, Victoria and Ottawa appointed the McKenna-McBride Commission to reconsider BC Indian lands. Settlement pressure had increased, and provincial officials wanted to 'reassess' the location and size of existing Indian reserves. The province refused to include Indian title in the commission's mandate, however, and the federal government concurred. As with the earlier reserve commission, this one also dealt with the fisheries.

The commission sat from 1913 to 1916. It visited every BC Indian community, much to the annoyance of the original chair, E.L. Wetmore. He resigned in the first year to avoid a round of journeys by canoe, horse, and stage-coach into the remote, fly-infested areas, where he would have to camp. He had been promised that 'the work would not be strenuous' and that 'BC is a nice place in the Spring,' and so he assumed that the commission would meet at convenient places!82 The commissioners apparently listened more to the local Indian agents than to the Indians themselves.[83] The commissioners recommended withdrawing lands from reserves in which the population had declined and adding to others. This process added twice as much land as it cut off, but the value of the 'cut-offs' greatly exceeded the value of land gained.[84] The commissioners recommended that the province finally convey title of the reserves to the federal government and affirmed some of the exclusive rights of Indians to fish in particular areas that had been granted when the reserves were laid out in the 1880s and 1890s. 'As fish forms the staple diet of a large percentage of the Indians of this province,' wrote the new chair,

N.W. White, 'the question of fishing privileges assumes a position of high importance.'[85]

Most Indian groups pressed their case for land and fishing (and hunting) rights, and many obtained promises of additional reserve lands for fishing stations.[86] Not all applications were successful, though, for the province continued to hand over land to non-Indians even as the commission conducted hearings. Also, the commission denied more requests for lands for fishing purposes than it approved. Ottawa did not adopt the commission's report (1916) until 1924, by which time the document had been modified and additional cut-offs had been made; title to BC Indian reserves was not actually conveyed to Ottawa until 1938.[87]

Without access to their traditional fishing sites, Indians would find, among other injustices, that it was impossible to conduct their own fisheries. Besides, not all groups thought that it was a good idea to cooperate with the commission. Some, the Skidegate, for example, demanded ownership rights to land and believed that accepting reserve lands would compromise their larger claim to aboriginal title.[88] The Kitwanga Band of the Nass Agency refused to answer the questions of commissioners unless comprehensive claims were discussed; Indians at Bella Bella, Bella Coola, Hartley Bay, and Kitkatla reacted similarly.[89] The commissioners gave assurances – falsely, as it turned out – to those Indians 'who identified with the movement for the recognition of Aboriginal Title' that their claims would not be jeopardized and 'did not permit this fact to militate against fair consideration of what investigation elsewhere shewed to be necessary and reasonable requirements of the Tribes.'[90] In other words, the commissioners allotted additional reserve lands to a number of local bands over the concerns and protests of those bands and congratulated themselves in the process.

Indian Food Fishing: Under Control

In this period, the Canadian government chose to balance Indians' privileges with respect to fishing for food with their rights to fish for commercial purposes, and the Indian food fishery became more vulnerable than ever to criticism and restrictions. When the Nass River canned-salmon pack was smaller than expected in 1891, the fisheries overseer said that 20 or more Indian villages and fishing stations lay between tidewater and the spawning grounds. He complained that Indian-owned dams and weirs obstructed the river and that the Indians of those villages were difficult to deal with, 'as they adhere very tenaciously to what they consider their privileges.'[91]

On Vancouver Island, a case against Indians having nets in the Cowichan River fell through early in 1894. The attorney general of Canada had decided that there was nothing illegal in the Indians doing so because they were simply fishing for food; there was no evidence of the fish being used for sale, barter, or traffic. But local fishery officers, who would have none of this, recommended a new regulation to 'remedy this fault' in the existing systems.[92] The new regulations (March 1894) specified that 'no Indian shall spear, trap, or pen fish on their spawning grounds or in any place leased or set apart for the natural or artificial propagation of fish, or in any other place otherwise specially reserved.'[93] Officially, only dip nets, never of widespread use by Indians, were allowed in non-tidal waters. And the regulations also required Indians to get the department's permission when fishing for food.

Indians were becoming desperate about protecting their traditional fisheries, as were many of the Indian agents and missionaries who sought their economic well-being. Typical of the complaints, residents of Village Bay Indian Reserve, on a salmon stream near Campbell River, protested in 1897 and for several years thereafter that a BC Mills dam and logging boom on their stream interfered with their fisheries and blocked canoe access to their village.[94]

Cowichan Bay was another 'hot spot.' At hearings by the 1902 commission, Cowichan Indians stated that reckless industrial seine-fishing in the bay and log drives on the spawning grounds killed their salmon; they wanted the bay reserved for themselves for food-fishing (unlimited) and for licensed industrial fishing.[95] Some gave evidence that food was getting short; white men with seines were taking chum and selling the catch to the Japanese, who salted it for foreign commercial markets. Meanwhile, the Cowichan went without food in winter. An Indian named Tsilpanult testified that there were no salmon on the drying sticks and the children had not enough to eat. Nonetheless, when the commissioners suggested that the Indians would have to give up weir fishing if seines were banned, one Indian, Sweehelt, said, 'I have come to ask a favor and not to give it.'[96] Other Cowichan witnesses claimed that they could no longer participate in the Fraser River industrial fishery: Japanese were taking their places. Fishing had actually ceased to be the major source of cash income for members of the Cowichan Agency by the early years of the twentieth century.[97]

In 1906, BC Indian chiefs protested to Ottawa that the chum-salmon fishery conducted by Japanese fishers prevented their people from securing enough of that salmon for their own needs; they asked government officials to reserve certain chum salmon streams for the benefit of Indians.[98] They also repeated their long-standing complaints about inadequate compensation for lands taken from them and about tougher federal fish laws and provincial game laws, which made it even more difficult for them to make a living within their tribal territories. Plainly, the facts were before the government officials.

Counter-arguments came, naturally, from the industry. As the canning industry grew and spread, processors demanded more, and different species of, salmon, especially the chum salmon that Indians traditionally caught in great numbers and preserved for their own needs. Canners wanted both a larger share of the fish and guarantees of harvesters and plant workers during the fishing season – two good reasons to get Indians off their food-fishing grounds and into the cannery camps. To comply, government officials decided that obstructions, including fishing barricades that Indians built on northern streams, were 'the most important matters concerning the conservation of the BC fisheries.'[99] Fish, however, had survived such mass-fishing devices for thousands of years. The fisheries department frequently offered estimates of the market value of salmon consumed by Indians in a year (usually about $3 million, though with calculations never explained), which must only have created more resentment within the industry. When inspectors cleared away Indian weirs and traps after these were prohibited, fishery guardians were hired to see that the laws were enforced in those areas.

The sweep through inland food-fishing grounds began in the 1890s in the Cowichan River – a major sports fishing ground for settlers. In 1897, and again in 1912, officers destroyed 'ingenious' dams and traps at waterfalls on the two most productive Indian salmon fisheries on rivers emptying into Quatsino Sound.[100] They even photographed the 1912 event. In 1904, officers raided and demolished a major network of Indian fish barricades in the upper waters of the Skeena watershed, on the Babine and Bulkley rivers; and in 1906, they conducted a 'crusade' against Indian barricades in Clayoquot Sound. In 1911, they eliminated Indian weir fishing near Stuart Lake, at the headwaters of the Fraser, and cracked down on Indian drag seining at Lac la Hache, in the Williams Lake Agency. In these and other cases, they were responding to complaints and rumours by coastal cannery operators or settlers arriving in the inland salmon-fishing areas about over-fishing and illegal sales of fish.

The most publicized and severe enforcement of the ban took place in the Babine Lake area, at the headwaters of the Skeena. Four or five new canneries were scheduled to open on the Skeena in the 1905 season. That meant about 1,000 gillnets taking fish at the mouth of the river; this and the Indian food fishery inland, reported John Williams, fisheries inspector for the Northern district, would destroy all the salmon before they had a chance to spawn.[101] Williams told his superiors that the Babine not only used barricades to fish for food but also preserved some of the weir-caught salmon for trade with other Indians and with miners who kept stores in the neighbourhood, which no doubt was true.[102] Peter Wallace of Wallace Brothers Packing Co. wrote to his member of Parliament that the upriver Indians had no sense of salmon conservation: 'They are killing both themselves and the industry,' he argued, and 'once the Indian gets what he wants he would never remove the barrier if there were fish dying by the millions ... It is not his nature.'[103] Untrue, but the fisheries department felt that it now had plenty of justification for eliminating the Babine barricades.

The Skeena River salmon needed to be conserved. But only a portion of the runs had to reach the spawning grounds. There was a surplus to be fished, so who would get it – the Indians or the cannery operators? For officials and canners the choice was clear. The Babine were fishing and using the fish for food and for exchange. But they fished principally at the end of the salmon's return journey to the spawning grounds. The industrial salmon fishery, being restricted to tidal areas, was first in line in the harvesting chain. For being last in line, the Indian riverine salmon fisheries would pay heavily.

Enforcement was swift and well publicized in the press. 'INDIANS WIPING OUT SOCKEYES' headed one newspaper story:

> A report in detail concerning the manner in which Indians at the headwaters of the Skeena and other northern rivers are striking at the very root of the life of the salmon-fishing industry in British Columbia, one of the greatest sources of the people's wealth, has been received ... No less than 2,000,000 salmon, most of them females full of spawn, were

killed in the Indian traps this year. That number of fish, if canned, would make about 142,857 cases, or 44,188 cases more than the total Skeena River pack of all classes of fish in 1903.[104]

The overseer's description of the Babine weirs in 1904 finds the traditional method of fishing and processing still being used. Hans Helgesen, like most non-Indian people who encountered major Indian fishing sites for the first time, could barely contain his wonderment at the ingenious technology. Two weirs barricaded the entire width of the Babine River, positioned 1 km apart. A section of the lower barricade was open to allow some salmon to escape to the upper barricade.

> A most wonderful sight met our eyes when we beheld the immense array of dried salmon. On either side there were no less than 16 houses 30 x 27 x 8 feet [9 x 8.25 x 2.5 m] filled with salmon from the top down so low that one had to stoop to get into them, and also an immense quantity of racks, filled up outside. If the latter had stood close together they would have covered acres and acres of ground, and though it was impossible to form an estimate, we judged it to be nearly three-quarters of a million fish at those two barricades, all killed before they had spawned, and though the whole tribe had been working for six weeks and a half it was wonder that so much salmon could be massed together at that time.[105]

Helgesen remarked sarcastically that it was amazing, given such fishing practices, that there were any salmon left in the Skeena system. Indeed! Like Peter Wallace, Helgesen was anxious to convince the government that Indians wantonly destroyed salmon to the point of extinction: '[Indians] are ever ready to kill and destroy all the fish and game within their reach,' he wrote to his boss, 'and are scarcely ever known to have any thought for the future ... [So the salmon] was practically exterminated.'[106] Such notions certainly fly in the face of common sense, but they were becoming widely accepted wherever Indians and newcomers competed for the same resources.

The Indians' explanation for the wholesale harvesting of Skeena River salmon that year is contained in the department's own annual report. The chief at Babine Village, Atio, told fisheries officials that Indians had had an 'indisputable right to fish for all time in the past,' and he thought it unfair that they be forbidden to sell the salmon taken in the Indian fishery when the cannery men sold all of theirs – and sent it out of the country.[107] The Babine undoubtedly understood the idea of escapement as a conservation measure; they pointed out to officials that the processors, not the Indians, had created the crisis. Development of the coastal fishery had transformed the fishery of his people. So many salmon were being taken in tidal waters for canning purposes that the Babine now had to take all the surplus that made it to their territory that year. The inspector says that he promised the Babine that he would make the Skeena River cannery operators allow more fish to reach Babine territory. There is, however, no evidence that the government ever undertook such a policy initiative – on the contrary.

Indians continued to object to having fishing limits placed on their rivers and made it clear to the officers that they needed fish for food and to sell. The more the pressure put on the resource by the industrial fishery, the more intense was the fishing under the Indian food-fishing permits and the more desperate was the economic situation for Indian groups.[108] Nevertheless, fisheries officers destroyed every weir around Babine Lake and closed the Moricetown Canyon on the Bulkley River to fishing except by dry fly. The Bulkley River arrangements proved disastrous: Inspector Williams reported his surprise the next season when he expected to find about 25,000 preserved sockeye at the Carrier village of Moricetown but found instead only 2,500.[109] This poor showing he attributed, unjustifiably and illogically, to what he interpreted as the destructive legacy of Indian canyon fishing in the river.

As compensation for destroying the Babine barricades, Indian Affairs supplied the locals with a few old gillnets donated by Skeena River cannery operators. These were rotten and next to useless, and so the food-salmon harvest was only a fraction of what was needed in 1905. The Indians rebuilt the salmon barricades for the 1906 season. Fisheries officials again attacked the barricades, arresting and imprisoning several Indians for illegal fishing under the Fisheries Act and for assaulting fisheries officers. Indians in Babine territory were up in arms; only a meeting in Ottawa between the ministers of the departments of Marine and Fisheries and Indian Affairs, Babine leaders, and a local priest, Father Cocoola, calmed things down.

Under what became known as the Barricade Agreements, 1906, Indian Affairs officials began supplying the heads of Babine houses with new regulation gillnets every few years to catch food for winter.[110] Use of these nets was subject to the same length and depth requirements as those for industrial fishers downriver, and, starting in 1909, fisheries regulations imposed a weekly closed period of 36 hours on Indian food fishing in the Upper Skeena.[111] The department also agreed to arrange for additional agricultural land for the Babine, which was slow in coming and ultimately amounted to very little. To the Indians' demand for commercial use of food fish, the fisheries minister was 'loath to commit' the department to such a policy, but he could not quite bring himself to say 'no':

> I am prepared, however to go this far: – Since it appears to be a fact that the Indians have hitherto to some extent trafficked in the food fish they have taken, I would not be disposed at the moment to interfere with the extent to which this traffic has prevailed: but this concession, so far as it may bind in future the policy of the Department, must be distinctly understood as a condition upon whatever action it is deemed advisable for the government to take upon the recommendations which will shortly be submitted by the British Columbia Fishery Commission ...[112]

Following this faint-hearted promise, the minister quickly approved plans for improving the tributaries of Babine Lake and erecting a salmon hatchery on one of them. This arrangement automatically banned Indian food fishing in the immediate area.

Stuart Lake provided the most extensive spawning grounds for the Fraser sockeye runs and thus, like Babine Lake, on the other side of the Fraser-Skeena divide, had long provided a major fishery. The local Indian agent expressed amazement that the Department of Fisheries – which he said must have been aware that the Indians of this area fished with 'fences and baskets' – would in 1911 destroy this traditional technology.[113] Fish was their main food supply, and they had no other means of obtaining adequate supplies 'for their purposes,' he wrote to his superiors in Ottawa.[114] It was bad timing, he said; any solution must be completely just, or 'nasty complications will occur.' Local settlement was restricting many of the Indians' old privileges and straining relations between them and settlers.

Dozens of letters passed within and between the departments of Indian Affairs and Fisheries. The same priest, Father Cocoola, who had intervened on behalf of the Babine fisheries interceded in this case, too. Ultimately, but very reluctantly, the minister of fisheries agreed to negotiate with the Indians of the Stuart Lake Agency. In return for the Indians' acceptance of the ban on barricade fishing on Stuart and Nechako rivers, and on Fraser Lake, Indian Affairs would meet their demands for gillnets, farm implements, and a boarding school for boys and girls, where, as the priest pointed out, the children would at least receive food.[115]

On Vancouver Island, the local fishery guardian, John Grice, met with West Coast Agency Indians in 1905 to forbid them fishing in Kennedy Lake, a salmon-spawning ground near Tofino, where the government had just built a salmon hatchery. They could still fish in the river, they were told, though not with spears or nets. Because they had received recognition of their fishing rights on this river, from the Reserve Commission in 1889, they were, of course, angry.[116] The local missionary observed that the Indians were furious and 'used abusive language to the Inspector, but they had to obey the law.'[117] In a series of letters to the district inspector of fisheries, Edward G. Taylor, Grice described his Helgesen-like crusade against spawning ground fishers. For Grice, 'it was a case of desperate diseases requiring desperate remedies,' and 'I came in for my share of abuse.'[118] What happened at Kennedy Lake was apparently only part of illegal-fishing scares and rumours in the Vancouver Island district, which were, according to Inspector Taylor, founded on hearsay. 'The Indian does not consider his methods of taking fish illegal,' reads Taylor's quite sensitive 1907 annual report, 'but looks upon them as his right, and we cannot expect to change his views on this delicate subject (the way to obtain his food) in one year.'[119]

Just how critical salmon was to the survival of Indians became clearer during the First World War. Railway construction along the Fraser resulted in blockages of the river and speeded flow, defeating spawning runs at Hell's Gate in 1913, in 1914, and for years thereafter. These events devastated the major Indian food fishery of the canyon and the waters above it. Leaders today recall elders describing mass movements to the canyon to fish, and to the coast, and serious hardships caused for so many villages by near-loss of a key resource.[120] The industry and government officials were aware of the famine of 1913 and 1914; their response was to protect the processing sector. Food fishing was immediately prohibited in the canyon and was soon curtailed throughout the Fraser system.

Indians may have had a right to a portion of the salmon stocks, but that right had become inconvenient; it was time to eliminate

Indian food fishing altogether. In his annual report for 1915, the chief inspector of BC fisheries tested the waters: 'Whilst the Indians may have a time immemorial right to certain fishing concessions, such concessions were granted under conditions entirely different from those of the present day, and with the ever-growing importance and value of the fishing industry of this province, it behooves the Government to make some other arrangements which will protect the salmon from molestation when they have practically reached the breeding stage and the breeding grounds.'[121]

According to government officials, there simply were too many industrial fishers and too many processing operations to allow Indians to capture salmon above tidal limits. They cited the large quantities of salmon caught in the Indian fishery and the inherent difficulty in regulating that fishery as justification for prohibiting Indians from taking salmon anywhere or by any means except under commercial salmon licence and in waters open for commercial fishing.[122] Clearly, with the canning industry no longer as dependent on Indian fishers as in the pioneer period, the fisheries department found it much easier to introduce and enforce strict regulations on Indian food fishing.

While the Indian food fishery has never been entirely eliminated, it became severely restricted at this point. New regulations in 1917 required Indians fishing for food to obtain a federal permit that was subject to the same types of restrictions (area and gear prohibitions and closed times and seasons) as was the industrial fishery.[123] It was already an offence for Indians to sell any of their freshwater food salmon harvest, or even to take any of it to the coast, and it now explicitly became an offence for anyone to be caught buying such fish.[124] These provisions have remained essentially unchanged since 1917.

In this crucial period, the late nineteenth and early twentieth centuries, Indians lost effective control of the salmon resource and of their labour to the rapidly growing fish-processing industry. Led by the powerful salmon-canning industry, the industrial fishery was capturing supplies of salmon and Indian labour through federal regulations and policies. Indians also lost land and other resources to industrial developers and non-Indian settlers. While it is tempting to assume that treaties might have protected Indian fishing rights, this is unlikely. The treaties protecting the fisheries of Vancouver Island Indians were ignored by government. For Ontario during the same period, Ottawa ignored the protection of Indian fisheries included in the Manitoulin Treaty of 1836, the Manitoulin Island Treaty of 1878, and Treaty No. 3; it pushed aside Indian fisheries in the name of resource conservation while non-Indian commercial fishers were permitted to destroy freshwater fish stocks in those treaty areas.[125] On the western plains, federal Indian Affairs policies prevented Plains Indians who were under treaty from developing a stable, independent economy based on agriculture.[126] The government never intended Indians to compete with white farmers on an equal footing. On the contrary, Indians there as elsewhere were to act as a pool of cheap labour for the development schemes of newcomers to their territories.

Because of excessive exploitation of fish stocks by an industrial fishery producing for an open-ended international market, even the subsistence fishery, which the government conceded only grudgingly to Pacific Coast Indians to keep peace, came under threat. The official justification was conservation. In telling fisheries officials that it was unfair to forbid Indians to trade or sell the salmon taken in their food fishery when the cannery men sold all of theirs, and sent it out of the country, the Babine had exposed a fundamental hypocrisy in state policy. Indians would continue to press this issue.

5 Battling a Revolving Door, 1919–1945

The interwar period witnessed significant changes in fleet size and gear type, coupled with an increasingly mechanized and diversified processing sector and the beginnings of a domestic market for BC canned salmon. Geographical expansion of the processing sector ended with the 1928 season, and a pattern of slow contraction and centralization of fish plants followed. Only the immense, guaranteed international markets generated by the food crisis of Second World War temporarily halted the process.

In 1922, the Department of Fisheries finally abolished restrictions on entry for the salmon fishery. Open access was deliberately granted to white and Indian industrial fishers at the expense of both Japanese Canadians, who had come to dominate in the fishing sector, and of the Indian food fishery, which the federal government attempted to eliminate. The new regime most seriously affected the Northern district, where gas boats could now operate. Although gillnetting still provided the largest part of the industrial catch and employment to the greatest single group of BC fishers, purse seining and trolling 'took off,' as did the pink and chum salmon fisheries. Thus overall production in the salmon–canning industry continued to rise. It peaked in the late 1920s, during a major round of business consolidations and new plant construction. Because salmon is so perishable, canning plants still had to be located relatively close to the fishing grounds, although centralization within each region had begun.

Federal officials tried to protect the industry through tougher restrictions concerning gear, area, and time in all branches of the fishery. They gave little weight to stock rehabilitation or environmental protection. Concurrently, in a series of court battles in the late 1920s, the federal department of fisheries lost the right to regulate fish-canning and -processing and to eliminate Japanese from Pacific Coast fishing and fish-processing.

The new approach of the 1920s benefited whites mostly, yet Indians remained a force in the industry for several more decades. Strong demand continued for Indian female shoreworkers, and many Indian communities wanted and needed to fish for their livelihood. The Indian population of the BC coast was now growing. A new pattern of relations involved strong personal loyalties between Indian families and canning companies, especially in isolated areas, away from non-Indian centres. Marginal operations in remote areas were the first to close – the very ones that depended on Indian labour almost exclusively. While independent Indian fishers owning powered vessels became more common during the 1920s and 1930s, most Indian fishers harvested in the Northern district, where they still operated the lion's share of the company-owned oar- and sail-powered gillnet fleet. Indian men and women joined Indian associations and non-Indian industrial unions to advance and protect their rights and access to resources such as salmon.

OPEN-ACCESS FISHERY

Boom Years: The 1920s

The restrictions on new cannery licences ended in 1919, and the federal Duff Commission in 1922 re-examined BC fishing restrictions.[1] After the First World War, export markets for BC canned salmon shrank. Until then, British Columbia packed salmon mainly for Great Britain and was one of its main sources of this commodity. But Japan's new canned-salmon industry was an unbeatable competitor; producers packed at a low cost, almost exclusively for export to Great Britain.[2] With the BC industry's permanent shift to the canning of species of salmon other than sockeye, the government amended its regulations in 1919 to accommodate the growing pink and chum salmon regions.[3] Yet expanding into new areas to offset depletion became more difficult – there were no new species or salmon-fishing grounds to tap.

Officially, the Pacific Coast fishery was to be opened at the expense of Japanese, who during the First World War had further consolidated their position in the fishing industry. In the post-war era of mounting anti-orientalism, the fisheries department dramatically reduced the number of fishing licences issued to people other than resident white British subjects and Indians. It wanted to eliminate persons of Japanese ancestry from the industry by the end of the decade. The Duff Commission was unequivocal:

> Our investigations have made it clear to us that all the interests concerned, excepting of course Japanese Fishermen's Associations and allied interests, profess to be at one as to the desirability of having white fishermen employed to a greater extent in the salmon fishery of British Columbia ... The question we have to consider in this connection is not whether Oriental licenses should be reduced in number, but what percentage of reduction should be decided upon in order to bring about the displacement of Orientals by white fishermen in the shortest possible time without disrupting the industry.[4]

Unlimited numbers of fishing licences could be issued to white British subjects or Indians. Political agitation in British Columbia led to limits on the entry of Japanese labourers into the salmon and herring salteries and to passage of the federal Chinese Immigration Act, 1923, which ended Chinese immigration – for several decades, as it turned out. In the 1920s, Ottawa and Victoria sought as well to restrict Chinese, Japanese, and East Indian employment in BC mining, railway, and public works projects.[5]

Regulations arising from the Duff Report also permitted gas boats in the Northern district, except for Japanese applicants.[6] Government officials said that they could allow this type of equipment because government agents, with or without use of gas motors, would now undertake 'conservation' measures in the north – presumably elimination of Japanese fishers and strict controls and production caps on the Indian food fishery.

The new policy resulted in record canned-salmon packs in the mid- to late 1920s, when BC production averaged about two million cases annually from over 50 canneries. These packs represented not a larger supply of raw salmon, of course, but rather full-scale exploitation of pink and chum salmon stocks and more intensive fishing for all kinds of salmon with larger, more efficient gear.[7] Everyone ignored the weekly closed time, closed seasons, and fishing boundaries.

By 1927, salmon-gillnet licences had increased over the previous four years by 53 per cent, salmon-trolling licences by 99 per cent, and salmon purse-seine licences by an alarming 128 per cent.[8] The growth in purse seining can be explained largely by the new pilchard- and herring-reduction seine fishery, sanctioned by Ottawa in the mid-1920s and discussed in chapter 8. The fisheries department allowed reduction seiners also to fish for chum salmon in fall, using smaller nets. This brought them into conflict with Indian fisheries. The department's annual reports chart the growth in seine fishing. In 1912, it had issued only 92 seine licences; in 1922, the first year of the open-door policy, 143; and the next year, 223. By 1925, the number had more than doubled to 329; in 1926, it shot to 445. Seines were about six times as productive as gillnetters. By then, as a matter of government policy, no seines were in the hands of Japanese fishers.

Seines underwent the greatest changes of any type of gear in the immediate post-war period. Motorized vessels of the first decade of the century were small, averaging about 11.5 m in length, with five-horsepower engines. By 1920, they ranged from 14 to 23 m in length, were powered by 45- to 110-horsepower gasoline or diesel engines, and required a crew of five. Power winches and power rollers allowed use of deeper and longer nets, permitting several more sets per day. In gillnetting, small, hand-operated gillnet boats were giving way to larger, gasoline-powered vessels. Most powered gillnetters and seines were privately owned, though often financed by processing companies.

The Department of Fisheries did adopt regulations to restrict fishing by the seine fleet. It subdivided districts 2 (Northern) and 3 (Vancouver Island) into several dozen areas, in many of which only gillnet or drift-net fishing, and no purse seining, was permitted. Regulations banned purse seining in the estuaries of the Nass and Skeena rivers, Dean Channel, Butedale, Namu, Bella Coola, Rivers Inlet, and Smith Inlet, for example. In fishing areas where purse seines were permitted, an allotted number was specified. In general, however, the department limited the quantity of fish caught each season simply by adjusting the closed periods.

The department reduced the number of licences issued to Japanese-Canadian fishers only until the 1926 season. By this time, it had eliminated 1,253 'Japanese licences.' The canning companies often chartered seiners and gillnetters from the Japanese owners who were unable to get licences and hired non-Japanese skippers and crews to fish them. The processors and Japanese-Canadian fishers forced the crown to end this openly racist policy in 1928, and the number of Japanese licence-holders was stabilized at the 1929 level. These fishers soon increased their efficiency and output with better boats and equipment.

This was only one of two critical shifts in fisheries policy – both resulting from a single case, *Rex v. Somerville Cannery Co. Ltd.* (1927, BC Supreme Court). Ottawa's exclusive privilege to regulate the BC processing sector came under renewed attack, this time by processor Francis Millerd, who was engaged in a series of business mergers. Millerd tested the federal power by intentionally canning clams at his Prince Rupert plant, Somerville cannery, without a licence from the federal fisheries department. The department charged Somerville cannery under the Fisheries Act, but on 25 March 1927 H.O. Alexander, a stipendiary magistrate, acquitted the firm on grounds that licensing fish canneries exceeded federal powers. In *Rex v. Somerville Cannery Co. Ltd.* (the *Somerville Cannery* case), the BC Supreme Court ruled against Ottawa's practice of regulating the fish-processing sector.[9]

Based on the questions raised in *Somerville*, the federal minister of fisheries took a reference on the constitutional validity of certain sections of the Fisheries Act to the Supreme Court of Canada. Specifically examined was Canada's authority over fish-processing and the minister's authority to refuse fishing licences to qualified individuals, such as Japanese Canadians. In *Attorney-General of Canada v. Attorney-General of BC* (1928), the court ruled that federal jurisdiction over fisheries ceased after the fish were caught and that the minister had no discretion to refuse licences to qualified fishers; in 1929, the Judicial Committee of the Privy Council in London agreed.[10] As the processors preferred, the provincial government alone could license, therefore control, an essential aspect of Pacific Coast fisheries management – the processing sector – and Japanese Canadians could return to the fishing grounds.

The triumphant BC premier, William Tolmie, assured a meeting of representatives from the fishing and fish-processing industries that the province would do everything that it could to cooperate with them: 'We should adopt a policy which will conserve this great industry for the future, and increase it where possible ... We are anxious not to load you down with restrictions, and not to make too frequent changes in our laws.'[11] His words met with applause. Fortunately for Indians, the province did not control the fishing grounds as well.

Having lost the power to regulate the processing sector, Ottawa turned to managing the fishing sector. Not only did it have, as was just, to accept the presence of the most aggressive fishers in the trade, the Japanese, but Canada remained unable to secure an agreement with the United States to share, and so increase Canada's share of, the Fraser River salmon runs.

Depression and War

The economic crash of 1929 and subsequent Great Depression severely weakened the salmon industry. Salmon canning declined by almost two-thirds in dollar value of annual output (and the number of canneries in operation fell dramatically) from its peak in 1930 to 1932, the bottom year of the Depression. The number of fish-boat licences rose, however: interest in fishing tends to grow during periods of general recession and unemployment.[12] But this was not a 'poor man's' fishery: sailboats and rowboats decreased in number by 1,089, while gasoline-powered vessels increased by an even greater figure, 1,690, over the same period.[13]

Other major changes in the industrial fishery during the 1930s altered its regional structure (Figure 8). Decline of the Fraser River salmon runs during the First World War left the Skeena the leading salmon river after the war. With an 'open access' fishery and the beginnings of spatial contraction and regional centralization in the processing sector (Figure 9), the Skeena runs peaked in the 1930s. Accordingly, plants in Port Essington had stopped operating by 1939, as had all other canneries on the Skeena River except Claxton and the four facilities (Inverness, North Pacific, Sunnyside, and Cassiar) on the north shore of the river close to Port Edward. Claxton closed in 1944. The Nass River runs had peaked in the 1920s; the last cannery put up its final pack in 1945, after which salmon from there went to the remaining Skeena–Prince Rupert plants for canning.

In the Queen Charlottes, where 15 salmon cannery sites had been established between 1911 and 1930, only one remained operating during the war, and it closed (for 10 years) after the 1944 season. Much of the salmon catch from the area was now processed in the Skeena–Prince Rupert plants. The long-standing Alert Bay cannery closed in 1933, and by the end of the war only one cannery continued to operate in the Johnstone and Queen Charlotte straits regions. No salmon canneries functioned in the Smith Inlet area after 1938; salmon from there was taken to Rivers Inlet, where after 1941 only one plant was still active. In addition, BC salmon-hatcheries had proven so inef-

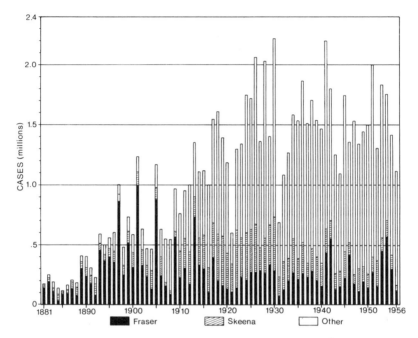

Figure 8 BC canned-salmon pack, by area (Fraser/Skeena/other), 1881–1956.
Source: Cicely Lyons, *Salmon: Our Heritage* (1969), 705–18.

fective that they were shut down. Under these tense and uncertain conditions, organization and unionization of fishers and shoreworkers, including Indian representatives, multiplied.

On the eve of the Second World War, conditions began to improve for the Fraser River salmon fishery. Canada and the United States finally ratified the long-awaited Fraser River Salmon Convention in 1937. This agreement provided for a joint body (The Pacific Salmon Commission) responsible for conservation of sockeye salmon (in 1957, pink salmon would be included). It divided the salmon caught in convention waters (roughly the Strait of Juan de Fuca and

Figure 9 Number of BC canneries licensed to operate for the season, by area, 1934–73. *Source*: BC, *Report of the Provincial Department of Fisheries*, 1934–73.

The decline in absolute number of active salmon cannery operations and the concentration of the industry in Vancouver and, secondarily, Prince Rupert, are evident. Wartime demand for canned salmon kept many 'out-of-town plants' in production until 1945.

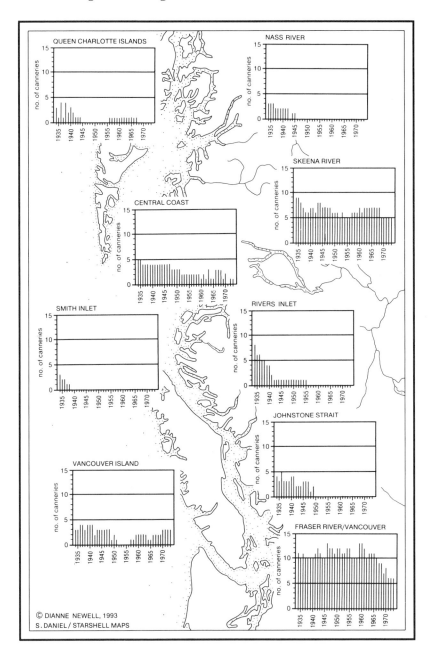

© DIANNE NEWELL, 1993
S. DANIEL / STARSHELL MAPS

southern Strait of Georgia) between US and Canadian fishers. It later did the same for catches of all stocks that spawn in Canada, travel through US waters, and are intercepted by US boats, and vice versa.

BC canneries operated at fever pitch as a protected wartime industry enjoying full, guaranteed markets. For the Pacific Coast fishery only, Canada banned all exports of raw fish and all fish-processing except the canning of salmon and herring, for which it relaxed all conservation measures, and the manufacture of fish-liver oil.[14] Despite feeble attempts to guard salmon stocks, virtually every catchable salmon was pursued, and almost every one caught went into a can. James Motherwell, federal head of fisheries for British Columbia from 1921 to 1946, wrote that production of large packs was more important than conserving fish stocks, confirming the government's position.[15] Federal officials and industry representatives wanted to cooperate with the British Ministry of Food in the hope that the Canadian industry would regain the large share of the British import market for canned salmon lost to producers in Japan between the wars.[16] Wars provide unique business opportunities; such concerns apparently outweighed the needs of conservation.

The Fraser had phenomenal sockeye runs in 1942 – the best since before the Hell's Gate disaster of 1913. Supported by favourable regulations, seiners ended up with 41 per cent of the sockeye catch that season, a trend that would continue after the war.[17] Seining no longer was in the hands of Japanese fishers, however, because in 1942 Canada removed 'persons of Japanese race' from the coast as an emergency war measure, and for almost a decade it forbade them to return.[18] For Indian men and women, large wartime markets for BC fish products and expulsion of the Japanese from the coast proved to be windfalls that temporarily boosted their participation in both fishing and fish-processing.

IMPLICATIONS FOR INDIANS

Industrial Fishery

The so-called open-door policy for the Pacific Coast fisheries in the 1920s actually did little to increase Indian involvement in the industrial salmon fishery in the inter-war period. Although Indians had opposed Japanese-Canadian participation and although Ottawa claimed that 'gradual elimination of the Oriental from the fisheries of the province was primarily for providing greater encouragement to white men and Canadian Indians to take up fishing for a living,' most licences went to whites.[19] This situation hurt the growing Indian communities on the coast.

The impact of the open-door policy on Indian fishers becomes clearest in specific categories of gear and regions.[20] Consider licences for gas-powered gillnet boats issued for the Northern district in 1923. Of the total in this category, 242, only 20 per cent went to Indians, and in Rivers Inlet, a mere 10 per cent. In the Fraser River district, Indians received only 5 per cent of licences issued for salmon gillnet fishing. This trend continued in the inter-war years. Indians in the north had opposed motors for the gillnet fleet. They had worried that remaining competitive would require further indebtedness to cannery operators, who would have to finance their new motors.[21] A few Indian villages took up motor boats right away. The Haida offer good examples. In 1925, Captain Douglas Edenshaw of Masset built an 18.5-m modern packer to transport fish bought by the canneries on the mainland coast. By 1926, the fleet of the Skidegate peoples included 30 motor-driven fishing boats. But these examples represent exceptions.

For the most productive gear – seines – Indians applied pressure to change long-standing, informal regulations that denied them seine licences.[22] It became an aspect of the open-door policy to give Indians equal privileges with whites in this type of gear and to deny such licences to Japanese.[23] Indians actually got proportionately few of the many more licences being issued for seining.[24] However, many Indians skippered and crewed on the salmon purse-seine boats chartered by the processing companies from Japanese owners refused licences, and Indians did receive an equitable portion of troll licences issued for the west coast of Vancouver Island.[25]

Indians needed the assistance of the cannery operators to get involved in seining or own any gas-powered fishing boats. Every aspect of advancement – from promotion to seine-boat skipper to receiving company credit for boats, nets, and other supplies – depended on a person's production record and ability to cooperate with company managers. Such paternalism aided a few high-ranking Indian fishers, such as James Sewid and Harry Assu, whose published memoirs record their experiences.[26]

James Sewid eventually got three of the coveted seine boats. As Chief William Scow told ethnographical field workers years later,

'Jimmy' got ahead by hard work; the cannery manager took a liking to him and gave him his first opportunity to buy a boat, with no down payment required. All the cannery operators had 'favourites' whom they helped, said Chief Scow.[27] Another Indian, Reggie Cook, 'got a break' when the Canadian Fishing Co. (Canfisco) assisted him in getting a vessel; he had a hard time meeting payments until the big Fraser River salmon run in 1942. After the war, Cook and Sewid were able to charter their boats to fishing companies.

Born into high-ranking Kwakiutl bands in 1913, Sewid grew up at the salmon canneries.[28] He spent summers at Knight Inlet cannery, owned by Anglo-BC Packing Co. (ABC), where he went fishing with his stepfather. His mother worked in the plant. By the age of 12, he was running the engine on a seine boat skippered by his grandfather, Jim Bell – ABC's first Indian skipper.[29] In safe waters, Bell let young James take the wheel, telling him where to go and what to do. Later, James ran the engine on a seiner skippered by his uncle, Henry Bell; Knight Inlet cannery owned it, too. James Sewid crewed with him for nine years, by the end of which time he had a family of his own. His wife, Flora, was a filler in the plant.[30]

In the 1930s, Sewid came into his own as a seiner. The longtime manager of the cannery let him skipper the company's best boat, the *Annandale*.[31] After running the vessel for a few seasons, Sewid bought a seine net on company credit for $1,700 – equivalent to his net profits in an average fishing season. He says that he was the first Indian to own his own net at that cannery. In 1939, ABC lent him another of its seiners, the *Frank A.M.* During the war, he and his uncle, Robert Bell, purchased it with a $5,000 bank loan (for the down payment) and credit from ABC.[32] The principal of the Alert Bay Indian residential school co-signed for the bank loan. Writes Sewid, 'It was a big favour to me because other people didn't trust the Indians.'[33] Sewid paid off his portion of the loan by borrowing from his wife's earnings at the cannery. His record catch in 1942 allowed him and his uncle to repay their debt to ABC. Sewid says that they were the first Indian skippers at this cannery to pay off a boat loan.[34]

Sewid was 'top boat' at the plant, so expert that the manager arranged for him to be exempted from military service during the war. He continued to be the 'highliner' throughout the boom years of the war, and so in 1944 he and Robert Bell bought a second seiner, the *Adele M.*, which Bell skippered. This one cost $12,000.[35] After the war, ABC Packers convinced Sewid to have a new seiner built for himself with company financing. *Twin Sisters* was completed to Sewid's specifications about 1951. Sewid skippered the new boat and leased the *Frank A.M.* to the company; his son, Bobby, skippered it.[36]

Harry Assu's family achieved similar success in the seine fishery. Cape Mudge was in the Vancouver Island district and not subject to the ban on gas boats before 1924. Harry's father, Chief Billy Assu, bought the first gas boat at Cape Mudge, in 1912. After the First World War, Billy Assu persuaded the local cannery owner to use Indian skippers on seine boats and, if none was available, to hire on at least two Indian crewmen, and he became active in the Native Brotherhood when it formed in the 1930s.[37] Harry Assu bought one seiner from BC Packers in 1941, after that firm bought the local cannery. His son skippered the seiner, and Harry was in charge of a company-owned seiner. The Assus became one of the most prominent fishing families – Indian or non-Indian – on Canada's Pacific Coast.

Such impressive success stories aside, for most Indians in the industrial fishery the old labour system prevailed. The majority of Indian fishers continued to fish with sail-powered cannery-owned boats, and in remote areas the populations of entire Indian villages still travelled to canneries during salmon-fishing season.

When Canada's famous west-coast artist Emily Carr made an ambitious sketching trip to northern Indian sites in 1928, she found the Nishga village of Greenville empty: everyone was away at a Nass River cannery.[38] Cape Mudge villagers took advantage of the canneries' longer operating seasons by dividing their time between the plants at Rivers Inlet (the fishers going in spring and the rest of the families, by Union steamship, in June), where an average of 11 canneries operated in the 1930s, and the local cannery, Quathiaski (for the fall fishing and packing season).[39] Billy Assu and Oscar Lewis hired the fishers for Wadhams; Tom Price, also of Cape Mudge, recruited for Strathcona. Indian women continued to labour on the canning lines and make and repair fishing nets.[40] Between the wars, the relative proportion of female piece-rate workers (mostly Indian, some Japanese) in salmon canneries rose, while that of male contractees (Chinese) fell steadily, as Figure 10 indicates. As in the past, BC cannery operators hired Indian fishers in order to guarantee the seasonal labour of the thousands of Indian women and girls needed in the cannery.

Female work for wages (Indian and some Japanese and white), unlike that at piece rates, was relatively unimportant until the Sec-

ond World War. With women taking on men's jobs and with unionization during the war, female wage labour became the norm in fish
plants. Most canneries had automatic filling machines by 1939. These,
however, were used for high-speed packing of the one-pound (454 g)
tall can, which the British Ministry of Food did not want. The small
sizes and odd shapes of cans ordered by the ministry had to be filled
by hand.[41] Indian women did this work.

Besides doing the more traditional jobs of washing fish and
filling cans, Indian women took on technical and supervisory occupations during the war. Lucy Smith, a Kwakiutl woman born in
Campbell River in 1931, spent the summers with her father and brothers and sisters at the Bones Bay cannery.[42] In 1944, at the tender age
of 13, she was on the upper floor making cans on the 'reform line' –
formerly a man's job. Her older sister, Ann Brochie (born 1926, in
Campbell River), was floor lady, or supervisor, on the canning line.[43]

Indians also were recruited for the busy plants of the Fraser
River district, after the expulsion of persons of Japanese ancestry in
the winter of 1941–42. When interviewed late in her life, Agnes
Alfred seemed to know little about the official evacuation of the
Japanese Canadians, which was the event most responsible for draw-
ing Indians back to the Fraser plants during the war. She remembered simply that the Indians got the 'nice dwellings' that the Japanese had been 'chased out' of at Steveston.[44] Her husband, Moses
Alfred, recruited Alert Bay women for BC Packers' Steveston cannery.
Agnes Alfred said that Billy Assu and his wife, Mary ('she was boss
for the women'), recruited the Cape Mudge fishers and plant workers. She reluctantly agreed to be a 'floor manager' at the Steveston
plant, hiring and supervising the female fillers. She spoke no English, only Kwakwala, and so had an Indian assistant and interpreter,
Lucy Brown.

The proliferation and spread of canneries and auxiliary operations into the 1930s permanently affected the movements of some
Indian people. Alert Bay was established in the 1870s as a salmon-
cannery camp to process the rich sockeye runs of the Nimpkish River.
By the twentieth century, it had become the centre of settlement and
education for the Kwakiutl people of the entire Queen Charlotte Strait
region. (It remains so in the 1990s, 60 years after the salmon cannery
closed.) The new, racially mixed, cannery-based communities of Port
Essington (1880s–1930s) and Port Edward (after the First World War

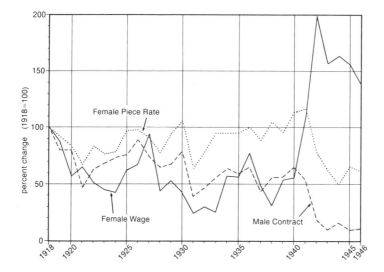

Figure 10 Relative changes in the BC salmon-cannery work-force, 1918–46. *Source:* Canada, Dominion Bureau of Statistics, Fisheries Division, *Fisheries Statistics of Canada*, 1918–46 (Ottawa, 1919–47), 2: 'Agencies of Production, Part 2, Fish Canning and Curing (c) Employees and Salaries and Wages.'

until recently) were in their day permanent centres for many Coast Tsimshian, Haida, and Nishga people who had jobs in the canneries and reduction plants there.[45] On Quadra Island, Indian families from around Ladysmith continued summer migrations to Cape Mudge, right into the 1960s, even though the Quathiaski Cove cannery burned down in 1941 and no cannery ever operated again in the Cape Mudge area.[46]

The same types of spatial changes occurred on the outer coast of Vancouver Island. At the time of contact with Europeans, the Nootka of Kyuquot Sound occupied 17 villages.[47] For many decades after the industrial fishery got launched in the 1870s, Indians from these villages travelled to take part in the industrial fishery each year, returning to their villages for the winter. Many Kyuquot men and women who had been employed in their youth at the canneries at Ceepeecee and Nootka had fond memories of stays at these camps, where 'the parties, the potlatches, and the lahal [gambling] games used to go on well into the night.'[48] Also remembered was the hard, often dangerous work. With the opening of a major, cooperative fish camp at Walters Cove in 1925, the Kyuquot began getting their own small trollers. They also could use these for travelling and living in, which reduced the need to maintain their own fish camps. The industrial fishery became the major employer of Nootka people, many of whom moved permanently into the racially mixed community of Walters Cove.[49]

In the Barkley Sound area, the Ohiaht had long worked at the Alberni Packing Co. cannery near the Indian village of Bamfield. The Ohiaht dominated in the local salmon fishery and in cannery jobs until the 1920s. At first, they seined and hand-trolled in the inshore grounds inexpensively, using their own dug-outs.[50] When BC Packers Ltd took over the Alberni cannery in 1926, consolidation of the Barkley Sound plants began. Rising costs of fishing led to company policies of extending large amounts of credit to fishers.[51] Some local Indians got modern vessels (some constructed by themselves), while others became crew members on the new salmon (and pilchard and herring) boats. Non-Indian fishers moved into the area; they operated from a distance or else settled at Bamfield. This racially mixed community became a major fishing centre and remained so into the 1950s. Meanwhile, Ohiaht dominance in the area's industrial fishery declined, particularly among owner-operators of fish boats. Several plants closed in the 1930s, leaving in business only the small herring-reduction plant at Ecoole and the Kildonnan cannery and reduction works on Barkley Sound. The Indian trollers attempted to get group financing to keep going.[52]

These changes took place in an industry riddled with conflict and racial prejudice. And while Indians resented Japanese-Canadian rivals to the point of discriminating against them, the feeling was probably mutual. One leading, old Japanese-Canadian fisher, Buck Suzuki, remembered that Indians were discriminated against in the 1930s by Japanese Canadians, who themselves had little power or voice in Canadian society: 'The Indian people had the full rights, as a matter of fact, they could do as they pleased, but there was a very subtle, insidious discrimination against people of all Native origin. It's, I would say, ten times worse than it is now [1976]. It's bad enough now, but it was a lot worse in those days. They were looked down as being, well I'll tell you the truth, even by the Japanese themselves, who were being persecuted, they were looked down as being inferior.'[53]

Indians Organize

The issue of Indian fishing rights got its first full airing in 1926, when the Allied Indian Tribes of BC seized the opportunity to air and advance their claims to land, hunting, fishing, and water rights in the province, to compensation, and to educational and medical rights. Nishga, Coast Salish, and Interior Salish had formed the organization in 1916, to oppose the McKenna-McBride Commission's findings on BC Indian lands.[54] Groups on the North Coast and many in the interior eventually joined it. Leading the Allied Tribes were Andrew Paull and Peter Kelly. Paull, a well-educated man of Squamish (Coast Salish) descent, had gained experience with government and legal procedures as an interpreter for the McKenna-McBride Commission. Kelly, a Haida from Skidegate, was a popular ordained Methodist minister who served coastal communities.[55]

The Allied Tribes had tried, unsuccessfully, to work with the provincial and federal governments. Ottawa's declaration in 1924 that the McKenna-McBride Commission's recommendations of 1916 represented a final adjustment of all matters relating to Indian affairs in British Columbia was a major blow to Indian rights. The Allied Tribes pressed for a full hearing of the Indian case by the Judicial Committee of the Privy Council in London. Before this was to happen, the Parliament of Canada formed a joint committee, with representatives from the Senate and House of Commons. Hearings were held in Ottawa in the spring of 1927. Kelly, Paull, their attorneys, and officials from the departments of Indian Affairs and of Fisheries testified.

The principal findings and recommendations of the joint committee went against the interests of Indians: the committee found no basis in fact for claims of unextinguished aboriginal rights to land in the province, and it urged immediate action to stop any person from obtaining funds in support of Indian claims in Canada. With adoption of this and other recommendations, including changes to the Indian Act, the Allied Tribes dissolved. Not until 1951 would section 141 of the Indian Act, which prohibited raising funds for pursuit of a land claims case, be repealed.

Despite the disastrous setback for pressing of Indian claims, the testimony on Indian participation in the industrial fishery makes for vital reading today. Having listened and responded to questions, Andrew Paull opposed the suggestions that Indian employment in the salmon-canning industry could in any way compensate adequately for the restrictions placed on aboriginal fishing rights.[56] For Paull and his Indian clients, the length of the Indians' presence in Canada entitled them to regulations that gave them as favourable treatment as possible. This suggestion met with acceptance from at least two committee members, who made their approval known on the record.[57]

Paull argued that it was not good enough to say, as some government witnesses had, that Indians enjoyed the same right to obtain industrial licences to fish as anyone else. Indians more and more had to compete with 'the Jap and the other foreigners' in a conflict-ridden industry.[58] Paull requested, as had several Indians and some Indian Affairs and fisheries officials in earlier years, that special areas be set aside in fishing districts where local Indian bands could retain exclusive right to conduct a commercial fishery.[59] On the comparison that Paull drew between this proposal and the already existing system of Indian land reserves (quantified in Table 5, for 1984), H.H. Stevens commented: 'There is good sound sense there, I think.' The federal director of fisheries, William Found, however, vehemently and repeatedly opposed any such Indian 'privilege' in the industrial fishery.[60]

Under questioning, Found had to admit, more than once, that for several decades the fisheries department had leased whole inlets to canneries and large, non-Indian fishing concerns, with no reciprocal rights for Indian fishers. However, he said, a decision by the Judicial Committee of the Privy Council had determined the public nature of the coastal fishery. In Found's opinion, it was no longer possible to 'grant' anyone exclusive use for commercial purposes: 'There is a public right of fishery in the tidal waters and the Federal Government is not in a position to grant exclusive rights to anybody.'[61] The notion that the crown grants, rather than recognizes, aboriginal rights was firmly entrenched by this time and would be difficult to shake. The Privy Council decision that Found had in mind must have been that of 1913.[62] He was challenged on the point, and a quick examination of the Fisheries Act convinced some members that the minister of fisheries had a right or power to set aside main areas for Indians.[63] The committee decided, however, not to get bogged down in these details, and the 1929 decision of the Judicial Committee of the Privy Council supported Found's claim.

Indians adopted new strategies in the 1930s. It was during the Depression, not long after the demise of the Allied Tribes, that they

TABLE 5
Indian reserves of BC coastal tribes, 1984

Tribes	No. of bands	No. of reserves	Total hectares	Hectares per capita	
				1929	1984
Haida	2	37	1,589.7	2.3	0.9
Tsimshian	17	255	36,068.6	10.0	3.4
Kwakiutl, Haisla, Oowekeeno, Haihais, and Bella Bella	17	170	10,666.4	15.2	1.7
Nootka and Nitinaht	15	168	4,958.2	3.0	1.0
Bella Coola	1	7	2,023.9	8.1	2.4
Coast Salish	52	234	25,069.6	5.8	1.9
Totals	104	871	80,376.4	6.5	2.2

Source: J.E Micheal Kew, 'History of Coastal British Columbia since 1846,' in Wayne Suttles, ed., *Northwest Coast* (1990), volume 7 of the Smithsonian Institution's *Handbook of North American Indians*, 161.
Note: The Indian population was growing during the period 1929–84.

organized specifically around the issue of fishing rights. A white fisher's union with some Indian members persuaded Indian fishers to join a strike at Rivers Inlet in 1936. Indians did, but they subsequently felt betrayed by the white strikers and so broke ranks with them.[64] This led Kwakiutl fishers to form the Pacific Coast Native Fishermen's Association.[65] Many Indians agreed to join it because they could no longer meet their boat payments and thus risked losing their main means of livelihood. The Indian organization won some immediate victories. It convinced the major packing companies to extend the loans of every fisher in the region who owed money on a boat, and it agreed to negotiate fish prices for all Indian fishers each year. When war broke out in 1939, twice as many Indian fishermen as white ones were organized in British Columbia (although not all were members of certified unions).[66]

During the war, Indians made unprecedented gains in numbers, per-capita income, and occupational status in fishing and fish-canning and -processing. They seem also to have benefited from high guaranteed wages because of unionization after 1942. But they won these gains, as I see it, largely at the expense of Japanese fishers and plant workers, who suffered grievances and mistreatment during the war that have recently been officially recognized by the government of Canada. Some Indian fishers obtained confiscated boats at low prices, and some were exempted from military service because of their value to the domestic war effort. One anthropologist, Michael Kew, suggests that the war years 'probably marked the peak of Indian participation as owner-operators in the fishing industry.'[67] As mentioned, cannery operators recruited Indian women and girls for all cannery work, including replacing Japanese shoreworkers and supplanting white males as machinery operators and floor supervisors. This often meant turning a blind eye to the cannery work of the juvenile children of the Indian women, so much so that the provincial departments of fisheries and labour dispatched special investigators to the plants in 1941.[68]

The Indians' struggle to maintain their fishing rights continued during the war. When Canada began taxing status Indians on their commercial fishing income, Pacific Coast Indians to whom the new policy applied protested on the grounds of their traditional right to the fishery and their lack of regular citizenship (although, as they said, they were expected to fight overseas, and many had). They directed their appeal to the Judicial Committee of the Privy Council and engaged, through the Native Brotherhood, in legal action against a packing company that was suing one of their members for back taxes (by suing it for collecting income taxes from Indians).[69]

It was largely over taxation that the Pacific Coast Native Fishermen's Association amalgamated with the Native Brotherhood of BC in the early 1940s. Andrew Paull, still a force in Indian political organizations in the province, is credited with influencing this move.[70] Formed by Indian chiefs in 1931 to represent coastal tribal groups, the brotherhood had been concentrating on Indian fishing issues. In 1943, the five companies in whose plants Indians formed the majority of the labour force (ABC Packing, BC Packers, Canfisco, Nelson Brothers, and Nootka Bamfield) signed labour agreements with the brotherhood.[71] Since 1945, the brotherhood has served alongside the more militant United Fishermen and Allied Workers' Union as the chief bargaining agent for Indian fishers and, to a much lesser extent, Indian processing-plant workers.[72]

Indian Food Fishery: No Longer Needed?

Between the wars, government officials applied the same draconian approach to the Indian food fishery that they had to Indian land claims. The 1917 regulation requiring permits for the Indian food fishery, with restrictions attached, was the next best thing to banning

the food fishery altogether. In the 1920s, Canada was also suppress-
ing aboriginal culture and economies (and badly treating Japanese,
Chinese, and East Indian workers, as indicated earlier). Throughout
the decade, Ottawa stongly enforced the anti-potlatch law of 1884.
For obvious economic and cultural reasons, BC peoples had not abandoned this core institution of their societies. In 1924, Ottawa had
unilaterally declared that the province had satisfied all the obligations
of the British Columbia Terms of Union (1871) respecting provision
of lands for Indian reserves (although Victoria did not reciprocate by
conveying title to the reserves until 1938), and in 1927, Canada in
effect forbade all claims-related activities by Indians.

The food-fishery restrictions were first applied in the most critical region for Indian fisheries – the Fraser River. Indians in the Upper Fraser still suffered terribly from lack of salmon caused by destruction of runs to that region caused by the Hell's Gate slides in
1913. According to the Department of Fisheries, the Fraser River bands
were so desperate that they wanted Ottawa to purchase their fishing
rights in that region.[73] Whether or not this is true, fisheries management, beginning in 1920, prohibited Indian food fishing at the prinicpal
Fraser River sites of this traditional activity. All the while, the industrial fishery remained open on the Fraser River estuary. When fish-
processing rebounded after 1922, the tough restrictions on fishing for
food on the Fraser were soon applied to river fishing elsewhere in
the province.[74]

Indians continually spoke out against erosion of their fisheries. At hearings by the Duff Commission (1922) in Prince Rupert,
Tsimshian objected to having to request permits to fish for salmon
for food and, like BC Indians elsewhere, asserted their claim to the
exclusive right to salmon creeks controlled by their ancestors.[75] The
Indian agent for the Nass River Agency stressed the economic importance of the aboriginal fisheries for Indian people, calling on government to abolish the red tape that had crept into the process over
the years.[76] The requirement that Indians get a permit for food fishing, he said, was impractical for northern Indians. He explained that
for the Fraser River the fisheries department issued all Indian food-
fishery permits through Indian agents, who sent the department 'a
list of all those deserving, and these are mailed to them direct.'[77]
What a mixed blessing for the region's Indians.

The chief inspector of Indian agencies, W.O. Ditchburn, asked
that the commission's recommendations place no burden on Indians,

who were, after all, wards of the nation. While at least one commissioner voiced his disapproval of giving Indians 'special treatment,' chairman Duff reassured Ditchburn that 'the aborigines certainly have an unalienable right to live, and to take their accustomed food in their usual manner, in my opinion.'[78] This curious statement came a generation or more after the period when Pacific Coast Indians could legally take their 'accustomed food' in their 'usual manner.'

As at earlier hearings, a common complaint before the commission was that non-Indians invaded the fishing grounds attached to reserves, preventing Indians from exercising their fishing rights. Ditchburn mentioned that the fisheries department had further eroded those rights by issuing exclusive commercial licences to seiners in those areas. He talked about how the fisheries department had repeatedly undermined terms of the Douglas Treaties. In Saanich Bay, for example, the department had long outlawed Indian fishing with nets, a right that the treaties of the 1850s should have guaranteed, and now Indians were prohibited from fishing there altogether. A pair of Indian fishers from Bella Bella requested that two of their ancestral fishing creeks, Cullchuk (or Gull Chuck) and Howiat, be made off limits to all but local Indians, who needed access to the chum salmon for their own use.[79] This issue arose again at the joint parliamentary committee hearings of 1927 into the petition of the Allied Indian Tribes of BC. The Allied Tribes claimed that Indians had the right to take fish for food wherever and whenever they wanted to, without permits and without limit. Andrew Paull told the hearings that the Fisheries Act meant in fact that Indians were 'stealing' the fish that they took for food in inland waters.

Despite the centrality of the food fishery to Indian communities, fisheries officials and industry representatives would happily have eliminated it. When questioned during the joint committee's hearings, William Found argued that the Indian food fishery existed as a sort of favour to his colleagues at Indian Affairs: 'Notwithstanding the need for adequate fishery protection,' he said, 'it has been the policy and is the policy of our Department, to co-operate, as fully as we feasibly can, with the Department of Indian Affairs, to make it easier for the Indians in the more remote sections, where it is necessary and compatible from a fishery standpoint to obtain fish for food purposes.'[80] Found and his officials saw the food fishery as neither a right nor a privilege. It was a concession to be tolerated only when other sources of food for Indians had been either eliminated or exhausted and when no inconvenience to the fish processors would occur.[81]

The permit system begun in 1917 had spatial implications. Historically, the fisheries department distinguished only between tidewater and inland fishing. But the permit system added a further geographical distinction to the Indian food fishery. According to William Found, Indians in remote areas needed food fish; those closer to 'civilization' (meaning coastal cities) did not. That, explained Found, was why the department routinely denied Indian food fish permits to Indians living near Vancouver, and that is why Indian agents were asked to screen applicants for licences.[82] He did not mention that the Fisheries Act already prevented Indian food fishing in many remote inland areas, at sites near natural spawning grounds or hatcheries.

Because Indians on the most commercially important salmon rivers, the Fraser and the Skeena, always faced the most severe restrictions, a decision by the joint committee favourable to protecting Indian food fishing could have made a considerable difference. H.H. Stevens played the devil's advocate: 'The way it appears to me is this, the Indians ought to have the inherent right to catch fish for food. Then comes the question of how can we harmonize that inherent right with the safeguarding of the interests of fishing. Our effort has been to find out just where the rub comes in.'[83] Again, we see a concrete expression of the conventional wisdom that an aboriginal right, 'inherent' at that, is something that a government could grant. In the end, the joint committee called for closer cooperation between Indian Affairs and Fisheries, 'with the aim that a liberal interpretation of fisheries regulations be adopted, insofar as Indians fishing for domestic consumption were concerned.'[84]

Found discovered that Indians with fish-based economies were capable of interpreting their rights for themselves. When in 1927 he called a meeting at Alert Bay to discuss a departmental proposal for salmon conservation, fishers came out in full force. A petition from the Kwakiutl Agency called for government restrictions on the number of industrial drag-seine licences on the Nimpkish River, where three Indian reserves were located.[85] Non-Indians operated 27 drag seines and 30 purse seines in this relatively limited fishing ground. Only Kwakiutl should be allowed to fish on the Nimpkish. It also requested the banning of all trollers using gillnets on the Nimpkish River. The small 'combination' boats, it claimed, crept into the creeks and robbed the Indians of their food salmon. Also, it requested that the proposed damming of the river for hydro-electric development be prohibited. These and other such explicit warnings to government went largely unheeded.

From this discussion it is not difficult to conclude that the fisheries department was prepared to protect the processing sector from the Indian food fishery, but not vice versa. The department had effectively become the resource management arm of the fishing industry. When in 1929 the Fraser River's sockeye runs showed signs of recovering, Canada's chief inspector of fisheries for BC, James Motherwell, declared that the Indian food fishery was both a threat to the future of the industry and no longer necessary to BC Indians.[86] On what grounds he based the last claim he did not say – nor could he, for surely there were none. So much for the joint committee's recommended 'liberal interpretation' of the fishing regulations for the Indian food fishery. Citing recent intense fishing and increased value of salmon, cannery operators announced that 'the [food] catch of the Indians should be curtailed if not discontinued entirely.'[87] The assistant to the commissioner of fisheries for BC, John P. Babcock, officially suggested that the Indians' right to fish in the Upper Fraser be purchased from them.[88] It is not known whether any efforts at purchasing Indians' rights to fish for food were ever made.

Certainly there were attempts, pathetic ones, during the Depression to 'wean' Fraser River Indians from salmon. First, local salmon canners donated cases of canned pilchard (*Sardinops caerulea*, a product for which there was, justifiably, no serious export market) to targeted groups in 1930.[89] Would the Indians substitute canned pilchard for the salmon that they usually caught for food? Certainly not. Undaunted, cannery operators a year later tried factory-smoked chum salmon in some of the Indian villages along the Fraser.[90] This crazy scheme met with no greater success – and we hear no more about it.

It could be said, then, that the Indian food fishery was seriously reduced after the First World War but could not be eliminated. Indian Affairs was the feeble defender of subsistence fishing rights. In the industrial fishery, Indian fishers and female shoreworkers maintained a sizeable presence through the boom of the 1920s, the Depression, and, most impresssive, the war years. In the 1920s and again in the 1940s, Indians benefited from being located above the Japanese in the racial hierarchy. For the first few decades after the war, however, Indian participation would be effectively restricted to the remaining plants on the mainland to the north of Vancouver Island.

6 Cast Adrift, 1946–1968

After the Second World War, North American attitudes towards resource development changed profoundly. Economic theorists argued for concentration on net economic yield, as opposed to net biological yield. As a result, Canada sought to change the old so-called common property approach to fisheries policy.

Changes in technology in the 1950s and 1960s went largely unchecked by government regulations. Technological innovations increased the range, mobility, efficiency, and composition of the fishing fleet. They accelerated the centralization and closure of plants. And they altered the very nature of fish-processing. After the war, female employment in fish plants dropped to about half its wartime levels. Union contracts transformed the conditions and remuneration for plant jobs. The provincial government lost interest in coastal fish-processing, preferring instead to promote a sport fishery for tourists and fish- and shellfish-farming. The province simultaneously supported massive industrial and municipal developments that damaged salmon rivers and spawning grounds.

Wartime demand had seriously depleted the already depressed salmon stocks. So unrestricted structural and technological changes in the industry intensified competition for declining stocks. Competition for fish led to a continuous decrease in the supply, or at least quality, of salmon in nearly every region. Industrial catches on the Skeena, having peaked in the 1930s, reached their historical low in the 1950s. Logging booms, hydro-electric ventures, urban land-fill projects, and other destructive developments on salmon rivers further threatened the survival of the fish. Centralization and diversification in processing required larger and more mobile, hence very expensive, boats and therefore greater investments by individual fishers and processors. Centralization destroyed jobs for plant workers and small-scale local fishers who could not afford more mobile vessels. The heavy investment in vessels and equipment together with dwindling supplies of salmon drove up the price of the fish. Yield per boat steadily declined, more than offsetting the technological advances and resulting increase in each vessel's productivity and profitability.

Although Pacific Coast Indians were no longer major factors in the industrial salmon fishery, fishing and fish-processing continued to be their major commercial activity. Indian fishers devised many strategies for remaining involved. Consequently, they operated some of the most sophisticated and least sophisticated vessels on the coast. Yet only in the Northern district could they remain substantially involved. By the 1960s, many fewer Indians were active in industrial fishing and fish-processing. Indian communities also found it much harder to obtain enough salmon for food. In a post-war society that valued formally educated, full-time workers, Indians were disadvantaged. Meanwhile, federal policies on the future of Native communities changed. Welfare payments to reserve residents and a surge of migration from reserves to industrial centres transformed coastal Indian economies. This pattern could be found for Indians throughout the country.

POST-WAR TRANSFORMATION

Fishing

In 1954, the American economist H. Scott Gordon called for the 'bionomic' equilibrium of a commercial fishery – by harvesting of the amount of fish that was the most profitable without threatening stocks. He called this outlook 'a maturation of economists' thinking on the question of efficient exploitation.'[1] And he had mathematical models to persuade policy-makers. Department of Fisheries officials liked the ideas of Gordon and his followers: 'The optimum intensity of fishing,' noted the Department of Fisheries and the Fisheries Research Board in a 1956 report, 'is that which maximizes the difference between costs and returns, and this normally is somewhat less than the level of intensity that maximizes the yield in physical terms.'[2]

Because of the common-property, biological nature of fishery resources, the theory went, the equilibrium of a fishery at optimum level was unstable, economically inefficient, and vulnerable to over-exploitation. Events in the Pacific Coast fisheries made little economic sense to resource economists such as Scott Gordon.

What *was* happening in the Pacific Coast fisheries? Technological advances during the Second World War altered the world's fisheries. Rapidly changing techniques and improved equipment required larger investments in boats, gear, and auxiliary equipment. In the 1950s, investment per person in the primary fishing operation in British Columbia doubled over that of the 1930s.[3] Large-scale adoption occurred of innovations in underwater fish-finding apparatus (first, echo sounders and, later, radar and depth-sounding gear), hydraulic gear (including powered winches), navigational and communication aids, refrigeration units, and in high-speed, all-weather, all-purpose transport. The refrigerated seawater method of conserving fish over longer travel times, adopted in the late 1950s, eliminated the need to locate processing plants so close to the fishing grounds.

These innovations speeded up centralization of the industry and increased the mobility and catching power of the fleet. Because echo sounders allowed effective exploration of deeper water, fishing effort was directed at more distant grounds. Wind and strong tides became more of a problem as all boats now ranged the entire coast and often fished in offshore as well as inshore waters. Fishers increasingly had to purchase expensive new navigational technology, such as loran (long-range navigation) radar, to stay competitive.

Technological changes affected each gear type differently, and no unilateral shift to a single type took place. With adoption of the power block in the mid-1950s and power-driven mechanical drums for setting and hauling in the mid-1960s, all net gear became more effective (and more expensive). The light-weight, tough new nylon nets that became popular after the war were more durable and easy to handle and maintain than the natural fibre ones that they replaced. Faster setting and net-retrieval allowed vessels to make up to six times more 'sets' a day than was possible in the 1940s.

Purse-seining boats expanded rapidly in number, size, and efficiency, displacing old-style gillnetters. Processing companies owned or financed most of the seine nets and vessels. There were significant changes in gillnet vessels, too; gillnetters were larger, much faster, and more mobile than before the war. With introduction of the powered gillnet drum, these vessels could be converted to small-scale seining. The more efficient gillnetters replaced old-style purse-seines. Consequently, gillnetting predominated in industrial fishing: gillnet boats as always took the most salmon and employed the most people. Processors owned the bulk of the gillnet fleet.

Trolling also changed dramatically and, with the assistance of legislation, grew in importance within the industry. With refinements in lures and flashers, troll fishers could be more selective in their catches. High-speed diesel engines, hydraulic gurdies, and multi-strand stainless-steel fishing lines permitted more fish to be taken per hour. Trollers could therefore participate more profitably not only in the cohoe and spring salmon fisheries, as in the past, but in both the offshore and inshore pink and sockeye fisheries. And they could round out the fishing season by mounting a small table-seine on their vessels for the fall chum fishery. Over the period, prices paid for troll-caught salmon grew more quickly than minimum prices for net-caught fish.[4] Rapid expansion in troll fishing reduced stocks of pink, however. Extra trolling for pink, plus the change in pricing, beginning in 1945, that emphasized weight rather than volume of individual troll-caught salmon, contributed to over-fishing of the largest stocks and hence smaller individual pink salmon. Within 25 years, runs from Alaska to Vancouver declined by about 220 to 680 g in average weight.

The fisheries department responded to the increased efficiency of the gillnetters and seiners by reducing fishing times and fishing effort in the net fishery, not by discouraging or limiting capital investment in boats. It established four- and five-year closures of certain areas and applied in-season management to restrict elsewhere the productivity of gear, beginning in 1956.[5] In future, salmon-fishing openings would last for as little as a few days at a time. Overall, the regulations encouraged even heavier capital investment in fishing, which raised fishing intensity and further threatened the resource. By 1964, the local chum and sockeye salmon stocks in Clayoquot Sound were so depleted that the government in effect closed the area to net fishing for ever. In contrast, regulations for the troll fishery were exceptionally lenient. Increasing post-war commercial demand for fresh and frozen fish led to exemption of trolling from the net-fishing openings and seasons in many areas, especially offshore.

Counteracting the regulations was a new practice on the coastal

fishing grounds: many gillnetters and some seiners invested in trolling capacity. These multi-gear salmon fishers had the flexibility to
move into troll areas when the net fishery closed. The historic relationship between method of capture, places of capture, and final
disposition of catch thus weakened.[6] Also, year-round fishing with a
single boat and convertible gear became standard for the Pacific Coast.
All this presented fresh problems for fisheries management.

Even more difficult to control was massive destruction of salmon
habitats. The colossal hydro-electric dams built in the 1950s blocked
the access of salmon on their way to and from inland spawning
streams. These projects, actual and planned, were highly controversial – what the fishing-industry advocate and long-retired canneryman
Henry Doyle angrily called the 'hydro-electric power vs. salmon fisheries dog.'[7] The most notorious case was the development by the
Aluminum Co. of Canada (Alcan) of a smelter complex and new
town of Kitimat; to attract this project to British Columbia, the province gave Alcan complete control of the flows of the Nanika, which
joins the Skeena system, and the Nechako, which joins the Fraser
system, for its hydro-electric development, known as Kemano. The
spread of logging operations into new areas of the interior scoured
and silted the spawning beds and diverted and blocked salmon
streams leading to them. Saw mills, pulp and paper plants, and mining operations on the coast and coastal tributaries discharged harmful levels of chemicals into salmon rivers and often altered the water
temperature of those rivers to lethal levels for young salmon. And in
area after area, industrial, municipal, and agricultural demands for
water lowered levels and rates of flow in the salmon habitats beyond
the point where the spawn and juvenile fish could survive. Victoria
showed little interest in cooperating to protect the coastal salmon
fishery against these dangers, as Geoff Meggs's investigations have
shown.[8] It was left to federal departments, Indian groups, processors, international fisheries bodies, fishers' organizations, and conservation groups to goad the province into a more protective role.

Processing Sector

After the war, work in the fish plants changed and the market for
Canada's Pacific Coast fish (including canned salmon) shifted from
export to predominantly domestic. Flash freezing and later, irradia-
tion, are examples of post-war innovations in food-processing that

transformed fish canneries and fish-processing. Frozen filleted fish represented a market opened up by introduction of novel processing techniques and home freezers. Expanded markets for new, cheaper products such as frozen breaded fish sticks and canned tuna led to further diversification in processing (and fishing). These changes, combined with technological developments in transporting fresh fish to plants, speeded consolidation of canneries into fewer and larger, more profitable, centralized and diversified, or 'combination,' plants able to operate year-round. Combination plants, like combination boats, changed the industry.

A dozen of what, under centralization, had become known as 'out-of-town' salmon canneries closed in the 1950s and 1960s. Yet construction of additional plants and expansion of older ones to include salmon-canning kept the absolute number of salmon-canning plants steady from 1948 to 1968, averaging 22 annually. Still, when we look at regional impact, we find big changes. Packing companies began closing down their older and most remote operations after the war. None of the existing canneries functioned on the Nass River after the 1945 season, or in the Johnstone or Northern Georgia straits areas after 1949; the single cannery remaining active in the historic Rivers Inlet canning area closed in 1955. On the west coast of Vancouver Island, no plants canned salmon in the years 1952–56, after which only a few operated each season. Most other types of fish-processing there had not survived wartime suspension of operations. In the Queen Charlottes, no plants were canning salmon between 1945 and 1955. The Masset shellfish cannery briefly returned to salmon-canning in 1956.

Reactivation of a salmon cannery in the Queen Charlottes reflected interest in pink salmon, the species that made up over 60 per cent of British Columbia's annual canned-salmon pack by the 1960s. In spectacular runs of pink salmon in the north central coast, more fish was caught in 1962 than the plants could handle, and again in 1966. In contrast, promising big runs of Fraser River sockeye and pink in the 1940s and 1950s did not recur in the 1960s. As a result, the industrial fishery of the central coast grew. New salmon canneries were built at Shearwater (Millbank Industries), close to Bella Bella, and at Port Hardy. The old Namu cannery, destroyed by fire in 1962, was rebuilt at great expense. Generally, however, construction and expansion took place only in the two urban fish-processing centres: Vancouver and Prince Rupert.

Consolidations and closures, complete automation of the canning line, and the shift from canning to fresh and frozen processing destroyed many jobs in shore work. Also, unionization of shore work brought attacks on the old labour contracts and piece rates and an end to both. The union secured monthly wage rates for the privileged positions – in the skilled (male) sector. Together with the Native Brotherhood, it eventually won benefits, job security, and racial equity for the hourly wage employees (women and casual male labourers).[9] Senority provisions created job security but tied workers to a single company. Mechanization, unionization, and plant consolidations facilitated a shift to year-round processing and resulting 'decasualization' of employment. Unfortunately for Indians, seasonal employment was disappearing not only in fishing but also in every primary industry in which they were involved.[10]

The Sinclair Report, 1960

In 1959, the same year as a crippling, industry-wide strike in the Pacific Coast fishing industry, Ottawa commissioned a quick investigation to determine how to apply the new economic theories of fisheries management – those promoted by resource economists such as James Crutchfield, Scott Gordon, and Anthony Scott – to BC salmon and halibut. Sol Sinclair, an agricultural resource economist from the University of Manitoba, headed up the study.

The Sinclair Report (1960) operated within Scott Gordon's theory of optimum economic yield.[11] The root of the problem, thought Sinclair and his colleagues, was the common-property approach to fisheries. There had been too much sentimentality and not enough sound economics in government regulations for the fisheries. The goal of protecting the livelihood of so many part-time and marginal fishing people and fishing communities was noble but economically inefficient. For resource economists, the Pacific salmon fisheries were a study in irrational conservation and a prime example of what biologist Garrett Hardin popularized in the 1960s as the 'tragedy of the commons.'[12] It was not economically rational to allow everyone to have a 'piece of the action.' 'Injustice,' wrote Hardin, 'is preferable to total ruin.'[13] Other scholars have since shown that privatization of open-access resources produces greater economic and social problems and that harvesters of such resources as fish do indeed have incentives to conserve the resource.[14]

The Economic Service Branch of the Department of Fisheries had conducted a survey of the earnings of west coast salmon fishers in 1953 and 1954.[15] The study suggested that about a quarter of the annual income of fishers came from employment other than fishing and that annual net incomes from fishing, especially gillnetting and trolling, were poor. Sinclair identified two routes to exploit more profitably and fully the BC fisheries without destroying the resource: either place the fisheries in government sole ownership or continue to operate them as common property but severely restrict entry of fishers. He favoured the latter.

Sinclair's report led to a radical new government policy. But that had to await another eight years of debate and election of a majority government in Ottawa. As we see in the next two chapters, the so-called Davis Plan (1968) became the most controversial and unpopular federal policy ever for the Pacific Coast fisheries – that is, until policy arising from the *Sparrow* decision of 1990.

IMPLICATIONS FOR INDIANS

The Sinclair Report of 1960 did not mention the condition or future of Indians in the commercial fisheries. Sinclair did concede, however, that their 'proper rights and privileges should not be interfered with'; no person would be refused a licence, he said, and so no Indians would be obliged to stop fishing.[16] This assumes the old 'equal footings' myth that the fisheries department had been peddling for eighty years. Indians had never been on an equal footing with others in the industrial fishery of the Pacific Coast.

Climate of Policy for Indians

The Canadian Parliament made massive changes to the Indian Act in 1951 to reflect the growing reality that the Indians in Canada were not vanishing, as was once expected. Indeed, the 1941 federal census had shown them to be the fastest-growing group in the country. By the 1960s, their numbers were expanding by about 3 per cent per year. A surge of migration to urban centres and the beginnings of a welfare economy on Indian reserves began about this time, as did the rapid growth of government bureaucracy and funding in the name of Indian people.[17]

Indian Affairs sought to adjust its old assimilationist policies to new conditions. In 1954, it commissioned a pilot study; the report, by Harry Hawthorn, C.S. Belshaw, and S.M. Jamieson and entitled *The Indians of British Columbia: A Study of Contemporary Social Adjustment*, appeared in 1958. In the 1960s, it commissioned a much fuller, nation-wide project; *A Survey of the Contemporary Indians of Canada: Economic, Political, Educational Needs and Policies*, edited by Harry Hawthorn, came out in two volumes in 1966 and 1967. These documents influenced the Trudeau government's 1969 White Paper, *A Statement of the Government of Canada on Indian Policy*, announced by the minister of Indian affairs, Jean Chrétien.[18] Intended originally as an aid to amending the Indian Act, the White Paper actually proposed terminating all special rights for Indians, including the Indian Act, the Indian Affairs department, and Indian status, reserves, and treaties.[19] The proposal proved so unpopular that the government shelved it the next year, with its credibility among Indian leaders in tatters.

Hawthorn, Belshaw, and Jamieson's recommendations of the 1950s reflect much more than a new approach to Indian policy; they disclose an ideology of 'growth centres' that came to dominate regional planning theory and practice throughout the Western world after 1945.[20] The idea was to centralize industries and services in core urban centres and eliminate older, smaller, especially remote, communities, which planners considered economically inefficient to service. Centralization was also applied to Indian communities; government departments withdrew or withheld crucial services such as post-secondary schools and health facilities from remote communities and encouraged the inhabitants to relocate.[21] The proportion of registered Indians who lived off reserve in coastal British Columbia was negligible in 1954. This situation changed with government incentives for Indians to relocate and with displacement of Indians from local industries, especially fishing. Within a few decades, many coastal reserves had half or more of their registered population living off reserve and many of the old villages had to be abandoned.[22]

The Industrial Fishery in the Indian Economy

Some Indians make an argument that has been current since at least the early 1950s: although comparatively few Indians in Canada have benefited from the economic system and industrial way of life that emerged after Confederation, the Indians of Canada's Pacific Coast could at least depend on the fisheries. Because of the industrial fisheries, wrote the late economic historian Percy Gladstone, himself an Indian, '[BC] Indians have managed to carry over the skills and aptitudes of their tribal culture and acquire new techniques to a degree that enables them to compete successfully with whites ... Here, to a degree rarely found in other occupations or regions on the North American continent, native Indians have been able to adapt the special experiences and skills of their traditional cultures to the new requirements of a dynamic, technologically advanced industry.'[23] It was, however, at about this time, the 1950s, that Indians no longer held their own against whites in the fisheries. And as we shall see, keeping Indians involved in the industrial fishery was no longer a priority for the federal departments responsible for either the fisheries or the Indians.

After the war, many Indians remained in the industrial salmon fishery, which was crucial to their economy and culture. Fishing and fish-processing offered employment and livelihood (cash income) for BC Indians – most notably for women. And although contraction and centralization within the industry had been under way for several decades, the fishing industry still shaped life in Indian communities over much of the coast. A 1954 occupational census of BC Indians found 10,558 Indian fishers and fish-processing workers plus dependants involved.[24] Of these, more than 2,000 derived their main source of livelihood from fishing – fish-patrolling, gillnetting, trolling, seining (operators and crew members), other fishing, fish-packing, boat-operating, and managing fish camps – and another 1,000 or more, mainly women, from fish-canning and other processing. This one industry provided over 45 per cent of primary employment for BC Indians, and more than 20 per cent of supplementary employment.

Even more telling are the band-level statistics. Commercial fishing and fish-canning and other processing provided the principal livelihood for a record 61, or one-third, of BC bands. They were the main supplementary source of employment for another 12 bands.[25] This is remarkable: unlike other primary resource industries, such as logging and saw milling, fishing was confined to an increasingly limited area along the coast. Hawthorn, Belshaw, and Jamieson regarded coastal Indian economies as very adaptive: 'The high concentration of employment in this industry represents, in part, a somewhat high degree of specialization of Indian bands in certain fishing districts along the coast where virtually the entire able-bodied population, male and female, is employed in fishing, fish-canning, or processing. At the same time, a small number of Indians in some of these more specialized bands, especially in the North Coast region, are engaged in a wider diversity of occupations than band members in any other part of the Province.'[26]

Fishing and fish-processing were the largest source of employment in all agencies on the northern and central coasts (Bella Coola, Skeena River, Queen Charlotte, Kwawkewlth, and West Coast) and the second largest in two major agencies in the Fraser region (Vancouver and New Westminster). Only in the interior agencies – Kamloops, Kootenay, Lytton, Nicola, Okanagan, Stuart Lake, and Williams Lake – was fishing not a main or supplementary employment.

The industrial fishery historically had enabled BC Indians to get higher social status beyond Native spheres than any other industry.[27] Hawthorn, Belshaw, and Jamieson found that many Indians in the fishing industry were self-employed or independent proprietors. Some, the seine-boat captains and cannery labour recruiters, for example, could be considered executives or employers. Several demonstrated widespread ownership and accumulation of capital: 'Some of the best seine boats that regularly make the biggest catches are owned and operated by Indians.'[28] James Sewid and Harry Assu were among those with 'management skills.'

Besides being a highliner with ABC Packing and eventually owner and skipper of three seine boats, Chief James Sewid also possessed a saw mill and store at Alert Bay. In 1955, the National Film Board of Canada selected him to appear in a documentary on the economic achievements of Canadian Indians. 'They called [the film] *No Longer Vanishing*,' explained Sewid, 'because I understand that some people thought the Indian people were going to disappear.'[29] The seiner featured for many decades on the Canadian five-dollar bill was owned by Chief Harry Assu. In the background is one owned by two of his sons, Don and Steve. BC Packers told Assu that his boat was chosen for the 1958 engraving because he was such a productive fisher and because he was the oldest skipper in the fleet, having worked for BC Packers for 49 years.[30]

Indians and the Industrial Fishery

How important were Indians as a group to the industrial fishery? Not very. In 1951, only one-third of BC's industrial fishers were Indians. Except for salmon drag-seine licences, all nine of which were held by

Indians, almost all licences, in every branch of industrial salmon-fishing, were held by non-Indians.[31] Many Indian women and families still worked in the canneries in the central coast and northern areas.[32] But this situation would change each year as fish-processing became more automated and concentrated in cities. Even a modification as simple as replacing linen fish nets with nylon after the war eliminated most of the net-mending jobs for Indian women.

The geography of participation is worth close examination. Indian fishers had long been replaced in the Fraser River district. Even though gillnetting and purse seining still predominated in that district, Indians held a mere 71 of the 2,882 gillnet licenses in 1953.[33] There was only one licensed Indian purse-seine captain, and there were no Indian crews. Fish-plant work was centred at Vancouver and Steveston, yet special reports by Indian superintendents showed that the dozen or so canning plants there employed less than 100 Indians from the Fraser River agencies.[34]

The Japanese returned to the Fraser after the government allowed them to do so 1949, and BC Packers recruited many fishers from among this group. Two of the men whom the company approached in Alberta, unsuccessfully, were Tatsuzo Yamashita and Tono Ohama.[35] Yamashita remembers receiving generous offers of loans, fish boats, and housing if he would return to the Fraser. Ohama recalls hearing from those who, unlike himself, went back to the coastal fishery that they got any type of licence to fish in any district they preferred. A third, Buck Suzuki, remembers things differently and from first-hand experience.[36] He was a fishing union activist who served in the Canadian armed forces and then joined the first wave of Japanese-Canadian fishers to return to the Fraser; he recalls that the government restricted the number of Japanese Canadians who could fish in that district.

Wartime jobs for Indian women in the Fraser plants proved temporary; local white women (mainly post-war immigrants) replaced Indians after 1945.[37] Before 1939, Indian women and families from the lower mainland could work in the canneries of the central and northern districts.[38] But now cannery closures there eliminated those opportunities.

In the Vancouver Island district, Indian participation in fishing and fish-canning and -processing was declining. Here, trolling and purse seining, which required much more capital than gillnetting, had been dominant since the 1920s. The total number of fishers grew between 1945 and 1953, but Indian numbers fell. On the west coast of the island, Indians met with stiff competition from white fishers, who generally had better access to credit for the expensive equipment now required. Indian fishing communities tried to stay competitive. Among them was Ohiaht. Demand for canned herring and salmon during and immediately after the war had brought in more Ohiaht fishers and increased their indebtedness to the fish-processing companies. Fishing companies support in building and outfitting modern troll vessels had been easy for them to get during the war. By the late 1940s, most Ohiaht families had a fishing vessel of 8.5 to 10.5 m.[39] Credit became tighter after the war, and so the men who stayed in fishing reverted to day-boat fishing or stuck with the old-fashioned ice boats. Most Indian fishers on this coast found it harder to make a living from fishing with these simple vessels. On the east coast of Vancouver Island and the islands and mainland opposite, however, Indians made small gains as salmon purse-seine captains and crew members and in salmon-trolling. And those with small boats and relatively inferior equipment could operate effectively in the sheltered waters of the leeward coast.

The fish plants of the Vancouver Island district had traditionally depended on Indian family labour and fishers. Closure of the salmon canneries there eliminated scarce jobs for Indian women (only 26 Indians, all registered in the Cowichan Agency, were employed in fish-canning and -processing in the district in 1953, though probably none of them in salmon-canning) and reduced the ability of kinfolk who fished to market their catch locally.[40]

Hawthorn, Belshaw, and Jamieson found that only in the Northern district did Indians still control fishing and fish-processing jobs. In the sockeye areas – the Nass, the Skeena, and Rivers Inlet – gillnetting and purse seining prevailed, while around the Queen Charlottes, trolling and purse seining took the lead. More Indians were fishing, and fewer whites, having been replaced mainly by returning Japanese Canadians. In 1949 and 1950, Skeena chiefs and the local northern branches of the Native Brotherhood had spoken out against the return of Japanese Canadians to the North Coast.[41] Processors still hired Indian fishers in order to obtain the labour of their female kin. Even in this district, however, remote canning plants were closing for good.

The sorts of gains made by Indians in purse seining during the war continued into the 1950s, and Indians also stayed in gillnetting.

By 1953, Indians far outnumbered whites in all branches of purse seining in the Northern district. But there is more to the story. Harry Hawthorn and his colleagues found that most of the white seine-boat captains were owner-skippers, whereas most of the Indian seine-boat captains had simply been hired on.[42] For gillnetting, the number of licences held by Indians in 1953 remained high, but the boats and equipment that they owned or rented from canneries were often old, technically inadequate, and in poor condition. In other words, Indians were there, but mostly at the margins. As far as Hawthorn and his fellow researchers were concerned, 'The license figures may really indicate, not that many Indians have held their own in gill-net fishing, but that they have held on, in the face of shorter fishing seasons, smaller catches per boat, declining incomes and standards of living, deterioration of equipment, and a rising burden of indebtedness. In other words, many Indians in the north have continued gill-net fishing under conditions that have driven a large number of Whites out of the industry entirely.'[43] The Sinclair Commission of 1960 was either unaware of or ignored this crucial observation about Indian economic strategies.

Regardless, the new fisheries regime about to be announced by Ottawa in 1968 eliminated precisely these marginal, older, inexpensive, often rental fishing-boat operations. Because these were owned or rented mainly by Indians, Indian fishers and their communities would soon be without boats. And under the new approach, once one left, it was almost impossible to get back in. That was the official goal.

With opportunities for part-time fishing and shore work diminishing, and with plants and cannery sub-districts closing for ever, what options did Indians have? Some communities, it seems, turned to other coastal industries, such as logging. Some Indians, encouraged by government policies, moved to urban centres to go to school or seek a livelihood. Once there, they had little economic incentive to return home.

To shift from fishing and fish-processing to other local industries was possible only in regions where such opportunities existed for Indians. Even in these cases, new employment was available seldom to Indian women – only to the men. Take the Kitamaat Band. From the 1880s to the 1930s, almost every able-bodied male earned at least part of his living as a fisher for the canneries of Rivers Inlet, and the females worked in the plants there.[44] Industrial fishing and cannery work continued to be the economic mainstay until the mid-1950s, when the last of the Rivers Inlet canneries closed. About half the Kitamaat fishers and plant employees then shifted to the remaining canneries on the Skeena and at Butedale, Klemtu, and Namu.[45]

Butedale cannery was the closest to Kitamaat, but it lay 209 km to the southwest. Two-thirds of the fishers worked aboard the seven seiners that operated from the village. The rest were on gillnetters. The canning plant at Butedale shut down shortly after the war, and later the herring-reduction plant collapsed and was not rebuilt. These events caused serious hardship for the Kitamaat salmon and herring fishers and plant workers. In the 1960s, the Klemtu plant operated only sporadically. Soon it also closed. Namu remained functioning but employed mainly fishers and shoreworkers from Bella Bella. With the building of Alcan's smelter complex and new town at Kitimat located a few kilometres away, the smelter and the town offered more employment to the Kitamaat Band than fishing and fish plants.[46] Meanwhile, the massive power project severely damaged the inland food fisheries of Carrier occupying the territory on the other side of the Kitimat range.

Credit Breeds Debt

Debt is no stranger to any fisher, but the debts of Indian fishers after the war were uniquely difficult. Indians had limited sources of credit: they could not normally get credit from banks. The Indian Act prohibited them from using their interest in reserve property as collateral. Despite the obstacles, many Indians remained in the fishing sector through social bonds and credit arrangements with the fish-processing companies. As newer and more efficient, and therefore costly, boats and gear came in after the war, they tended to be owned by individuals rather than canneries. Indians who purchased vessels and were highly regarded by cannery operators continued to get credit from the companies. This type of debt became considerable in the 1950s.

Indians who were indebted to a cannery were expected to fish or work for it until their debt was paid off. And it was a two-way street. Canners were obligated to accept all the fish of these indebted fishers. Through these reciprocal obligations, Indians could stay in the industry – so long as canneries did not close down. As we have seen, however, canneries were shutting down. There are parallels here with the traditional fur trade, which was a credit-barter system. Arthur Ray's study of the subarctic fur trade suggests that the decline of this legacy of the mercantile age by the early twentieth century left local Indians dependent on state support to supplement their inadequate income.[47]

The system of company credit on the Pacific Coast began to sour. The small and indeed decreasing number of Indian seine-boat owner-operators in the 1950s reflected large debts to the canning companies. In addition, routine indebtedness to cannery stores for groceries and fishing supplies curbed the amount that they could spend on new vessels or repairing and upgrading their current boats and equipment. The high operating costs of these vessels and several poor fishing seasons led to Indian seine-boat–owners either chartering or selling their vessels to the processors and then leasing them back for fishing. While this lowered profits for the Indian vessel-owners (the boat and net shares that normally went to the owner would go to the company), it also reduced their short-term financial risks. This growing financial obligation made it harder for Indians to initiate or join with others in strikes against the processing companies.

Indian Affairs bankrolled only a few Pacific Coast Indian fishers in the 1950s. It lent money to those who were willing to become independent through the Revolving Fund, which issued small loans to Indians across Canada, to a maximum of $10,000 per individual, for a variety of economic activities.[48] But in the early years of the program, a disproportionate amount went to support agricultural projects, depriving Pacific Coast Indians of needed capital.[49] In fact, only about $16,000 of Revolving Fund loans went to these Indians between 1949 and 1954.[50] At a time when a well-equipped gillnet boat would cost from $5,000 to $10,000, and a seine boat over $30,000, the government's funding was woefully inadequate.

Post-war alterations to the structure of the industry and new government policies reduced the fishing-based economies of whole Indian villages from a source of community wealth to a sign of community poverty. The Masset had always been major boat builders on the coast. Percy Gladstone described the situation at Old Masset village in 1953: 'One finds one of the largest and finest seine-boat fleets of any community on the coast, valued at $350,000 ... The same village also boasts a modern boat-building yard.'[51] Philip Drucker conducted field work about the same time; he discovered that almost none of these people owned their seine boats outright. Often fish-packing companies had financed the boats, or at least the most expensive item – engines.[52] Most Masset trollers owned their own boats, although some were indebted to the fishing companies that had financed them.[53] Two years earlier, Canfisco had replaced six of its old, low-speed gillnetters with high-speed versions. The company took the old ones over to Masset and sold them to Indian troll fishers there for $600 each.[54]

In the 1950s, the whole community participated in the fisheries. Drucker even speculated that Masset might not be a good place to do ethnographic field work, because the locals were too busy: 'It is said that practically every able-bodied person there who is not fishing is employed in the local shellfish packing plant.'[55] When the salmon fishery failed around the Queen Charlottes in 1953, it hit the Indian villagers of Skidegate and Masset so hard that they had to ration food for winter.

An anthropologist who conducted field work at Masset in the 1960s, Mary Lee Stearns, saw the 1950s as good years for the Masset, but she knew that the situation was soon to change:

> The largest fishing companies financed construction [of the big seine boats] by Indians who operated them under an agreement to deliver their catches to the company at the end at the offered price ... In the recollection of many persons now in their fifties and sixties, these were happy days. Many Indian women were cooks when the boats skippered by their husbands ranged along the entire coastline of British Columbia. Often several of the Masset boats with wives and children aboard journeyed to the fishing grounds together. The fleets visited the villages of other coastal tribes along the way, enjoying great hospitality and sociability. All these boats were later repossessed by the companies.[56]

By the next decade, Masset fishers would return to the small-boat pattern of previous decades. The small boats would be eliminated from the fleet by the Davis Plan after 1968.

Hawthorn, Belshaw, and Jamieson warned in 1958 that for Indians in the industrial fisheries, which were so crucial to many of them, the future looked hopeless: 'In contrast to the generally successful history of Indians in the fishing industry of British Columbia, however, a number of current trends make their future in this field problematical. While some branches of the industry may offer opportunities for greater income and employment to Indians, in other branches their opportunities are shrinking. Already several hundred Indians in some areas face the immediate problem of destitution and what appears in the long run to be permanent displacement from fishing.'[57]

It is difficult to know if this study influenced the dramatic changes in fisheries policy and regulations of the late 1960s. Although the report acknowledged the importance of fishing in Indian economies, its recommendations proposed steps to increase the flow of Indians to urban centres and to secondary or service industries. Of less importance would be protection for those who remained in traditional fields of employment in 'competition with whites.'[58] The authors concluded, oddly, that the Department of Indian Affairs ought to find something else for Indians to do – such as encouraging them to work in forestry, especially in logging. There was no future in fishing.[59]

The BC fishing industry was indeed in difficulty in the 1950s, but recommendations more sympathetic to Indians could have been drawn. Twenty-five years later, a federal commission on the fishing industry headed by Peter Pearse would draw the opposite conclusion: Indians should have priority rights in the fishery. So, although Hawthorn and his colleagues were working at a critical time for Indians in the Pacific Coast fishery, their recommendations undermined the Indians' very future.

Crisis in the 1960s

The 1960s witnessed a major transformation and decline in the coastal fishery. This affected all fishers but the evidence gathered through contemporary studies and commissions shows that Indians suffered disproportionately. Intermittent and permanent closures of canning and fish-reduction plants, and repossession of Indian-owned fish boats, threatened entire villages. Temporary closure of the salmon cannery at Klemtu in 1960, for example, brought hardship and uncertainty to the 300 Indians who fished or worked there.[60] On the Queen Charlottes, the Skidegate people were no longer very active in the industrial fishery; for the women and girls, even summer employment in the mainland canneries was no longer available.

In spite of the setbacks, strong cultural and economic pressures kept many Indian communities in the industrial fishery. Fishers from the Kwakiutl village of Gilford maintained close identity with industrial fishing.[61] They had always preferred to own or at least operate gillnetters rather than work on the seiners, although most of the men had seined at one time or another. Several villagers who had once owned gillnetters had recently lost them to the fishing companies, principally through failure to meet mortgage payments. These people now served on gillnetters as crew members. No one skippered his or her own seiner during the regulated salmon season. Although Indian Affairs officials encouraged the men to log, few took up the challenge: 'Most [Gilford Indian men] identify themselves as fishermen and prefer fishing to other occupational pursuits.'[62] Mary Lee Stearns found that similarly, in the mid-1960s, 'one could still say that the [Masset] Haida identify themselves as fishermen ... The general expectation in the village that a man will fish goads even the lazy ones into action.'[63] After the plant at New Masset stopped canning salmon in 1966, the local salmon-fishing fleet made a long, arduous journey across Hecate Strait and back, to take the catch to mainland canneries.[64]

The Masset had once dominated northern seine fishing, both as skippers and as crews, but by the mid-1960s contributed only 38 per cent of the local work-force.[65] For one thing, after repossession of Masset-built seines by packing companies, the centre of seining shifted away from the Charlottes, and, generally speaking, mainland crews replaced Haida. The beach at Masset was idle; the village wharf, big enough to fit sea-going vessels, had fallen into disrepair; and the Haida Boat Works boat-house stood empty.[66] Any remaining privately owned seine boats specialized in the crab fishery for as much of the time as possible. Gillnetting was less important for industrial fishing in the Queen Charlottes than in many other areas of the coast, so there was only a small gillnet fleet. Masset Band members owned a mere three out of the fourteen local vessels. New Masset Indians owned four; whites, seven. Masset Band members still owned the bulk of the local trolling fleet (10 trollers, or 58 per cent), however.[67] Many trollers had been built there years earlier and passed on from father to son. Typically, these were two-person vessels, somewhat older (from 10 to 36 years old), and smaller and had less-powerful engines than those owned by whites. They did not carry fish-finding devices or two-way radios.

The most common type of fishing boat owned by members of the Masset Band was the small outboard-motor boat – the mosquito fleet – used for a variety of fisheries. These had been built with special loans and government-supplied material. They averaged 5 m in length, had a small cabin and an 18-horsepower engine, and could easily be operated by one person. Worth about $1,000 each, they would be rigged with poles for trolling spring and cohoe salmon and fitted with rollers for use with a half-length of gillnet for sockeye. They were also used to jig for halibut during the subsistence fishery and for transportation. They were no good for professional fishers, however, being suitable only in good weather and sheltered waters. But they were versatile, required little capital, and afforded economic independence to their owners. The Masset could thus fill a niche in the industrial fishery and maintain their self-sufficiency. Unhappily for them, the Davis Plan sought to eliminate small boats.

A key to survival of industrial fishing in the Masset area was continued operation of the local cannery. Old Masset Village (Masset Band) was the one Indian fishing-based community and reserve in the Queen Charlottes that retained its fish-processing plant after the war. Nevertheless, there were big changes. In 1958, the original cannery at Old Masset closed and a new plant opened at the white village of New Masset (founded c. 1908), several kilometres away. Even so, in 1965 the cannery remained the largest employer of Indian wage labour and a major market for the produce of local Indian fishers.[68] Of the 135 shoreworkers employed, 87 (or 64 per cent), 52 of whom were female, were members of the Masset Band. In addition, 27 were men and women of Indian background who lived at New Masset. Also, some of the supervisory and technical staff were Indians. Cannery work accounted for 98 per cent of the principal occupations for Indian women living on the Masset Indian Reserve in the spring of 1966, and 89 per cent of all Indian workers had earned at least part of their income during the previous year in the fishing industry.[69] 'Part-time' producers included children, women, and men with other employment who dug for clams or borrowed a boat on weekends to go fishing.

Then in 1966, the Vancouver-based giant, BC Packers Ltd, bought out the operation and put an end to the canning of salmon at New Masset and, hence, in the Queen Charlottes, eliminating 75 Indian jobs. The seasonal nature of the local economy, the marginal state of local fishing equipment, depletion of fish stocks, and government restrictions on fishing times and places prevented most people here and in many other Indian communities throughout the coast from earning enough to support a family during winter.[70]

With talk of licence-limitation in the air, the Native Brother-

hood of BC, among others, warned the fisheries department that declining opportunities in the industrial fishery would continue to damage the economies and self-image of this and other coastal Indian
communities.[71] Citing a drop of 33 per cent in the number of Indian
fishers between the mid-1940s and the mid-1960s, the brotherhood
recommended that Indian Affairs and the fisheries department institute financial assistance directed at this group.

James Sewid, by then a vice-president of the brotherhood, recalls a hopeful trip to Ottawa in May 1964. He and other representatives told parliamentarians about BC Indians' concerns over their
future in the Pacific Coast fisheries:

> [What] we talked to them about at that time was the law they were
> going to pass that all skippers of fishing boats had to be certified as
> captains. I was kind of worried because the Indian skippers like my-
> self didn't have enough education to pass those exams. I didn't feel
> that it was necessary for the Indians because the Indian people knew
> the coast. We really knew those waters because we were born fisher-
> men. They were also talking about limiting the number of fishing li-
> cences that they were going to give out, and we talked to them about
> letting the Indian people have the same number of licenses and not
> cutting them down.
>
> In our spare time we went and visited different leaders. I went
> in and saw the Minister of Indian Affairs and told him that we would
> like to see some money available to start some Indians in their own
> businesses, such as building boats, canneries, or some other kind of
> industry. I told him what was happening was that the Indians were
> going to the Indian agent for relief, and it would be better to employ
> them if [sic] they had some little industries up along the coast. He was
> very sympathetic with what we were asking for and we had a very
> nice visit with him.[72]

This 'nice visit' and other lobbying by BC Indians paid off. When the
Department of Fisheries got permission to introduce licence-limitation
in 1968, fisheries officials almost simultaneously announced the Indian
Fishermen's Assistance Program (IFAP)[73] – a multi-million-dollar incentive scheme of direct grants and government-backed loans to increase
the size, quality, and safety of the Indian fishing fleet. It plainly sig-
nalled the government's recognition that the new policy for the Pacific
Coast might in fact eliminate Indians from the industrial fishery.[74]

Because the new special treatment would be hard to sell to the fishing industry, the public justification given was, as always, economic hardship. The Minister of Indian Affairs, Arthur Laing, pointed to the 'indescribably bad' conditions faced by Indians in some areas and argued that the money provided by the IFAP was 'not an important sum compared to what is required each year for Indian welfare payments.'[75] It was the old story – assistance to Indians if starvation were the only alternative. So Ottawa granted Indians special privileges in the fishery, not as acknowledgment of aboriginal rights or recognition that Indians wanted economic independence, but because Indians were poor. Rather than assisting economic development, the state-sponsored programs promoted economic dependence.

The Indian Food-Permit Fishery: Needed More Than Ever

In the post-war period, Indians came to rely on the Indian food fishery more than ever. Hawthorn, Belshaw, and Jamieson's report in 1958 found that this fishery yielded real income to Indian families far beyond what might appear to be the case: 'It would be difficult to evaluate such items as [fish and game] in money terms because they cannot be purchased in the market except in the form of expensive and inadequate substitutes such as canned salmon and fresh or smoked beef or pork.'[76] Fish, especially salmon, provided the largest component of Indian food supplies not bought from a store.[77]

Without question, traditional Indian salmon-fishing had persevered, although aspects of it had changed. Home-canning outfits and home freezers revolutionized food preservation in coastal communities in the 1960s. Nevertheless, traditional techniques simply incorporated available technology. Even though, for example, at least half the households of the Masset Band had purchased home freezers by 1966, the largest freezers could not hold a winter's supply of salmon for a large family. Some of the salmon had to be canned (fresh or smoked) in jars or tins; some was, as always, dried or smoked without further processing.

In Masset territory, the seasonal cycles of salmon and life-cycles of the villagers still shaped food fishing activities. In the 1960s, Masset Band members fished the small spring sockeye and late-autumn chum salmon runs, which the government had reserved for them nearly a century earlier. At the Yakoun River in Masset Inlet, for instance, entire families were camping and netting 'bluebacks,' or 'creek cohoe.'

These they smoked or canned. Only the Haida were permitted to catch them here, according to Florence Edenshaw.[78] When Edenshaw was growing up in Masset, around the turn of the century, her busy family had traded for or bought its fall salmon from other Indians.[79] She, as a young mother who worked at the local cannery, and her husband had little time to make trips to the Masset's sockeye salmon rivers to preserve fish for food. However, in later years they did. When interviewed by Margaret Blackman in 1979, Edenshaw was about to leave for the annual sockeye run; she was 82.

At the Indian village of Kitamaat, field workers for Hawthorn, Belshaw, and Jamieson discovered that even though not all families, or everyone in a family, could go to the summer villages to fish, and canning had replaced smoking or drying for preserving the food catch, fishing and the annual pilgrimage still took place:

> Two or three villagers have nets in the water in front of the village. In these they catch spring salmon, coho, and sometimes halibut. Almost every week for the first two or three weeks of fishing two or three village seine boats will return to the village for about six hours. During this time crewmen and villagers busily carry and wheel loads of fish to the homes, where they will be smoked and canned. Gillnetters who return to the village on weekends almost always bring one or two [commercially caught] fish home for their wives to can. One of the main reasons for families moving to Butedale in the summer, now that the cannery itself has closed down there, is that the movement provides a good opportunity for the women to can fish themselves. Mrs. A. said that the average family of about seven members would can from 12 to 15 cases of fish a year (12 two and a half pound [1.1-kg] tins per case). Added to this would be the fresh fish caught from November to March.[80]

Approximately 150 cans, for a total of 425 lb (190 kg) of fish, would last a family of seven through the winter.

Things were a bit different at Alert Bay. The local Indian council appointed James Sewid to head the community's drag-seining operation for sockeye. At the mouth of the Nimpkish River, Sewid and his crew set the net in reserve waters. 'We weren't allowed to drag seine just anywhere we wanted,' writes Sewid, 'but only on our own reserves.'[81] Other Indians took turns going over to the river to catch food fish for distribution to villagers for canning. There is a sad footnote to Sewid's story: after a few years, the Alert Bay Band had to give up this custom because there were no longer enough fish in the river to make the trip worthwhile.

Inland from the coastal waters, closer to the spawning grounds, the Indian fishery also remained central to local Indian economies. In the Upper Skeena and Babine Lake area, the major source of food for Indians in the 1950s continued to be fish, 'particularly the salmon caught as it reaches the spawning grounds from July to November.'[82] The average annual catch from 1946 through 1953 was 90,142 lb (40,925 kg) of edible weight (82 kg of edible fish per person). Although they used various fishing methods, the 50-year-old tradition continued of fishing with standard-sized gillnets supplied to each family head every few years by Indian Affairs.

The Bulkley River salmon fishery was another story. Salmon-fishing with set nets was impractical; fishing at canyons with traps, gaff hooks, and jigs was the tradition. In the 1950s, the fisheries department blasted out sizeable, ancient fishing sites at the Moricetown and Hagwilget canyons and installed fish ladders. Over Indian protests, the department said that this would improve the salmon runs, but it did not. The runs of sockeye – the major fishery here – immediately fell off and never recovered over the long run.[83]

Although government officials knew that the traditional fishery kept Indian communities alive, and could have interpreted the rules liberally, they decided on strict enforcement of the Indian fishery regulations. In court, BC Indians who were charged with fishery violations pressed the crown to recognize their hereditary rights to fish in the province. While the magistrates' decisions in lower courts are rarely the basis for any legal precedent or trend, they illustrate local judicial attitudes and arguments.[84]

Section 88 of the Indian Act provides, among other things, that, subject to the terms of any treaty, provincial laws of general application apply to Indians. Hunting regulation, under section 92(13) and section 92(16), is a provincial subject area. So in specific hunting cases in British Columbia, such as the well-known *White and Bob* (1964), where Indian defendants who came under the Nanaimo Treaty signed in 1854 with Sir James Douglas were charged with violating provincial hunting laws, they could point to a treaty right that exempted them. Non-treaty Indians could not have used this defence and would have had to rely on their aboriginal rights. In fishing cases, charges would have been laid under federal law, and treaty rights are not a defence against a federal charge. Aboriginal rights were a weak argument prior to the 1980s; however, as discussed below, section 35(1) of the Constitution Act, 1982, and the Supreme Court of Canada's judgment in *Sparrow* (1990) are changing this situation.

In *Regina v. Cooper*, in the BC Supreme Court, 1969, the appellants, all Indians, had been convicted and fined in 1968 under the Fisheries Act for unlawful possession of salmon on the Sooke River at a time when fishing was prohibited.[85] They claimed treaty-protected rights to fish, citing the treaty made in 1850 between their ancestors and Sir James Douglas. The accused attempted to prove that the fish were taken 'as formerly,' in order to employ the treaty as a defence. Mr Justice Brown referred to the Douglas Treaty as a 'larcenous arrangement' that must have been drawn up by or on behalf of the Hudson's Bay Co., and 'so any ambiguity must be construed in favour of the exploited Chiefs.' Yet he upheld the conviction. He ruled that the Fisheries Act had later taken away the rights claimed.[86]

Nowhere was the issue of the Indian fishery more pressing than on the all-important Fraser River, where over half the BC Indian food-permit salmon was caught.[87] New fisheries regulations for British Columbia for the 1967 season closed Fraser River fishing from Mission Bridge to Lytton from 3 to 25 July, citing the need to protect the crucial early sockeye run at Stuart Lake. Officers conducted 24-hour patrols, arrested Indians, and confiscated Indian nets – all in the name of fish conservation. But conservation for whom? As Indians were quick to observe, the industrial salmon fishery on the Fraser estuary remained open during this period.[88]

In a series of meetings of representatives from both shores of the Fraser, Indians agreed to press Ottawa on several fronts. They wanted legislation defining their aboriginal rights to fish the Fraser. They wanted an Indian spokesperson appointed to the advisory board of the International Pacific Fisheries' Commission, the Canadian-US body that managed the Fraser River sockeye and pink salmon fishery. And they protested the length and timing of the Fraser River closure and what they saw as harassment of Indians by fisheries officers.[89] The press reported Chilliwack Band Chief William Mussell on the issue: 'In the past, Indian organizations have not consistently fought to have their rights recognized. [On the Fraser] we ended up having a three-day week to fish and the most recent thing has been the July closure. Families that rely heavily on salmon as a diet during

Friendly Cove (Yuquot), Nootka Sound, from an engraving published in London, 1798. Eighteenth-century explorers noted fish-drying racks at such coastal summer villages. Here, Indians trolled for salmon; ocean-going canoes had sails of skins or red cedar mats. Fishing and fish-processing were communal and family-based. Hand-crafted technology was adapted to local conditions, and custom governed access to fish, with no distinction made between harvesting for subsistence and harvesting for exchange. 'It also appears that they must have had,' writes Wayne Suttles, 'besides technology and organization, sufficient means of describing and interpreting what we call space and time to be – often enough – in the right numbers, with the right gear, at the right place, and at the right time'; *Coast Salish Essays* (1987), 68–9.

Indian dip-net fishing on the Fraser River, n.d. Large, Fraser River dip nets are attached to rings of bone or shell slipped around the hoop at the end of the shaft. The operator kept the net open by pulling the line taut and released the line when a fish entered the net. The rings slid down the hoop ('pursed'), closing the net and trapping the fish inside. Federal laws permitted Indians continued use of this technology in their upriver fishery.

Salmon Weir on the Cowichan River, c. 1867–70. Sections of a wooden
lattice fence were placed against a framework built across shallow rivers.
The downstream current helps to hold the fence in place. Openings led
migratory salmon into one of two long parallel-sided traps on the upstream
side, here being tended by a boy. Despite a relatively small drainage, the
Cowichan River supports, in addition to chinook and cohoe salmon, three
species of trout, two of char, and spring and fall runs of steelhead. Struggles
between the Cowichan people, who claimed treaty protection for their
fisheries, and non-Indian sports and commercial fishers (who wanted
Indian weir fishing banned) began as early as the 1880s.

Smoke-houses at Hagwilget, nineteenth century. The raised cache (centre) stored preserved fish, and open-air drying racks were strung with fish. Indians have always preserved massive quantities of salmon for food, ceremony, and trade.

Salmon trap at Hagwilget Canyon, from a postcard postmarked 1914; Indians operated elaborate traps here on the Bulkley River. Nineteenth-century federal fishing regulations prohibited this technology, and in the 1950s the fisheries department even blasted out major ancient fishing sites here and at Morice Canyon and installed fish ladders.

A Haida family fish camp, Long Arm, Skidegate Inlet, Queen Charlotte Islands, 1901. The federal fisheries department and packing companies hoped that working for coastal canneries would replace Indians' pursuit of their traditional fisheries and even talked during the First World War of banning Indian food fishing altogether.

Haida woman dressing halibut meat at a fish camp, c. 1901. Food preservation was largely women's work. The flesh of this large fish is being sliced as thinly as possible on a decorated butchering block. After squeezing out most of the moisture with weights, she will drape the flesh over a drying rack. Halibut was a 'back-up' food resource for many aboriginal BC groups; for the Haida, it was a larger resource than salmon.

Ed Whonnock's mother drying salmon, Alert Bay, n.d. Even after the
Second World War, great quantities of Indian food fish, especially salmon,
continued to be dried or smoked in the customary way – the largest
component of Indian food supplies not bought from a store. Dried fish and
meat traditionally were eaten with carbohydrate-yielding oil extracted from
sea mammals, salmon, or eulachon. On the drying racks hang thinly sliced
salmon fillets and salmon chunks, which may later be smoked over a fire to
add flavour. To the rear, whole, split salmon are held firmly open in
anchored, wooden roasting tongs.

Federal fisheries officers, including district inspector E.G. Taylor, removing
a Kwakiutl salmon trap on Marble River, Quatsino Sound, Vancouver
Island, in 1912. This type of trap, just below a falls in a river, caught
migrating salmon tumbling back. Diversification and the spread of
processing throughout the coast after 1900 led to tough enforcement of
fisheries regulations to conserve the resource for packing companies.

Canada fisheries patrol vessel *Cloyah*, on the Skeena River at the North Pacific cannery dock, n.d.

'Songish chiefs sister with fish for sale.' Songish, more commonly
'Songhees,' is the English name used for Indian people in the Victoria area.
From 1888, federal regulations defined Indian fishing as food fishing and
prohibited sale or trade of fish so caught. Then it became an offence for
Indians to bring fish caught in non-tidal waters to the coast and, later, for
anyone to buy fish caught by Indians under Indian permits. After the
Supreme Court of Canada's decision in *Sparrow* (1990), the government
modified the ban on sale of 'food fish,' but commercialization of the Indian
food fishery remained a hotly contested issue.

The tug *Tyee*, towing a scow loaded with salmon (left) and a fleet of gillnet boats (mostly out of view) back to a Port Essington–area cannery on the Skeena River, probably at week's end, early 1900s. Tugs or packers towed the oar- and sail-powered cannery fleets out to sea and back each week. Company packer boats visited the vessels daily to pick up the catch; at the sight of a load of fish, the cannery would be fired up for packing. Expansion of canning on the Skeena caused fishers to tap grounds farther out to sea. The Indian gillnet convoy remained a familiar sight until 1945.

Anglo-BC Packing Co. receiving salmon, Garry Point cannery, Fraser River, 1891. Indians fished the cannery-owned gillnet fleets in the mouth of the Fraser and inshore waters of the Strait of Georgia until Japanese Canadians began replacing them on the fishing grounds and in the plants of this district after 1900.

Interior, salmon cannery, Skeena River, c. 1890. Indian women traditionally cleaned fish ('washing,' usually reserved for older women) and packed them into cans ('filling'). Both jobs required considerable judgment, agility, and physical stamina and remained largely hand operations until after 1945. Here, women stand at wooden cleaning tables and cold water tanks, where they put in long hours washing, scrubbing, trimming, and scraping with remarkable speed thousands of freshly butchered and gutted salmon carcasses. Canvas strips protect forearms and hands from cuts and bruises and from exposure to the frigid water. Until unionization during the Second World War, salmon canneries were exempt from most provincial labour laws and regulations.

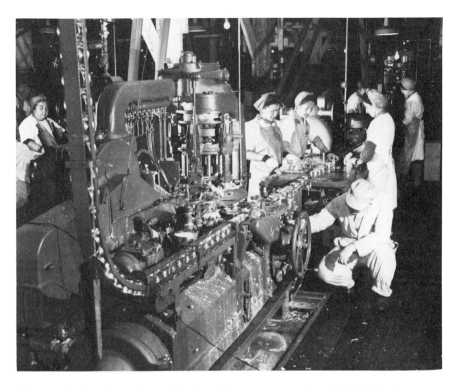

Automatic cleaning and canning line, Namu cannery, August 1945. During the war, Indians benefited from the fisheries' high demand for labour, especially after expulsion of Japanese Canadians from the Pacific Coast. Indian women took on most of the mechanical and supervisory jobs normally performed by men.

Students of St Michaels Indian Residential School, Alert Bay, drag seining salmon at the mouth of the Nimpkish River for food for the school, n.d. In the twentieth century, government restrictions and depletion of local stocks resulting from industrial fishing and destruction of fish habitats have undermined Indians' ability to fish for food at ancestral sites.

Mrs Dorothy Gordon and Mrs Ruben Mason drying herring eggs, n.d. Aboriginally an important item for local consumption and trade between villages and regions, herring eggs (roe or spawn) have always been harvested on pre-set or naturally growing plant material at hundreds of spots along the coast. The fisheries department licensed an industrial roe-herring fishery and roe-on-kelp harvest, beginning in the early 1970s. Only in these new, small-scale, highly regulated fisheries with Japanese markets are Indians strong participants.

Publicity shot, probably late 1940s: 'Maurice Barns, buyer for Francis
Millerd Canning Co. of Prince Rupert weighing clams, while young Sam
Lewis is making sure his mother is getting all that is coming to her.' Clams
have been canned on a small scale in the province since the beginning of
this century. Indians, mostly women, supplied clams to the canneries by
digging in the flats at low tide the Indian way, with a short, pointed stick,
and later with a small steel blade or a potato fork. They could reach a range
of small clam beds in their canoes, and when harvesting for their own use,
they and their families camped and dried or steamed clams on the beaches.
A popular type for canning was the butter-clam (*Saxidomus giganteus*).

Old sign found on the Fraser River near Hell's Gate, October 1982.

Haida commercial fishboats in Sedgewick Bay, Lyell Island, Queen Charlotte Islands, May 1986.

Drying salmon on the Fraser River, July 1987.

Federal fisheries officer and Indian dip-net fishers on the Fraser River, July 1978. The federal government introduced radical changes in fisheries policy for the Pacific Coast (the Davis Plan) in 1968. Government raids on Indian fish camps and communities, and accusations of salmon-poaching and black-market sales, led George Manuel, president of the Union of British Columbia Indian Chiefs in 1978, to declare the Department of Fisheries 'Enemy No. 1' of BC Indians.

'If you want to fish buy a license': protest fleet on the Fraser River, 27 August 1992. The Supreme Court of Canada's landmark decision in *Sparrow* (1990) found an aboriginal right to fish for food and ceremonial purposes in non-treaty BC areas and confirmed the priority of aboriginal fishing. During the Fraser River's salmon-fishing season in 1992, federal fisheries minister John Crosbie announced the Aboriginal Fisheries Strategy, including a pilot project to allow Indian groups to manage the fisheries and to permit commercial use of part of the Indian food fish allocation. This trial failed miserably and provoked near-riots within and among various groups of fishers.

Fishers picket BC legislature over Indian fishery, 27 February 1993.

Canned salmon label, c. 1900. The persistent, pervasive image of Natives as one-dimensional, natural beings existing in a primitive state – timeless, spaceless, and society-less – has made it easier for others to misunderstand the issues surrounding aboriginal rights.

the winter managed to catch only one-quarter of the larder they usually get.'[90] The protest provoked the Fraser valley's Indian leaders into submitting a brief to the federal government claiming aboriginal fishing rights on the Fraser and citing the Royal Proclamation of 1763 as their authority.[91]

When in the 1968 season the fisheries department again imposed a three-week closed season for the Indian fishery on the Fraser, Indian leaders urged an end to government regulation of their fisheries. They also warned that some Indian people would be disregarding the existing regulations.[92] Genevieve Mussell, former chief of the Chilliwack Band, was a prominent leader in the conflict: 'Indians fear they will lose all their fishing rights if there is not some definite recognition of an aboriginal right to the Fraser's fish resources,' she told reporters.[93] Indians challenged the arbitrariness of policy on their fishery and also the fact that they had had no voice in shaping it. Under this pressure, government officials reluctantly agreed to allow the Indians one 24-hour opening for sockeye-fishing during that year's three-week restricted period. What happened in the late 1960s on the Fraser River fishing grounds echoed the revival of the aboriginal rights issue in British Columbia and elsewhere in Canada. Indians were no longer content simply to pay a fine or go to jail silently.

Plainly, Indians devised many strategies for coping with the postwar transformation of the Pacific Coast fisheries. Many Indian families and even entire villages could still participate together in the Northern district. Sol Sinclair predicted in 1960 that Indians would not suffer under licence-limitation. But the processors knew otherwise. The response of the Fisheries Association of BC to Sinclair's report was prophetic: '[Under licence-limitation] the historic rights of the natives would be difficult to preserve. They would either be elevated to a place of extra special privilege or ultimately fall by the wayside.'[94]

In fact, both scenarios would be enacted. Limitation of licences would temporarily give Indians special deals, but, as the policy began to take effect, most Indians would find it impossible to make a living in fishing. Simultaneously, state policies and regulations hobbled the upriver Indian fishery – an essential resource for Indians. In the new national climate that favoured settlement of land claims and entrenchment of aboriginal and treaty rights, Indian fishing rights would remain high on the agenda of BC Indians.

7 Rights Reconsidered: From the Davis Plan to *Sparrow*, 1969–1993

The idea of the Salmon Vessel License Control Plan, or Davis Plan, announced in the fall of 1968, was to keep the Pacific Coast salmon fishery profitable for full-time, mobile fishers and large-scale, centrally located processors operating year-round. It incorporated Sol Sinclair's proposal of restricting entry to the salmon fishery through rigid licensing regulations, phasing out vessels, and promoting centralization and concentration of processing facilities. Implementation took place in phases and required many modifications, changes, and financial aid and special deals to overcome its obvious basic failures. The administrative tinkering seems only to have made things worse. Economic benefits to the industry have been mixed, and for most industrial fishers and fish-plant workers licence-limitation has been a disaster. As for the health of the salmon stocks, benefits have also been mixed.

While the new regulations and policies reduced the number of fishers and shoreworkers, as intended, Indians again suffered the greatest losses. The immediate result of the Davis Plan was that BC fishing and fish-processing employed less than half as many Indians as they had two decades earlier. The scheme hurt the Northern district, the only one where many Indian families had remained involved in fishing and fish-processing. Conditions temporarily improved for Indians in the mid-1970s when new markets and major financing from Japan opened for salmon and herring products. By then, unfortunately, a series of plant closures meant that fewer Indian families could find places in the industry. Schemes to develop Indian-owned fish plants turned into political nightmares. Rationalization of the fishery along centralist lines broke down the pattern of cultural persistence and adaptation that had continued long after Indians entered the industrial fishery.

In the new North American climate of Indian cultural renewal and political activism, BC Indian groups and several government departments and agencies devised many special programs in the 1970s to increase, or at least stabilize, participation by Indian fishers and shoreworkers. Dozens of studies and commissions have concluded that, despite special assistance, only the already highly successful have been able to stay in industrial harvesting.

Indian activism and legal action in Washington state led to the *Boldt* decision (1974), which guaranteed Indian fishers up to 50 per cent of the allowable catch of salmon. In British Columbia, similar Indian actions led to clashes on the fishing grounds and unprecedented numbers of raids and court actions over the Indian food fishing regulations. Fish-based Indian groups have attempted to negotiate land claims with fishing rights as a critical feature of them, and recently some have taken the crown to court in light its failure to negotiate.

Canadian governments and the Fisheries Act consistently refused to recognize any special fishing rights in Indian peoples beyond meeting their own food needs. But a comprehensive federal investigation of the Pacific fisheries headed by Peter Pearse in the early 1980s recognized the intimate traditional connection between Indians' fishing for food and their fishing for commercial and other purposes. Pearse recommended that the government cooperate with Indians to guarantee their aboriginal prior claim on the salmon catch. Also, because of their different economic and political circumstances, Indians should be allowed, band by band, to develop ways to take economic advantage of their allotments of fish. Until the 1990s, the state resisted acting on these recommendations, and through its policies and in the courts it persisted in its long-standing refusal to acknowledge aboriginal rights to a commercial fishery. Constitutional entrenchment of aboriginal rights in 1982 and the Supreme Court of Canada's decision in *Regina v. Sparrow* (1990) are changing the law and public policy on Indian fishing.

THE DAVIS PLAN

In September 1968, the new minister of fisheries, Jack Davis, himself an economist, announced Ottawa's goal for the Pacific Coast fisheries: to improve the fisheries' economic performance and increase fishers and shoreworkers' incomes by restricting and reducing the number of licensed salmon vessels, over-capitalization, and 'excess labour usage' in the salmon industry. By lowering costs of production, the program would create profits and thus raise the level of return for individual fishers and compensate the government for the costs of managing the industry and the resource.[1] The first branch to be affected was the salmon fishery. While Davis lost his seat in the 1974 election, his policy has survived under the half-dozen subsequent fisheries ministers.

Davis intended to implement the plan in four phases, over several years. First, a system of licensing would freeze the fleet at a stable level. First-class salmon (A) licences would be issued to vessels with large recorded catches (over 10,000 lb [4,540 kg] in fish landings in 1967 or 1968). Second, the government would buy back and scrap fish boats to shrink the fleet ('Buyback Program'). Third, Ottawa would improve the fleet's efficiency through quality-inspection, with the hardship provision of cheap, temporary salmon licences (B) for substandard vessels. Fourth, 'economically optimal' gear and area regulations would maximize mobility in the fleet and improve the quality of the catch by reducing the river catch of salmon to a minimum and shifting commercial harvesting out to sea. The government also created a category-C licence for non-salmon fishing. The C licence was not subject to limitation, but most of the fisheries in this category soon came under licence-limitation also.

The First Few Years

The Davis Plan initially reduced fleet size and employment in the salmon fishery. However, over-capitalization became a greater problem than ever.[2] Tonnage increased as did the price of boats, partly because of introduction of A salmon licences – permanent licences, and hence the most costly and difficult to obtain. Every time a class-A fishing vessel changed hands, its value soared. Before the Davis Plan, buyers and sellers valued only the hull, engine, and electronics, but after limitation, the market value of a licence (averaging about $4,000 per ton) figured into the price.[3] Those building new boats could try to assemble and combine more than one B licence to produce a single class-A vessel with many times the fishing power. Construction was dauntingly expensive, with a 15-m freezer troller, fully equipped and licensed, costing around $200,000 in the mid-1970s. In 1978, consolidation of licensing regulations ended the practice of combining tonnage by prohibiting replacement vessels from exceeding either the length or the tonnage of the vessel being replaced.[4]

Other reasons for the high price of boats included permanent withdrawal of vessels from fishing through the government's Buyback scheme.[5] Also, a massive injection of new capital in larger and more expensive gear resulted from development of the government-promoted roe-herring industry, beginning in 1972, followed by an excellent salmon-fishing season in 1973.

In general, the new fisheries policy had a differential effect on each type of fishing. Although entry was not permitted under licence-limitation unless a licensed vessel were retired, the seine fleet grew at the expense of the gillnet fleet, the licences of which were purchased and combined to allow construction of higher-capacity vessels and licensing of new seine boats. This trend undermined the objectives of licence-limitation. The government promulgated a ton-for-ton replacement rule, so that introduction of one seiner required retirement of six to seven gillnetters.[6] This slowed down, but did not reverse, the tendency towards over-capitalization in the fleets. As had happened repeatedly in the industry, fisheries policy was also an intentional bonus to the processing companies, which owned fleets of otherwise-worthless, dilapidated rental gillnetters.

For trolling, the story was different. Under the Davis Plan, the total number of trollers in the province did not rise much above the numbers of the 1960s. There were 2,200 licensed in British Columbia in 1970. But the value of the troll fleet skyrocketed, from $28.1 million in 1966 to $41.5 million in 1969. A new type of troller, the freezer boat, appeared early in this period. Freezer boats replaced the old day trollers, which carried ice, and many gillnetters were converted to trolling-combination boats.[7] The new vessels could stay at sea for up to a month at a time, giving owners an incentive to install costly electronic aids and diesel power – which they did. But then new regulations shortened the troll-fishing season, reduced the number of lines in which trollers could fish, and banned barbed hooks, thus artificially lowering the productivity of these expensive vessels. In a conservation measure, the government further lowered productivity by implementing coast-wide maximum troll catches for spring salmon, the principal fish for this type of gear.

The West Coast Fleet Development Committee supported and

encouraged fleet rationalization under the Davis Plan. Jack Davis created the committee, composed of representatives of the fishing and processing sectors and the provincial and federal governments, in 1971–72 to shape the future of this perpetually troubled industry.

For the processing sector, the new fisheries policy was intended to promote a 'leaner' industry, where fewer plants operated but at maximum efficiency. Spatial and business centralization assisted the powerful fish-processing conglomerates. Processing was ruled by two big companies (BC Packers Ltd and Canfisco) and one big union (the United Fishermen and Allied Workers' Union).[8] The dozen BC packing companies controlled or owned 40 per cent (2,100 vessels) of the province's commercial fishing fleet.[9] Plants had closed in previous decades, but the closures in 1969 were, according to the Fisheries Association of BC, 'very noticeable because there were so many' and because major firms went out of business.[10] In 1969, one of the oldest on the coast, ABC Packing, sold its assets to the two industry giants, which then closed most of ABC's former plants. Next, BC Packers announced a merger with Nelson Brothers Fisheries Ltd (secretly a wholly owned subsidiary since 1960), closing many of the latter's plants.

On the Skeena, only the Cassiar (independent) and Port Edward (BC Packers) canneries operated after 1968. The North Pacific cannery operation ended when ABC Packing sold it to Canfisco. Canfisco immediately consolidated its northern operations at its old Oceanside plant in Prince Rupert.[11] BC Packers, owner of Sunnyside cannery, declared that operation obsolete and transferred production to its Port Edward plant, which it enlarged to handle the additional pack. BC Packers and Canfisco announced shutting down of the J.H. Todd Co. plants at Sooke and Rivers Inlet, which they had operated as a joint venture since 1954. In the central coast region, only two of the original five fish-processing plants (Namu and Millbank, near Bella Bella) kept running, though only temporarily. Canfisco and BC Packers closed nearly all their troll camps (which supplied ice and bought fish) on the west coast of Vancouver Island, which events severely threatened small-boat salmon-fishing there.[12] These deals may have been lucrative for investors and company executives but not for the men and women who fished and worked in the industry.

Fishers' marketing cooperatives changed under the Davis Plan. Marketing coops had appeared (and disappeared) in the 1920s and

1930s as a means for fishers, mainly trollers, to bypass traditional controls and ties between fishers and cannery processors.[13] The most successful coops fished on the margins and turned out products that did not compete in a major way with cannery operations. Members were not unionized. But after introduction of licence-limitation, coops started full-scale production of all fishery products and so entered into direct competition with company processing firms, union-affiliated fishers, and unionized shore-plant workers. Only one coop substantially involved in the industry – Prince Rupert Fishermen's Cooperative Association, chartered in 1931 and operated as a local collecting organization – has survived to the 1990s as a major diversified processing plant that unionized.[14]

Taking Stock in 1976

When licensing came under review in the mid-1970s, the findings were alarming: the cost of fishing had soared without the anticipated comparable rise in returns for fishers or processing companies.[15] The total number of vessels had dropped from 7,000 in 1968 to less than 5,000 in 1976, but these figures reflect mostly elimination of small gillnetters and day trollers from the provincial fleet. The government cancelled the Buyback Program in 1974, having purchased 354 vessels. Total capital investment quadrupled between 1969 and 1980, yet the size of the catch remained the same. Salmon prices rose accordingly, but this made it difficult to market the canned product and so threatened overall profits and plant jobs. More important, the Davis Plan had failed to respond to the threats to salmon conservation and management caused by powerful industrial interests and a growing sport fishery.

To bolster stocks and handle the crisis in salmon conservation caused by over-investment in the fleet and damage to habitat in the salmon rivers, the federal and provincial governments together introduced the multi-million-dollar Salmonid Enhancement Program, which began in 1977. Ottawa funded the program, and Victoria provided technical service. Most of the effort went into developing hatcheries – which by the 1990s some fisheries experts viewed as 'expensive failures' that may have harmed the wild stocks – rather than into habitat rehabilitation.[16] Simultaneously, Ottawa toughened provisions in the Fisheries Act against polluting or contaminating fish habitats. But Geoff Meggs's study of the decline of the BC salmon fishery has revealed the federal government's shamefully poor record of enforcement of such regulations in the province.[17]

The 1980s: The Pearse Commission

The period 1980–84 has rightly been called one of the worst for Pacific Coast fishers since Confederation. Heavy indebtedness and low profits created spiraling debt for fishers: processors went bankrupt, leaving fishers unpaid but still financially obligated to the companies.[18] Cuts in prices and a fishing strike that forced the industry to miss an entire herring-roe season in 1980 triggered another amalgamation in the processing sector and another round of plant closures. BC Packers Ltd became the unchallenged leader that year when it acquired all the northern holdings of its principal competitor, Canfisco. Canfisco concentrated production at its Vancouver plant. BC Packers quickly closed the last of the remaining plants in the Skeena River area, including the Port Edward cannery, which it dynamited, and consolidated its northern operations at its recently acquired New Oceanside plant in Prince Rupert. (In the 1985 season, New Oceanside produced a half-million cases of canned salmon, the largest pack ever at a single BC plant.[19]) That left only the Cassiar in operation on the Skeena. It closed after the 1983 season, having operated continuously for an unprecedented 80 years. That same year, BC Packers shut down its large fish-processing plant at Tofino. A handful of plants still operated in Prince Rupert, but it became common practice to truck some of the catch south to the Vancouver plants for final processing. Vancouver was the main centre of the industry.

When the economy headed into recession in the early 1980s, continuing anxiety about the state of the fisheries and about government regulations led the new fisheries minister, Roméo LeBlanc, to convene the Commission on Pacific Fisheries Policy in 1981. The head, Peter Pearse, was a resource economist at UBC and had been heavily involved in ongoing planning for licence-limitation.[20] Pearse and his fellow commissioners travelled extensively in the fishing districts and received volumes of written and oral presentations from Indians and others with an interest in the future of the industry.

The commission's report (*Turning the Tide*) in 1982 proposed sweeping measures for licensing commercial fishing, rationalizing fleets, and creating mariculture leases (ocean ranching). It showed that levels of salmon abundance were only about half what they had been between 1894 and 1913 and blamed over-fishing. Hatchery programs were no solution. They only posed an added threat to survival of wild stocks. The report criticized the many federal and provincial programs supplying subsidies, loans, and tax incentives to boat-builders, fishers, and fish processors; these had not helped to conserve fish or to create an economically efficient industry.[21] It also recognized the enormous catches taken in the sport fishery in recent years. Up to 300,000 anglers fished annually in tidal waters without a licence, and highly profitable sport-fishing charter-boat operations represented an expanding but unregulated industry. The report also noted weakening of the historic pattern of control of fishing fleets by processing companies and saw this trend as desirable in the interests of conserving fish. To forestall reversal of that trend, but also to acknowledge the special position of Indian people in the Pacific Coast fishery, the commission strongly recommended stricter regulation of access to fish for industrial and sport fishers, and a better deal for Indians.

IMPLICATIONS FOR INDIANS

When the government announced the new fisheries regime in 1968, Indians, politicians, and many others had warned that licence-limitation would eventually eliminate Indians from salmon-fishing and fish-processing.[22] Over time, governments, the industry, fishing organizations, Indian organizations, and other bodies would commission dozens of studies into the impact of the new regulatory regime on Indian people. Collectively, these studies show that Indians have been hardest hit by licence-limitation, particularly by the higher licence fees and more stringent licensing requirements involved in fleet reduction, as well as by plant closures in the Northern district. Indian men and women, often entire villages, lost their boats and their fisheries jobs. Indian fishers from the ancient Clayoquot Sound village of Ahousaht were not alone when they challenged Commissioner Peter Pearse to do something about it: 'Nobody here thinks their fate is sealed,' they said; 'we all believe in struggle.'[23] Indians' struggles to maintain their fish-based cultures were more public than in the past.

New Pattern of Indian Involvement

Government-sponsored studies show that the increasing competition and capital-intensity in the fishing industry caused by licence-limitation pushed Indians out of the industry. Indian participation declined substantially in the period 1969–71, stabilized for several years under government assistance, and then fell again after 1980. For those Indians who lost their boats, the Davis Plan hurt them in many areas of their lives. They lost vessels that they depended on for food fishing, for maintaining vital transportation links with other communities, for transporting tourists, freight, and beach-combed firewood and timber, and for conducting hunting trips.

In 1969, poor runs of salmon and permanent closure of seven large BC canning operations, five of them in the north, cut Indian participation in the industry.[24] Only 15 plants canned salmon that season – the lowest number ever. Half of them were located in the Fraser River district, where very few Indians were working for the industry. In 1970, there were 18 salmon canneries licensed to operate – more than in any year that followed. Of the 3,700 people employed in BC canneries that season, about 40 per cent were Indians.[25] But as was true of Indians who fished, the number of Indian shoreworkers now was less than half what it had been two decades earlier. Nonetheless, Indians in the Northern district remained active in the processing sector until the early 1980s, when most of the remaining northern plants shut down.[26]

Out-of-town canneries closed partly because of pressure to bring cannery operations into compliance with federal regulations regarding fresh-water supplies and cannery housing for Indians into compliance with provincial Industrial Camp Regulations announced in 1968.[27] Indian housing sat on pilings above low tide and was vulnerable to fire, subjected to discharges of raw sewage, and plagued with substandard toilet and fresh-water facilities. This situation, however, was hardly new. Now, health officials declared 50 per cent of the units to be beyond renovation or repair. The provincial rulings coincided with announcement of the Davis Plan, and the province may well have been deliberately speeding up centralization in the processing sector. In the past, the cannery operators had obtained exemption from such regulations.

Compliance with health standards required costly renovations that the packing companies estimated would cost more than $100,000 per site.[28] Initially, a few firms said that they were willing to invest in the upgrading of some of their Indian housing but would board up and eventually demolish the rest. The owners of Cassiar and Sunnyside, on the Skeena, and Namu, on the north-central coast, intended to keep these old plants operating. In private memos, they wrote that only by keeping alive the tradition of a 'summer village' for Indian fishers and plant workers could they do so: 'There has been a long tradition of inter-dependence between [the Skeena] canneries and the Skeena River Indians and between Namu and the Bella Bellas, and we are anxious that this should continue.'[29] At the cannery village of Port Edward, only about half the 505 Indians who worked or fished at the cannery lived in cannery-owned housing, and so the owners decided to get rid of the Indian village there. Another company took this opportunity to get out of the fish-processing. ABC Packing left when it did partly because of the need for 'large expenditures of capital for non-productive improvements at a time when the company's (and the industry's) profit capability is seriously low.'[30]

Whatever the reasons for them, cannery closures ended seasonal jobs for many Indian fishers and shoreworkers. Fisheries department studies revealed that in 1969 alone closure of two Skeena River salmon-canning operations (North Pacific and Sunnyside, permanently) and three central-coast plants (Klemtu, permanently, and Millbanke and Namu, temporarily) left over 720 Indian shoreworkers, most of them women employed on the canning lines, without cannery employment.[31] This number represented more than 70 per cent of everyone who lost jobs in the fish plants that season. Most of the Indians hit were members of bands in the Upper Skeena and Nass rivers and the Bella Bella Band.[32] Relative to population, Klemtu and Hartley Bay bands were hurt worst of all. Not surprising, Indian welfare rolls on the central coast grew dramatically. There was little alternate employment, especially for young people and women.[33]

The processing industry's own survey of what happened to employees and fishers in the large canning plants operating in the Northern district between 1968 and 1971 shows the long-term trend for upcoast Indian women and men.[34] In 1968, when all seven of the district's major plants – from north to south: (old) Oceanside, Port Edward, Cassiar, Sunnyside, North Pacific, Klemtu, and Namu – operated, they collectively employed over 1,700 Indian plant workers, well over half of whom were female, and over 800 fishers, a few dozen of whom were women. Four seasons later, in 1971, when only three of these plants packed salmon (salmon-canning ended at Namu that year), 37 per cent fewer Indian men, and 45 per cent fewer Indian women, worked in them. A government study confirmed that in 1971 more Indian men were taking part in cannery work once done by Indian women.[35] The men took up plant jobs once they discovered that they could not make a living from fishing.

Fourteen per cent fewer Indian males were fishing for the plants.

Those who gillnetted suffered most. Fishers in this category decreased by 18 per cent for independent vessels and 13.6 per cent for rental boats.[36] Licence-limitation policies and regulations also hurt the Indian fleet. Between 1964 and 1973, the number of personally licensed Indian fishers fell by 44 per cent (as opposed to only 12 per cent for all BC fishers), and the number of vessels in the Indian fleet (vessels owned or operated by Indians) decreased by 40 per cent. Indian participation dropped most dramatically between 1968 and 1969. The situation was serious, since salmon accounted for roughly 90 per cent of the total value of the Indian industrial catch.[37] Even-numbered years, when the northern runs of pink salmon were strong, were better for the Indian fishery than odd-numbered ones.[38]

Especially at risk were Indians who operated the rental gillnet fleet. As government officials and politicians were aware when they drew up the Davis Plan, Indian fishers were the major operators of cannery-owned rental and charter fishing boats in British Columbia. Under the Davis Plan, processing companies had to reduce their own salmon-fishing fleet in direct proportion to the total decrease in privately licensed salmon vessels. 'Since most of these [rental] vessels are fished by Indians,' admitted the Fisheries Association of BC in 1972, 'most of those without boats are Indians.'[39] The firms sold off or retired their rental vessels faster than required, and at considerable profit.[40] The company-owned fleet in 1969 consisted mostly of old gillnetters. The number of gillnetters rented to Indians tumbled from 482 in 1968 to 202 in 1971.[41] Company-owned gillnet vessels withdrawn in 1971 were seldom returned to the fishery.

Indians suffered further hardship when companies tightened up on credit. Besides directly owning of fishing vessels, fish-processing firms financed the Indian vessels. In the spirit of the Davis Plan, plant operators withheld credit from any but the most productive fishers – including Indians.[42] When they closed down a plant, the owners expected those with debts to the operation to clear their obligations. Banks were replacing processing companies as the predominant source of vessel financing, but because the Indian Act prevented Indians from using their interest in reserve property as collateral, most Indians did not qualify for bank financing.[43] So processing companies – by withdrawing the opportunity for Indians to continue to fish, with vessels owned, financed, or chartered by processors; by refusing personal credit; and by closing plants – made it impossible for the many Indians heavily indebted to them to repay their debts.[44]

With their lines of credit stripped away, Indian fishers who managed to hang on to their boats lost their traditional manoeuvrability.

Many Indian-owned vessels, though initially categorized as first-class vessels for purposes of licensing, were small producers. The Masset mosquito fleet, described earlier, is a good example. Most small producers were heavily in debt to processing firms. The jump in licence fees hurt them, forcing many of them to leave the fleet. Some Indian vessels that had qualified for ordinary (A) salmon licences were soon sold through the government Buyback Program before it was discontinued in 1974. Others failed to meet the initial landings qualifications required to obtain a salmon licence and so never even qualified. Still others were disqualified for A licences later, when fisheries officials tightened regulations in 1973 by requiring inspection for quality standards. In that year alone, 25 Indian-owned boats were declared ineligible.[45]

Special Deals for the Indian Fleet

In the larger context of government subsidies, assistance, and incentives to fishers, boat-builders, and fish processors, Indians, too, received some special deals. Ottawa assisted Indian vessel owners in 1971 by offering them a choice of licences. They could pay the high fees for A licences and participate in the Buyback operation. Or they could take out a special 'Indian only' salmon-fishing licence (A-I) at token annual costs.[46] Indians who held temporary (B) licences, which became invalid after ten years when the vessel involved would be withdrawn from fishing, could upgrade them to A-I status. In 1972, the fisheries department decided to convert all B licences held by Indians to Indian licences with no time limit. Although vessels with special Indian licences were not eligible for Buyback, the licences were transferable to other Indians or could be converted to ordinary A licences and then transferred to non-Indians by payment of a financial penalty. To stem further losses of vessels from the Indian fleet, the government eliminated this loop-hole as of 1980. Indian Affairs purchased some licences for the Indian Fishermen's Assistance Program tonnage bank. And the government introduced non-transferable band licences for the benefit of band members. These government interventions were mainly to keep vessel licences from leaving Indian hands and ran against the general trends of licence-limitation. Nevertheless, the rigidities and single-mindedness of the

Davis Plan made the entire industry generally less flexible towards Indians, and Indians continued to lose their fishing licences and their boats.

The government also attempted several temporary forms of financial assistance to Indian fishers.[47] Through two regular Indian Fishermen's Assistance programs (1968–73 and 1974–78) and one emergency assistance program (1980–82), officials at Indian Affairs granted special loans to build new fishing vessels or purchase used vessels, to rebuild or convert fishing vessels, and to buy fishing gear and equipment. This was a response to pressure from Indian groups and others. The assistance was originally intended to last only a few years. Because the Davis Plan reduced fleet size but created a fleet composed of large, mobile, efficient, and expensive vessels, Indians would need even more time and money to catch up. A second assistance program was required.

A government-sponsored evaluation of the first program (1968–73) noted that fewer Indians were leaving the industrial fishery.[48] The grants had encouraged a few Indians to upgrade their vessels and some Indian fishing communities to develop facilities, such as net lofts and boat works.[49] Yet, while the grant-supported vessels tended to be equal to or above the BC fleet average value, vessel values of the non-assisted Indian fleets remained well below the corresponding BC fleet average. Also, the total income of the Indian fleet did not rise.

The second program (1974–78) had a bigger budget and a lower minimum age for applicants to allow younger Natives entry into the industry as owner-operators, and it aimed to encourage fleet mobility. Largely as a result of this program, the Indian fleet declined more slowly than the BC fleet as a whole. In fact, the Indian salmon fleet (Indian-owned and -operated salmon vessels rented from processing companies) rose as a proportion of the provincial fleet between 1973 and 1977.[50] Unfortunately, the appearance of success was illusory. Only a handful of Indians benefited, and, besides, the proportion of Indian fishers within the BC total was less than half of what it had been 20 years earlier.[51]

While assistance was not intentionally confined to wealthy vessel owners, this is what happened, just as it had in the larger industry under the Davis Plan. Overall, the Indian fleet in the mid-1970s took on relatively more seine vessels; almost no Indian-owned seine boats left the fleet in the first 15 years of licence limitation.[52] Seiners were better able to attain production minimums and meet vessel-inspection standards than smaller vessels.[53]

A mere handful of prominent Indian seine fishers continued to account for most of the Indian catch for all gear types.[54] In 1974, 96 predominantly seine and large gillnet vessels registered to the Johnstone Strait region, comprising only 12 per cent of the active Indian fleet, accounted for an estimated 30 per cent of the total landed value of the Indian salmon catch.[55] In the Nass, Skeena, and central-coast home ports, a significant proportion of fishing revenues from Indian-owned vessels was (and still is) realized not by band members who live in these regions, but by off-reserve Indian fishers living permanently in Vancouver.[56] Their incomes do not necessarily benefit the Indian fishing communities.

Two sociologists, Keith Warriner and Neil Guppy, recently concluded that the Davis Plan did not damage coastal fishing communities.[57] This is not true for Indian communities. Fleet mobility, an explicit objective of phase 4 of the Davis Plan and of the second IFAP, proved especially harmful to them. Mobility made it possible for non-Indians to fish in Indian fishers' home waters, 'no matter how isolated their villages.'[58] According to Chief Harry Assu of Cape Mudge, non-Indian seines invaded the local grounds, destroying the fishing industry and forcing out of business some Indians whose ancestors had fished there for thousands of years.[59] Indian fishers, too, had to range over a wider area, moving away from their home waters and thus losing time for fishing for food.

In 1980, in response to the crisis in fishing that year and to the growing numbers of Indian vessels leaving the fleet, the government devised the Indian Fishermen's Emergency Assistance Program to protect Indian fishers against further losses. The Department of Indian Affairs, the Native Brotherhood of BC, and 13 bands of the Nuu-Chah-Nulth Tribal Council (Nootka) administered grants, loan guarantees, and direct loans. The program ended in 1982.

Overall, the three programs of Indian assistance generally did make the Indian fleet more efficient and mobile and helped sustain the relative position of Indian fishers in the industry. But they helped principally the few Indian fishers already doing well before they began. As throughout Canada, unemployment was a growing issue for Indians. In British Columbia, coastal fisheries were crucial to solving the problem. Although Indian fishers represented only 3.2 per cent of status Indians in the province in 1976, they accounted for 12 per cent of the 13,620 Indians in the provincial labour force.[60] Twelve per cent may not seem like much. But considering the rate at which the coastal Indian population was growing, and that unemployment for them averaged between 50 and 60 per cent, the industrial fishery remained a major source of income and jobs.[61] It also provided cultural continuity and economic purpose. Because the assistance programs had the same inherent biases as the Davis Plan itself, they ultimately worked against the interests of Indian fish-based communities and favoured the highly successful vessel owners and processing conglomerates.

Other examples of special deals for Indians in the 1970s are the Indian Fisheries Development Board (1971) and the Salmonid Enhancement Program (1977). The Development Board was designed to dispense assistance funds for Indian fishers to purchase boats and gear so that they could operate independent of the processing companies. Yet two crucial expenses – down payments on boats and gear and vessel licences – were not covered.[62] The Salmonid Enhancement Program was not created just for Indians, but it was supposed to offer employment to Indians who had suffered under the Davis Plan. We could call it a semi-special deal for Indians. Initially, it was the major urban processors and not small producers, fishers, or coastal Indian communities that benefited most, even though Indians eventually became involved in planning salmonid enhancement.[63] Some bands found jobs with the enhancement projects through the Community Development Program component, though only 10 per cent of the program budget was set aside for this work. So, as with other special government deals for Indians, the more affluent Indian fishers received the bulk of the economic benefits, while the poorer ones, even those who fished full-time, received little help and so lost ground.[64]

The Indian Cannery Experiments

The goals of the government's new Pacific Coast fisheries policy were at odds with the economic and social plans of many Indian communities on the coast. Dianne Draper's graduate research shows that the cannery project at Port Simpson, an Indian fishing village, is a painful example of what happened when Indians entered into direct competition with non-Indian fish processors.[65] In December 1973, the newly elected NDP government in British Columbia approved payment of a $3 million grant to the Pacific North Coast Native Cooperative for construction of a fish cannery at Port Simpson. This project reflected three years of effort by North Coast Indians to get government assistance for their scheme to provide employment in the area. It also would allow them to participate in a vital social and cultural activity for North Coast Indian communities. The cooperative had formed in May 1970 as an affiliate of the North Coast District Council, itself conceived in 1968 to counteract the effects of plant closures and company consolidations in the fishing industry. The council represented 5,000 members of nine northern Indian reserve communities and about 3,000 Indians who lived off reserve.

The council consulted with engineers, economists, and provincial departments about the best location for a plant; Port Simpson was the largest concentration of Tsimshian people and is quite close to Prince Rupert. The council negotiated with Indian Affairs for funding from the new Indian Development Fund (set up in 1969), but Indian Affairs decided in 1970 not to get involved in the project.

The coop spent about $75,000, mostly from the BC government's First Citizens' Fund (also founded in 1969), on a feasibility study that targeted Port Simpson. Indians thought that the cannery project would receive financing from a special new program of the Agriculture and Rural Development Agency (ARDA), within the Department of Regional Economic Expansion (DREE), as a joint federal-provincial project.[66] The BC Department of Agriculture nominated and supported the proposal for ARDA funding in 1971. Minister of Fisheries Jack Davis spoke out against the scheme, however, vowing never to issue fishing licences to a cannery at Port Simpson.[67] A new plant would undermine the goals of the Davis Plan, he said. Davis's rejection carried weight with Jean Marchand, who was minister of DREE. Marchand announced that DREE would be happy to consider for funding other proposals for Indian economic enterprises on reserves, such as logging and saw-milling.[68] This must have sounded disturbingly familiar to the Indians.

There were rumours that Davis was trying to protect the big fishing companies, which resented the idea of new, government-assisted competition. This may have been true. Certainly the coop's application for ARDA funding in 1971 triggered strong reaction from the fish-packers and their organization, the Fisheries Association of BC. A letter from A.E. Macmillan, managing director of Cassiar Packing, to Cyril Shelford, BC minister of agriculture, typifies this reaction: 'We take violent exception to any proposal that would finance the construction of any production plant that would be in direct competition with ourselves and thus reduce our earning power.' He added, 'It is wrong for the government to support competition for us out of public funds.'[69] Ken Campbell, manager of the Fisheries Association of BC, wrote directly to Jack Davis, claiming that 'studies' showed that new jobs for Indians were not likely to accrue from the fishing industry.[70] The studies that he seems to have had in mind included one conducted in 1970 for the Joint Consultative Committee on Manpower, headed by Dr Noel Hall of UBC, and one undertaken in 1972 by the Fisheries Association of BC itself.[71] Noel Hall's analysis of jobs lost with the closing of plants in 1969 trivialized the industrial fisheries vis-à-vis Indian economies: 'The Industry in no way possesses the growth potential necessary to provide employment for the growing Indian population.'[72] The Fisheries Association reached the same conclusion as Hall. Both echoed the recommendations of Hawthorn, Belshaw, and Jamieson in the1950s.

The Fisheries Association sent proposals to Jack Davis, Cyril Shelford, and R.J. McInnes, director of the BC Indian Advisory Committee, for 'new employment which may be made available to Indian people.'[73] Most were fishery-related activities. These included maintenance of salmon streams ('with the Indian's knowledge of their home areas and their natural skills in the wilderness, it would seem a natural thing to enlist them as stream guardians'); construction, operation, and maintenance of artificial spawning channels; employment in salmon hatcheries ('[Indians] have inherited skills which many non-Indians do not possess ... The exacting and tedious work of fin-clipping tiny fry at Fulton River is done best by Indian women'); aquaculture development; government-subsidized harvesting and processing in underdeveloped fisheries; seaweed harvesting; and manufacturing fishing lures as a cottage industry. Other suggestions concerned tourism: promoting Indian carving and crafts and developing outdoor recreation projects, such as construction and maintenance of hiking trails and creation of Indian heritage parks, which the association suggested 'might also be the means of helping to preserve the Indians' culture.' (In other words, Indians should preserve their culture by fossilizing it.) Last came forestry-related projects on reserve lands, such as pulp mills, reforestation, and Christmas-tree farming. Indian reserves in the coastal areas were tiny, created to support fish-based economies. To suggest that Indians abandon fishing activities and exploit the forest resources on reserve lands was both impractical and gratuitous.

The processing industry thought that Indians should service the commercial and sports fisheries and other industries in marginal capacities rather than fully participating, hence competing, directly in them. This reflected concern not for the welfare of Indians or conservation of fish but for control of the industrial fishery:

> [The] Association feels strongly that projects undertaken by Indians, or on their behalf, should have a good opportunity for success and should be as non-competitive as possible with established industry. We say this because it would be self-destructive to simply set up new operations based on a resource already fully utilized. It could be argued that Indians have as much right to utilize it as anyone but unless it is made exclusive to Indians and denied to others, then the entry of the new factor only makes it less economic for everyone, including the Indians. So we strongly advise that Indian projects in the fishing industry should involve new production, or under-utilized resources.[74]

It could also have been argued that Indians had the greatest right of all to salmon. In the 1980s, when one Indian community tried to expand its involvement in herring roe on kelp, an 'under-used' resource, the Department of Fisheries and the Pacific Fishermen's Alliance, representing non-Indian fishers, backed by the federal trial court, blocked its way.

Canada backtracked. The minister of fisheries said that he would consider other proposals for Indian canneries, especially revival of the idle plants.[75] This statement provoked another deluge of complaints and reproaches from North Coast Indians and their supporters. The Port Simpson cannery had been intended to help communities to remain intact and regain their economic and social health. It was a carefully planned initiative, but no federal agency would back it.

Not until March 1975 was the $12-million Pacific North Coast Native Cooperative Seafoods processing plant at Port Simpson up and running.[76] The troubles had only just begun. The coop faced formidable odds at every turn. The leadership of the Native Brotherhood pledged its support, but its members would not promise to fish for it.[77] Then the American Can Co. reneged on its original agreement to lease machinery and equipment for three canning lines. Coop members believed that pressure from the canning companies lay behind both organizations' decisions.[78]

Between 150 and 180 Indians found employment with the operation, but the business was unprofitable.[79] Certainly, there were problems with management and in recruitment of skilled labour, but the coop had trouble getting an adequate supply of reasonably priced fish. Members of the Native Brotherhood would not cooperate fully, and the United Fishermen and Allied Workers' Union blacklisted the operation because non-unionized coop members fished during an industry strike in 1975.[80] The coop eventually attracted many Indian fishers, but it never did get the most successful ones, especially the seiners, who were the backbone of any successful processing enterprise.

The operation limped along. It was the second-newest plant on the coast, with some sophisticated machinery and equipment. Also, Japanese interests supported it so as to secure supplies of Pacific Coast frozen salmon and herring roe.[81] But in 1982, Japanese trading companies began withdrawing their investments in the BC fisheries. Because of industry pressures and internal operational difficulties, the Port Simpson plant did not can salmon until 1988, under management of a non-Indian enterprise, the Prince Rupert Fishermen's Cooperative Association, but the facility soon closed.[82] In 1992, some North Coast Indian officials regarded the operation as a potential 'gold mine.'[83] It has excellent ice and cold-storage facilities and good local people. The Prince Rupert Coop is willing to provide it with custom processing for a few years, to allow Port Simpson to secure long-term commitments and establish custom processing of its own.

The Central Native Fishermen's Cooperative and the Bella Bella Band also proposed viable Indian canneries. The coop formed in Bella Bella in June 1975 as a response by independent members of the local seine and troll fleet to announced cutbacks at the Millbanke Industries cannery (Shearwater), near the Indian village of Bella Bella.[84] It wanted to buy and operate the Millbanke plant with a bank loan. Members would raise the down payment, and the owner of Millbanke fisheries would provide a second mortgage.

Meanwhile, the Bella Bella Band had petitioned Victoria for a $3-million grant and a similar sum as a loan to finance a band-owned, year-round, multi-purpose fish plant at the village. The proposed cannery – a modest combination gillnet-troller venture of 60 to 70 boats (purchased from the BC Packers fleet) and a freezer plant – formed the cornerstone of the band's five-year plan for community service and economic development. It was intended to provide steady employment for about 330 shoreworkers and 90 fishers who were band members.[85] Given its own objectives, the band argued strongly against the coop's proposal for Millbanke. It claimed that the plant had never had much to do with the Bella Bella community and nothing would change under the new owners, most of whom were not members of the band.[86] The band believed that the operating philosophy of the Native coop conflicted with its own. Profit-oriented, urban Indians dominated the coop, whereas the band was prepared to operate on a break-even basis, especially in the labour-intensive, low-profit fisheries, just to create local jobs.[87] The coop raised equally strong objections to the Bella Bella proposal.

The Department of Fisheries officially opposed the Bella Bella proposal for the same reasons that it had objected to the Port Simpson project. Because of existing over-capacity in salmon-canning, said officials, it would not support a new salmon-canning development. DREE and the provincial Social Credit, returned to power in 1975, supported this position.[88] The province was more interested in the coop's scheme to take over an existing plant and make profit. In a private memo to 'file,' the acting provincial deputy minister responsible for fisheries noted that it could be politically dangerous for the government to buy 'too many losers,' although there could be 'pressure to recommend this *specific* proposal,' by the Bella Bella Band.[89]

Thus the coop's proposal won out over that of the Bella Bella Band. The coop bought the Millbanke operation, renaming it the Central Native Fishermen's Cooperative. It also acquired a medium-sized plant at Ucluelet. A powerful Japanese trading company (Marubeni) spent about $7 million on these projects, under a sales agreement for salmon, salmon roe, and herring roe, and a special ARDA program towards economic development of BC Indians contributed $1 million in 1978.[90] The coop faced such stiff competition for supplies and so much financial difficulty that by the mid-1980s its creditors persuaded it to lease its plants to a consortium of private companies.[91] Eventually, the coop's plants had to close. With structural changes in the industry, falling markets, withdrawal of Japanese investment in BC processing, federal policies and regulations that favoured centralization and consolidation, and differences in the objectives of Indian groups, remote undertakings such as these could not survive.

The Crisis in the 1980s

High licence values in 1978 and 1979 led some Indians to sell their vessels for a profit. Indian participation in 1979 was a mere 8.8 per cent of the total provincial salmon fleet, down from 10.5 per cent at the beginning of 1977.[92] Poor incomes in the 1980 fishing season – because of falling prices, strikes, and cannery closings – and record-setting high interest rates left many Indian vessel-owners with heavy loan commitments that few could meet. When researchers for the Native Brotherhood of BC asked a sample of Indian fishers in 1981 why they had sold their boats, the main responses were as follows: 35 per cent cited financial problems; 30 per cent, below-standard vessel condition; about 10 per cent, being tired of fishing and wanting another business; and 6 per cent, repossession.[93] Thirty-three per cent had sold their vessels to non-Indians and said that they received good prices. They needed the cash. Generally, Indians sold off gillnetters and trollers; they said that they could not make a living from fishing. A few sold their seiners, usually because they fetched such high prices.[94]

The Pearse Commission of 1981 was the first and, in truth, the only inquiry into the Pacific Coast fisheries to consider seriously the testimony of Indians. The commissioners called on Parliament to give stronger legal recognition to aboriginal interests.[95] Collapsing Indian participation in the fishery should be, in the view of the commissioners, reversed. Submissions from Indian groups had convinced them to recommend a broad definition of the 'Indian food fishery,' which they agreed was a continuation of a traditional Indian fishing practice that 'extended well beyond its food value.'[96] And they concluded that the inadequacy of Indian reserve lands in the province was tied to the issue of fisheries. Most BC Indians were in the double bind of having neither guarantees of their traditional fisheries nor control of land-based resources sufficient to maintain economic self-sufficiency. The commissioners offered crucial official recognition of the complexity and economic importance of traditional Indian fisheries and of the intimate historic link between Indian fisheries and BC land claims.

Officials of the Department of Fisheries boldly assured the commission that Indians had, within their fishery, prior claim on the resource, subject only to the paramount needs of resource conservation. However, government officials pleaded the old conservation argument: Indian river fishing was at the end of the harvesting chain for salmon. How could the department maintain proper escapement levels in the province unless it curtailed the Indian fisheries?[97] The commissioners disagreed and proposed a reasonable – if revolutionary – alternative: define quantitatively the Indians' prior claim on the catch and negotiate separate arrangements with each band.[98] This proposal went nowhere. For one thing, Indian groups differed on these issues. Also, processors and non-Indian commercial fishers did not then and do not now want to see Indians given the right to sell fish caught in the Indian food fishery or have Indian claims settled with allocations of salmon – thereby shifting, in their view, the cost of claims settlements onto the fishing and fish-processing sectors.[99]

In 1983, the active Indian-owned and -operated salmon fleet comprised 664 vessels (a drop of 37 from 1976), of which only 396 were privately owned; 59 were rental vessels, and 209 were fishing under an entitlement to the newly created Northern Native Fishing Corp. (NNFC). The tribal councils of the Nishga, the Giksan-Wet'suwet'en, and the North Coast (Coast Tsimshian and Southern Tsimshian bands) had formed the corporation in 1980 to acquire (through Indian Affairs) and manage the BC Packers' gillnet fleet of about 225 vessels, to lease vessel licences, and to sell vessels to Indian fishers who previously had rented them from cannery operations. Ottawa spent millions on the deal, which it saw as creating jobs for several hundred Indians. Most of the gillnetters from BC Packers were relics of Canfisco's old northern fleet, and profits from the sale allowed BC Packers to upgrade its existing plants – an undertaking that one sociologist, John McMullan, said 'eliminated Native jobs in the process.'[100] Many NNFC members could not pay the $1,000 licence rental and so, in order to fish, had to borrow directly from BC Packers. This transaction re-established debt obligations and assured the industry's control of a portion of the Indian fleet. Similarly, the Native Fishing Association was formed under the umbrella of the Native Brotherhood of BC about 1986, to administer low-interest loans and training programs for Indian fishers. But, again, when Indians are unable to meet these debt obligations, they have to go back to the processors for loans. The processors have kept their grip on the Indian fleet.[101]

Because of the NNFC's purchases, and also the traditional Indian preference for gillnetting, gillnet and gillnet/troll combinations were predominant in the Indian fleet in the early 1980s.[102] However, li-

TABLE 6
Ownership of BC Indian licences (salmon), 1991

Licence category	Indian licences			Total salmon licences issued	Percentage issued to Indians
	Reduced fee	Full fee	Total		
Salmon gillnet/troll	474	49	523		
Salmon seine	62	6	68		
Salmon NNFC	254		254		
Salmon B	1		1		
Total salmon	791	65	846	4,472	18.9

Source: Files, Native Brotherhood of BC, Prince Rupert Branch Office.
Note: Numbers of full-fee licences are estimates and do not include Indian-owned vessels leased to non-Indians. A vessel usually had more than one type of licence, and so the total of licences over-represents the size of the fleet, Indian and other. The source does not give a breakdown by licence category for the last two columns.

cence-limitation favoured seiners over gillnetters and trollers, and so many Indian communities that had once had substantial gillnet fleets lost them, as was true for the village of Gilford. Also, processing companies in some Indian villages with a purely rental fleet effectively dropped all Indian fishers despite their individual competence. This happened at Nootka, Klemtu, and some of the smaller villages in the Alert Bay area.[103] Trolling persisted on the west coast of Vancouver Island in some Indian communities that had long been active in this branch of fishing. The Ahousaht of Clayoquot Sound, for example, operated 38 of the 85 licensed trollers owned by the Nuu-chah-nulth Tribal Council in 1981 and also 'informally' operated 15 to 20 small trollers, which they called 'putters.'[104]

Between 1985 and 1991, Indian ownership of licensed salmon vessels hovered at 18–19 per cent of the total (see Table 6, re 1991).[105] About 40 per cent of these belonged to the NNFC.

Although Vancouver was the main centre of the industry, only Prince Rupert offered numerous jobs for Indians.[106] Indians constituted 58 per cent of the processing work-force there, and only 5.5 per cent in plants of the lower mainland.[107] Elsewhere, companies shut down one plant after another; only Seafood Products at Port Hardy remains. When Mary Lee Stearns returned to Old Masset Village in the spring of 1980, she found the beach idle; only eight band members still owned fishing boats.[108] The cannery at New Masset had become no more than a fish-buying station for a large Vancouver company.

Aquaculture was seen as an alternative to the industrial fishery in the 1980s. Indian Affairs created an aquaculture task force in 1982 to develop pilot projects and management training, but in 1990 only six bands were involved in aquaculture (three operated salmon farms, three practised oyster or shellfish culture) and the task force had been disbanded.[109] By 1991, financial difficulties resulted in closure of two of the three band-owned salmon farms.

The Indian Food Fishery: A Battle Zone

For BC Indians, fishing for salmon for subsistence and cash became more important than ever, as their opportunities to earn income from fishing shrank and cash incomes generally withered. They fished on the Fraser River system, up the Skeena and along many other salmon-carrying rivers, and in Indian communities and at fishing stations along the coast and islands.[110] The Fraser River, which as always housed over half the BC Indian bands, was the major Indian fishing area in numbers of people fishing and of fish caught; sockeye comprised the bulk of the catch. The salmon harvest there increased sharply from 1965 to 1973, although salmon counts are based mainly on fishery officers' informed guesses.[111] According to them, in 1973 estimated gross returns (or landed value) of the food catch under individual or band permits was $1.7 million, or 10 per cent of Indian industrial salmon returns. Sharing networks ensured, as they do today, distribution of salmon and other food among households. Many families had smoke-houses, home-canning outfits, or freezers for preserving fish.

The new fisheries regime heightened conflicts over fishing rights in the 1970s and 1980s. South of the border, 'fish-ins' and court action led to the celebrated *Boldt* decision of 1974 (*United States v. Washington*). *Boldt* guaranteed to Indian tribes in western Washington state with whom nineteenth-century treaties had been signed the right to take 50 per cent of the harvestable annual runs of salmon.[112] These peoples had fought in the courts for recognition for Indians' treaty fishing rights since the late 1890s.[113] Similar battles took place a few years later over the Indian salmon fishery on the Klamath River of northern California.[114] Today, in the early 1990s, the western Washington and Klamath River Indian fisheries remain sensitive and potentially explosive issues of economics and race.

In British Columbia, Indian groups with and without treaties have struggled equally long to win legal or political recognition of aboriginal rights to commercial and food fisheries. Until the 1990s, Canadian fisheries officials and the lower courts, rather than acknowledging such rights, challenged Indian salmon fisheries in major spawning tributaries. Restrictions and harsh enforcement in the 1970s and 1980s fuelled the fight for aboriginal rights in British Columbia. Tactics of resistance included mass rallies, sit-ins, road and rail blockades, and court injunctions and law suits against private resource companies and the crown over resource rights, management, and use in Indian territories.

Pearse commented that Indian food-fishing communities deeply resent what they see as arbitrary and insensitive enforcement of fishing laws that they had no say in creating: 'Indian people (have) experienced harassment, intimidation, unjustified confiscation of fish, cars, and gear, unnecessary and fruitless court action pursued at great expense by Fisheries personnel, constantly using emotionally loaded terms such as "massive poaching," "illegal possessions," etc.'[115] In court, the crown continued to argue, as in the 1960s, that aboriginal fishing rights never existed in the province, and that if such rights had existed they would have been extinguished by enactments and/or regulations passed over the years to conserve fish.

In the 1970 salmon-fishing season, the *Vancouver Province* reported a 'fish-in' by 100 young Indians near Chilliwack; federal fisheries officers ignored the action.[116] Indians defied another ban when members of the Penticton Band fished for spawning Kokanee (landlocked sockeye) on a creek in which, they claimed, their ancestors had been fishing for 1,000 years.[117] Apparently, when asked about Indian rights to fish here, the local fish warden, A.M. Hames, said: 'We do not recognize ethnic groups.'[118] He expressed surprise at how things had blown up that year when he ordered a few Indian women to stop fishing. In the past, he said, it was enough simply to chase Indians off this fishing ground. Leading the protest was Louise Gabriel, who informed reporters that 'this little creek is where the older women can go to fish ... This is what bothered me so much: I thought "I have to protect my women".'[119] Indians and fisheries officials alike wanted the matter settled. Indians held a massive 'fish-in' on 4 October, during which Chief Noll Derriksan was arrested.[120]

In the court case that followed, *Regina v. Derriksan* (1975), the crown charged the chief under the Fisheries Act with catching salmon for food off a reserve.[121] Derriksan claimed an aboriginal right to fish in the area, as guaranteed by the Royal Proclamation of 1763. The court found against him. Both the BC Court of Appeal and the Supreme Court of Canada upheld the trial court's conviction.[122] The *Derriksan* case decided that aboriginal fishing rights were subject to regulations under the Fisheries Act. Those rights therefore were subject to legislative control or regulation.[123]

With the well-publicized government crack-downs of the late 1970s on alleged contraventions of the Indian fishery regulations, Indians' resistance to interference with their traditional fishing rights intensified. In 1977, federal fisheries officials established the massive undercover 'Operation Roundup' to enforce provisions in the Fisheries Act against poaching and illegal sales of salmon by Indian fishers. First to be targeted were the Gitksan and Wet'suwet'en fishing communities of the Upper Skeena and Nass systems.[124] Charges were laid against 23 individuals. Unlike in the past, however, Indians from these communities did not plead guilty and pay a fine: the Gitksan-Carrier Tribal Council provided legal defence in a move to press the case for fishing rights. In the court battles that followed, the crown was unable to obtain any convictions.[125]

Things reached an impasse late in 1978, in the midst of stalled negotiations over comprehensive claims in British Columbia. At a meeting of the Union of BC Indian Chiefs, the president, George Manuel, articulated a long-standing feeling among his people that the Department of Fisheries was 'Enemy No. 1.'[126] Manuel and others spoke of the harassment that Indians received from Ottawa's fisheries officers; they proposed that Indians ignore federal fisheries regulations and prepare their own rules for their territories.[127]

Raids and accusations of salmon-poaching and black-market sales continued. No one would deny that some Indians sold food-fish salmon. Long-time BC residents say that until the 1970s it was easy to order up a few salmon from Indian friends and neighbours or to buy 'Indian' salmon out of the trunk of parked cars on the back roads. The former chief of the Cowichan Band, Wes Modeste, is reported as having said that crippling unemployment forced Indians, especially young ones, to sell some fish taken in their food fishery.[128] Illegal sales of salmon provided the only source of income, apart from welfare, for many of them. Many Indians, said Modeste, would prefer to have licences to sell the fish that they caught on their reserves. They have always denied, however, being engaged in large, black-market rings, as fisheries officials and the non-Indian commercial fishers have alleged.

On the Musqueam Reserve in Vancouver, another fisheries department 'sting' operation took place in the early 1980s. A pre-dawn strike was accompanied by a flock of reporters and television crews. Again, there were no convictions. Department of Fisheries officers led another armed raid against Indian people in 1986. That summer they invaded a Gitksan fish camp. The Gitksan-Carrier Tribal Council had filed a formal comprehensive claim in 1977. Because under federal comprehensive claims policy years would have elapsed before their claim, already accepted for negotiation, would get on the table, the hereditary chiefs sued Victoria and Ottawa for ownership of and jurisdiction over their House territories. This case came to trial in 1987 as *Delgamuukw et al. v. The Queen in Right of BC and the Attorney-General of Canada*. Meanwhile, the summer river-salmon fishery remained central to the economy and culture of these people.

Neil Sterritt, president of the Gitksan-Wet'suwet'en Tribal Council (a reformation of the Gitksan-Carrier Tribal Council) during the 1986 raid, reports that about three dozen fisheries officers, 'armed with shotguns and flak jackets and with helicopter [and RCMP] backup, were prepared to invade the Gitksan fish camp.'[129] The officers charged Indians with fishing without Indian fishery permits and during a closure in the river. 'The Gitksan maintained, as they always have, that they owned the fish in the river, and had the authority and responsibility to harvest the fish,' according to Sterritt.[130] About 100 Gitksan and their supporters formed a human barricade around the site that the officers were unable to penetrate and pelted the retreating men with marshmallows. This interesting example of Gitksan humour, the famed 'marshmallow-throwing war,' drew national attention to the Indian fishery. Eventually there were arrests, but, again, no convictions.

Recent Case Law: Sparrow *and* Delgamuukw

A key element in post-1982 Indian fishing disputes was the Constitution Act, 1982, section 35(1) of which expressly recognizes aboriginal people and rights.[131] In *Regina v. Sparrow*, Ronald Edward Sparrow, a prominent elder of the Musqueam Indian Band, was charged on 25 May 1984 under the Fisheries Act with fishing with a drift net longer than permitted by the terms of his band's Indian food-fishing licence.[132] The defence argued that Sparrow was exercising an existing aboriginal right to fish in a section of the river and that the net-length restriction was invalid because it was inconsistent with Section 35(1) of the Constitution Act, 1982. The crown argued that the band's original right to fish had been extinguished under regulations of the Fisheries Act, which over the years became increasingly stringent.

Sparrow was convicted at trial. The judge found that an aboriginal right could not be claimed unless it were supported by a specific treaty. Since the Musqueam Band was without treaty, section 35(1) of the Constitution Act, 1982, had no application in this case. An appeal to county court was dismissed for similar reasons. In 1986, the BC Court of Appeal overturned the decision, unanimously ruling that section 35(1) meant that an aboriginal right to fish for food continued to exist in non-treaty areas of British Columbia.[133]

In a unanimous, landmark decision rendered on *Sparrow* on 31 May 1990, the Supreme Court of Canada found that the crown, having relied only on past regulation as evidence of extinguishment, had failed to prove extinguishment.[134] The court ruled that there was nothing in the Fisheries Act or its detailed regulations that demonstrated a clear and plain intention to extinguish the aboriginal right to fish. An aboriginal right is not extinguished merely by its being controlled by regulations under the Fisheries Act. Food fishery permits were a manner of controlling fisheries, not of defining underlying rights.

The Supreme Court confirmed the priority of aboriginal harvesting, noting that government policy with respect to the BC fishery already provided that, in allocation of the right to take fish, Indian food fishing is to be given priority over the interests of other groups of users. And the court endorsed the priorities as previously cited by Mr Justice (as he then was) Brian Dickson in an earlier BC Indian fishery case before the same court, *Jack v. The Queen* (1980) – first, valid conservation measures; second, Indian fishing; third, non-Indian commercial fishing; and fourth, non-Indian sport fishing.[135] It stated that even legislation aimed at conservation and resource management must be justified if it detracts from any aboriginal right protected under section 35(1): 'The special trust relationship and the responsibility of the government vis-à-vis aboriginal people must be the first consideration in determining whether the legislation or action in question can be justified.'

The Supreme Court anticipated that this interpretation might give rise to conflict with the interests of others, given the precariousness of the stocks. Without question, the decision threatened deeply entrenched interests, including those of members of the fisheries department. The open interest and involvement of the fishing industry in preventing recognition of aboriginal fishing rights are evident from the list of intervenors against Ron Sparrow. Intervenors included the BC Wildlife Federation, the Fisheries Council of BC, the Pacific Fishermen's (Defense) Alliance, the Prince Rupert Fishermen's Cooperative, the United Fishermen and Allied Workers' Union, and nine other, gear-specific or regional organizations of BC fishers.[136]

Despite the opposition, the future of aboriginal fishing rights in the province seemed promising. Federal fisheries authorities publicly announced that the *Sparrow* decision would bring about a major change in policy regarding allocation of fish, and that the prior rights of Indians within the highly competitive salmon fishery would be honoured. In November 1990, the Pacific region's director, Pat Chamut, reported that Pacific Coast Indians would gain control over salmon at the expense of the province's commercial fishers: 'In my view,' the *Vancouver Sun* reported him as saying, 'Indian people will have a larger role in fisheries management and they will be catching a larger share of fish ... The only uncertainty in my view is when it will occur and how it will occur.'[137] Veteran aboriginal rights lawyers and legal scholars optimistically predicted that the right of Indians to sell the fish that they caught in the licensed food fishery might be returned to them in the future. BC Indians also interpreted the decision in that way and hailed it as confirmation of their right to use their salmon as they saw fit. And so it appeared as if the Pearse Commission's recommendation – to broaden the official definition of Indian food fishing to include commercial use – may have been confirmed through the *Sparrow* decision.

Lawyers and lobbyists for non-Indian fishers and the processing sector saw things differently. One cheerfully predicted that the courts 'will subsequently reduce the implications of the Sparrow case.'[138] Within months, this had occurred, with the BC Supreme Court's decision on the Gitksan-Wet'suwet'en comprehensive claim to and jurisdiction over a 57,000-km² territory in the upper part of the Nass and upper and middle parts of the Skeena systems. In *Delgamuukw et al. v. The Queen et al.*, the 51 plaintiffs, all Gitksan and Wet'suwet'en hereditary chiefs, laid claim to ownership of the beds and banks of the rivers and lakes within their territories, which ownership was said to carry over to the fishery.[139] At least one of the Gitksan villages, Gitwangak (or Kitwanga), hoped to establish an inland commercial fishery. This remarkable trial lasted three years.

On 8 March 1991, Chief Justice Allan McEachern of the BC Supreme Court completely dismissed the action against the crown in right of the province and the plaintiffs' claims for ownership of and jurisdiction over the territory and for aboriginal rights in the territory. He favoured assimilation for Indians. On the possibility of broadening the scope of *Sparrow* to include an aboriginal right to commercial use of food fish, the chief justice offered the 'early judicial opinion' that 'the purpose of Aboriginal rights was to sustain existence in an Aboriginal society' and concluded that land-based commercial enterprises cannot be regarded as an aboriginal right. The ultimate impact of the decision remains to be determined, for on 25 June 1993 the BC Court of Appeal released judgments in eight appeals related to aboriginal rights and associated issues. On *Delgamuukw*, it allowed the appeal in part, ruling against the trial judge's conclusion on 'blanket extinguishment,' but left the scope and content of the plaintiffs' unextinguished, nonexclusive aboriginal rights, including rights to fisheries, to be determined. Five of the remaining appeals concerned aboriginal claims to the right to fish without a licence or to barter, sell, or trade 'food fish' catch. Although the majority of the five justices who heard the appeals rejected those claims, the extensive dissenting opinion in each case could make a difference, should any of them reach the Supreme Court of Canada.

The *Sparrow* decision forced the government to respond to a partly defined and evolving aboriginal right to fish as protected by the constitution. The crown wanted to prevent further litigation over claims. In 1991, Ottawa launched its Aboriginal Fisheries Co-operative Management Program, with some 150 agreements entered into with Indian communities across Canada. Meanwhile, the blueprint of the BC Claims Task Force for addressing Indian claims suggested interim agreements to provide for aboriginal fishing, pending full, negotiated settlements. Indian leaders pressed their advantage with Ottawa, although the federal government failed to achieve a single, comprehensive fisheries framework agreement with all Indian communities.

On 29 June 1992, with the salmon-fishing season under way, federal fisheries minister John Crosbie announced yet another in an endless stream of programs, the Aboriginal Fisheries Strategy (to run 1992–8), including a pilot project to assign Indian groups responsibility for managing fisheries and to commercialize the Indian food-licence fishery in British Columbia. The fisheries department got a few groups to sign one-year trial agreements, including Indian bands in the lower Fraser River area (the Musqueam, Tsawwassen, and Stalo Nation bands, organized as the Lower Fraser Fishing Authority). These provided specific allocations of salmon for the Indian food fishery and allowed sale of a portion of the catch.

Processors were outraged to see Indians able to compete on an equal footing in processing and marketing, and they repeated their long-standing opposition to giving Indians the right to commercial use of their fish caught under food licences. Non-Indian commercial fishers, through the Fishermen's Direct Action Committee, threatened to boycott fish plants that accepted this catch. The United Fishermen and Allied Workers' Union also openly opposed the new arrangements. The opponents claimed that Indians would not stick to the quota, would continue black-market sales, and, in the end, would destroy the resource and hence the fishing industry. One can see their point; there are 93 Indian bands along the Fraser system alone.

The Indians involved in the new arrangement on the Fraser dismissed these allegations as a smokescreen for chronic bias against Indian claims and Indian fishers. They were pleased with what they regarded as a significant moral and economic victory. 'They've actually acknowledged that we do have a right to sell our fish,' declared one woman who fished under the new agreement.[140]

There were problems, however. Fewer fish returned to the Fraser than predicted, more salmon died in the rivers than expected, and numbers arriving at the spawning grounds fell far short of the fisheries department's target. Government officials shut down the regular industrial fishery, and then the Indian food-licence fishery, but it was too late. Then came the news that about 500,000 fewer salmon than expected reached the spawning grounds. This provoked near-riots within and among groups of fishers and rekindled the controversy over commercialization of the river fishery. Indians themselves were divided on the issue. Many Indian industrial fishers simply do not support commercialization; the same can be said for some upriver Indian fishers.[141] One Indian leader from Stuart Lake, close to a major sockeye spawning area, spoke out angrily and publicly against what he saw as the lower Fraser Indians' selfish disregard for the lives and aspirations of Indian people living in the interior.[142] There was no end to accusations – of poaching, abuse of fishing agreements, and incompetence by the fisheries department. Everyone demanded an independent inquiry. After much resistance, the fisheries minister brought in Peter Pearse to conduct a brief inquiry on the government's behalf.

Pearse reported in November 1992 that the bulk of the 'missing' half-million sockeye could be explained by unrecorded, largely uncontrolled fishing by Indians and others in the river between Mission and Lytton, which was partly within the agreement area and partly beyond it upstream, and that much of the catch was sold illegally.[143] Besides, the department had not properly prepared for implementing the fishing agreements, which had been made too late and in a season with the smallest runs in the Fraser's four-year cycle. Meanwhile, the Lower Fraser Fishing Authority sponsored its own inquiry and blamed slack enforcement of Indian food fishing and extensive over-fishing of Fraser salmon at sea by Canadian and US commercial fleets and in the upper Fraser by Indians and others.[144] And a third report, commissioned by non-Native fishers, predicted that a large-scale government allocation of salmon-fishing rights to Indians was imminent, could devastate the fishing industry, and was an over-simplification of the issue: 'You effectively destroy a viable commercial industry in the name of economic opportunity for Indians.'[145] This sort of ignorance, wilful or genuine, of the implications of *Sparrow* did not hold true for the minister of fisheries and oceans. Responding to the findings of the Pearse inquiry, John Crosbie reaffirmed the government's commitment to proceeding with commercial salmon-fishing agreements with Indian bands, suggesting that the department had no choice – Indians had rights. To the department's credit, it kept its promise to Indians for the 1993 season, despite the series of rulings from the BC Court of Appeal on 25 June 1993 to the effect that aboriginal rights do not include the right to sell Indian 'food fish,' and regardless of the storms of protest and threats of legal action from industrial fishers, who interpret these rulings as killing any justification that the department may have had to allow Indians to sell a portion of their food fish catch.

Without question, the Davis Plan initiated major systemic change in Pacific Coast fishing and fish-processing. Nevertheless, Indians in the 1970s and 1980s acquired a 'fallback' position. A former fisheries enforcement officer, J.R. McLeod, suggested in the early 1980s that 'eventually there will be comprehensive claims settlements, and through this means they will attain their authority and rights within the Canadian Constitution (1982),' which will, he said, 'give them the *force majeure* that has been missing in their arsenal to date.'[146] The delays that Indians have experienced in negotiating claims and the judgments received in *Delgamuukw* suggest that winning of aboriginal fishing rights through claims settlements and claims litigation could be a long and costly process.

8 Vanishing Alternatives: Halibut and Herring

In the aboriginal fisheries, halibut and herring were next in importance to salmon but were strictly tidewater fisheries. A major industrial halibut fishery started up in the inshore banks of the Pacific northwest in the 1880s, shortly after salmon-canning began. Historically, white fishers have controlled longlining for halibut and the markets have always been North American ones. The fishery left in its wake a succession of depleted halibut grounds. Yet until 1924 the halibut fishery was virtually unregulated. The early industrial fishery relied heavily on Indian assistance, but as that fishery became more profitable and increasingly capital-intensive, Indian halibut fishers were relegated to the margins. Indians made headway in the 1950s by part-time halibut- and salmon-fishing using combination gear. When halibut came under licence-limitation in the late 1970s, however, no Indians met the requirements for licences. The fisheries department instituted special programs for Indian fishers. Nevertheless, by the 1990s, Indians had been largely eliminated from this fishery.

The history of Indian involvement in the herring fishery is more complex and appears more successful. Pacific herring is a shore spawner. The aboriginal herring fishery was concentrated in shallow water everywhere along the coast. This coastal inshore fishery was predominant until the industrial fishery eventually eliminated it through stock depletion. The industrial herring fishery, which depended on purse seines, began in the late nineteenth century. By fisheries department design, it was conducted in only a minor way before the government in the mid-1920s permitted a limited pilchard-

and herring-reduction industry, which was centered on the west coast of Vancouver Island. Indians have generally occupied the margins of the fishery. Processing, by its nature, provided few jobs for Indians or anyone else.

Large-scale herring-seining, a product of the brief canned-herring industry that operated during the Second World War, represented a heavy financial investment that kept most Indian herring fishers out of the reduction fishery when it prospered again after the war. As with halibut, groups of Indians from fish-based economies devised strategies to increase involvement, and herring-fishing proved lucrative for the few who had licences. But just as Indians were beginning to make some advances, fears of resource depletion, which federal officials attributed to over-fishing, led Ottawa to end industrial herring-fishing altogether in the late 1960s. Recovery of stocks in the early 1970s coincided with establishment of a Japanese market for Canadian herring roe (mature roe and roe, or spawn, on kelp). This prompted Canada to allow and encourage limited herring-roe and herring roe–on-kelp fisheries, which revitalized several unused canning plants and led to conversion of others for processing herring roe. Only in these new, brief, highly regulated fisheries with Japanese markets are Indians currently strong participants.

HALIBUT

Aboriginal Halibut Fishery and Its Persistence

In the Pacific, halibut was found almost exclusively off British Columbia and Alaska. It was plentiful and also one of the largest (usually 14 to 18 kg and occasionally as much as 90 kg) to be caught there. Most coastal peoples took halibut, particularly when salmon was scarce.[1] A poor run of chum salmon or herring followed by bad weather that prevented cod- or halibut-fishing 'quickly brought privation.'[2] Halibut was a 'back-up' food resource for many Indian groups, and for the Haida, it was quantitatively the most important fish.[3] Haida were serious exploiters of bottom fish – halibut and deep water black cod (or sablefish, *Anoplopoma fimbria*).

Indians took halibut fairly close to shore, in waters of 15 to 30 fathoms or more, in late winter, spring, or summer. Some groups, such as the Kwakiutl, fished mainly in sheltered inshore waters, where a good catch could be made in winter and spring. But the deeper waters in the wild seas off the west coast of Vancouver Island and around the Queen Charlottes were the best grounds. There, fishing took place March through September. In early summer, the Nootka of the west coast of Vancouver Island moved en masse to sites near the open sea. There they fished for halibut and hunted marine mammals, such as seals, sea otters, and whales. They and the Haida maintained their traditional halibut fishery practices into this century. For these and many other groups, halibut-fishing formed a crucial link in the seasonal rounds.

Halibut-fishing often launched the year. Charles Moser, a Roman Catholic missionary stationed at Opitsat, in Clayoquot Sound, noted in April 1902 that all the Indians who had not gone out sealing went fishing in their canoes for halibut (they caught 847) and cod; on 16 May, six canoes with eight men in each went whale-hunting – to no avail; then in late summer, most left to work at the cannery at Clo-ose, and in late September or early October they departed for the Kennedy Lake area to put up their supply of smoked salmon.[4]

Similar seasonal migrations occurred for the Masset people. The Edenshaw family, like other Masset Haida, moved about frequently to fish, starting each new year with halibut.[5] The Edenshaws stayed at their ancestral halibut camp at Kung, site of a deserted Indian village in Naden Harbour, where they spent a month harvesting and drying halibut. At the beginning of April they left for Yatz (or Yatze), a Masset reserve and former aboriginal seal hunters' camp west of Kung. There the men fished for halibut and the women preserved it and planted their gardens. Other Masset people went to different halibut stations.

Indians traditionally caught halibut with intricate arrangements of baited stream-bent wooden hooks and anchored lines. Northern Indians made one- or two-piece V-shaped hooks, often with elaborately carved designs.[6] The tough U-shaped, steam-bent, wooden barbed hooks were the classic types used by the southern and central coast people for taking halibut. These they made of the stringy, tough part of the Douglas fir, balsam, spruce, hemlock, or yew, steamed until flexible, shaped and hardened in a mould. Some groups, such as the Nootka of Kyuquot Sound, continued to make and use such hooks in their Indian fishery until quite recently.[7] Halibut hooks were attached to strong fishing lines crafted of materials such as nettle, twisted deer sinew, kelp, spruce roots and inner cedar bark, and spruce or hemlock boughs, arranged in various ways and suspended in the sea with bladder floats and sinker stones. Since an individual halibut is so heavy, harvesters required great skill and endurance to haul these large fish to the surface, knock them out, drag them into the canoe, and guide the loaded canoe back to land.

Spring storms added to the risks. In the 1860s, Gilbert Sproat observed that the traditional halibut fishery of the tribes on the west coast of Vancouver Island represented an elaborate and dangerous procedure:

> The mode of fishing is to trail the line slowly after the canoe, the hook being sunk in deep water. Hundreds of canoes, with two or three men in each, start at midnight for the fishing ground, so as to arrive there in the morning. After a half a day's work, if the sea is moderate, the canoes are quite laden and the fishermen return. If the sea should rise during their progress to the shore, rather than throw away any of the fish overboard, the natives tie large inflated seal skins to both sides of the canoe to increase its buoyancy ... To get so large a fish as halibut into a canoe at sea is rather a difficult matter. Accidents, however, rarely happen, and the fish seldom gets away after being hooked. By using bladders attached to the line, and spearing the halibut when he appears on the surface, the largest fish is finally towed alongside the canoe, where he is killed by being struck on the head with a club.[8]

Typically Indian women preserved halibut by splitting, slicing, and smoking or drying the firm white flesh.

Unfettered Growth of the Industrial Halibut Fishery

The halibut fishery, as an industrial fishery serving North American markets, remained essentially unregulated in Canada and the United States from its beginnings in the late 1880s until 1924. Rapid, unfettered technological advancement and highly exploitative, indiscriminate yearly fishing threatened the profitability of the industry and the survival of the halibut. Then everything changed. In 1924, halibut-fishing came under strict, international regulation.

Halibut is quite different from salmon. For one thing, it is biologically more vulnerable to depletion under an intensive fishery. It grows very slowly; females do not mature sexually until about the age of 12. The gear used – anchored, set ground lines strung with hooks baited with herring – has never been age-selective. So immature fish are caught or destroyed during fishing. For another thing, the various stocks of halibut are relatively immobile bottom-feeders and hence are easily located and over-fished. Unlike salmon, halibut was destined wholly for the fresh- and frozen-fish trade – it was not canned. Processing involved icing or freezing the fish in cold storage.

Halibut-fishing in British Columbia for distant North American markets began in 1891. The fishery developed as a type of 'closed shop' with a remarkably homogeneous labour force (white immigrants of Norwegian ancestry, other fishers formerly from the halibut banks of the Atlantic region, and coastal Indians). Methods resembled the mothership-and-dory operations used in cod-fishing in the Grand Banks of the east coast.[9] While the longliners fished as far north as the Queen Charlottes, until 1910 most of them operated on grounds within a few hundred kilometres of Seattle and Vancouver.[10]

Opening of long-distance markets for halibut stimulated improvements in fishing and refrigerated transport. In turn, the fleet expanded in range and capacity to exploit fully the richer grounds in the deeper, more open seas. As early as 1903, gas-powered engines and powered winches were being installed in the old sailing vessels. Even so, the small fleet of two or three canoes or dories that fished from the halibut vessels were oar-powered and their lines handled by hand-powered winches. With depletion of inshore waters and introduction of larger, more efficiently powered vessels, the catch in the northern grounds off British Columbia had peaked by 1912.

Rapid depletion of the more accessible areas led halibut fleets into the deeper offshore waters and more remote northern areas, where fishing required larger, more specialized vessels and equipment. The small canoes and hand-operated dories faced dangerous seas. In turn, harvesting new banks with faster, diesel-powered main vessels eventually reduced stocks of the resource even further, and on a grander geographical scale. The outcome was dramatic. It became commonplace for a mere handful of vessels to fish out an entire halibut bank in a few days, with a single steamer taking home several hundred thousand kilograms of fish in one voyage.[11] Subsequent extension of the halibut fishery into Alaska resulted in a peak there about 1929.

Along with development of the commercial halibut fishery came expansion, in both British Columbia and Alaska, of cold-storage facilities for processing and storing halibut and other types of fish for the fresh and frozen trade. Companies located the plants near long-distance transportation and the fishing grounds.

Early on, Canada promoted unfettered expansion in several ways. First, it did not regulate the industry before the 1920s. Second, a federal subsidy from 1909 to 1919 supported establishment of a railway freight (refrigerated) service for fish products from both coasts to population centres, hence markets, elsewhere in Canada.[12] Frozen halibut and salmon were among the few fish products that could bear the high cost of rail-shipping charges over long distances. Third, completion of the Grand Trunk Pacific Railway to Prince Rupert in 1917 and a change in customs regulations to extend bonding and buying privileges to foreign vessels engaged in Pacific halibut-fishing quickly turned Prince Rupert into the major halibut-fishing centre on the coast.

Regulating Pacific Halibut in the 1920s

Reckless depletion of Pacific halibut stocks brought about international control of the fishery in the 1920s. The Duff Commission's recommendations in 1922 led to signing of a treaty for joint Canadian-US regulation of the halibut fishery (21 October 1924) and creation of the International Fisheries Commission (renamed the International Pacific Halibut Commission in 1953). The two nations implemented regulations made by the commission, which had no enforcing power. The commission established the first closed season to halibut-fishing, to cover the spawning months from mid-November to mid-February. As usual, it resulted in intensive fishing of remaining banks during the rest of the year and, in fact, to increased annual catch overall.[13] The practice of a main ship's deploying dories for longlining gave way in the 1920s to smaller and more productive, modern diesel-powered main boats, from which longlining was done directly. Concern over concentration of effort in very short seasons in the major regulatory areas led to a more sophisticated system of regulation, with catch quotas in geographical areas, size limits, gear restrictions and prohibitions, and continued closure of nursery grounds.

During the Second World War, demand for halibut livers, rich in vitamins A and D, kept this fishery going, but spawning grounds were permanently off-limits. After the war, decline of the Atlantic halibut fishery left the Pacific northwest suppling most of the world's halibut. By this time, two halibut fleets operated in British Columbia. Large, diesel-powered boats up to 22 m long had crews of five to eight and operated offshore in deeper waters; gillnetters and trollers half that size and rigged up simply for the halibut season had two-person crews and operated close to the main halibut ports. In 1954, when the harvest reached record highs, the international commission restricted the BC season to a mere 21 days. An external threat posed by foreign (Japanese and Russian) interests operating factory ships off the Northwest Coast created new, less manageable problems.

By the 1960s, environmental degradation and larger incidental catches by foreign high-seas trawling fleets further reduced stocks. When Canada and the United States finally agreed in 1979 to share the catch from remaining international stocks, the amount of halibut available to Canada dropped; halibut came under licence-limitation in Canada that same year. Applicants needed halibut landings of at least 3,000 lb (1,362 kg) in either 1977 or 1978 to qualify (or requalify) for a regular halibut licence (L). An individual quota system for halibut licences started on a two-year trial basis, beginning in 1992. Licence-holders must maintain catch based on the previous four years' levels in order to renew their licence each year.

Indians in the Industrial Halibut Fishery

At first, immigrant fishers operated steamers accompanied by fleets of Indians fishing from their own canoes, using the traditional long, baited lines. Continued Indian participation was limited to operating one- or two-person dories (the mosquito fleet), which replaced canoes and fished halibut primarily in spring.[14] White fishers exploited Indian involvement in order to learn the locations of richer, more distant fishing banks. The Indians fished for a fraction of this lucrative catch.[15] Elimination of dory fishers in the switch from dory fishing to direct longlining, which began with regulation in the 1920s, all but eliminated BC Indians.

After the Second World War, the number of Indian halibut fishers rose temporarily. Haida fishers from Old Masset village and Heiltsuk from Bella Bella, who had acquired larger seine boats, engaged in offshore halibut-fishing. Many Indians with small gillnetters or trollers operated within the inshore halibut fleet before the opening of each salmon-gillnetting season. In 1950, Indians held 263 of the 928 licences issued to captains for fishing halibut or black cod (only the captain of the boat, not the fisher, needed a licence).[16] But competing with them at the margins were returning Japanese-Canadian fishers. BC Packers recruited and outfitted a 10-boat Japanese halibut-trolling fleet as an experimental project about 1953, and, as in the salmon fishery, this raised alarm.[17]

Licence-limitation in the halibut fishery worked against the interests of Indians in the same way that it had in the industrial salmon fishery, and it wiped out gains made in previous decades. No Indian-owned vessel had landed the requisite 1,362 kg the previous year to qualify for a halibut licence in the first year under licence-limitation, 1979; 269 non-Indian vessels did.[18] Some Indians felt, justifiably, that the government had picked the minimum figure expressly to keep Indians out.[19] Because they fished for halibut only part of the season, their landings were below that figure. Government officials who handed out the licences under the new scheme gave no consideration to the halibut that Indians caught but did not sell. Indian appeals were rejected. When the government issued additional licences, as it did in 1980, when the international commission excluded Canadian vessels from the Alaskan halibut grounds, none went to Indians.

Once again, Ottawa engaged in 'damage control' by issuing special Indian licences for halibut. It once again offered too little, too late. By 1981, when the licensed halibut fleet had grown from 331 to 422 vessels, fisheries officials had issued a dozen special personal licences to Indian applicants 'who depended on halibut for a significant proportion of their incomes, but do not own the vessels they operate.'[20] Some Indians regarded the special Indian licences as just another type of benefit for the fishing companies, which owned the rental boats.[21] Unlike ordinary halibut licences, the special Indian licences were held individually and non-transferable. By 1983, only nine remained in Indian hands.[22] Nevertheless, 18 regular licences had been awarded to Indian-owned vessels. A further eight had been acquired in 1981–82 as part of the purchase by the Northern Native Fishing Corp. (NNFC) of BC Packers' northern rental gillnet fleet and administered on behalf of northern tribal councils. The 35 halibut licences in Indian hands represented merely 8 per cent of the provincial total. Indians held roughly the same number, for the same percentage, in 1991 (see Table 7).[23]

Despite special deals for Indians, by the mid-1980s only 35 Indians

TABLE 7
Ownership of BC Indian licences (other than salmon), 1991

Licence category	Indian licences			Total non-salmon licences issued	Percentage issued to Indians
	Reduced fee	Full fee	Total		
Roe-herring gillnet	351	6	357	1,327	26.9
Roe-herring seine	52	5	57	252	21.4
Total roe herring (H)	403	11	414	1,580	26.2
Abalone (E)			0	28	0
Geoduck/horseclam (G)			0	55	0
Herring roe-on-kelp (J)			26	38	68.4
Sablefish (K)			1	48	2.1
Halibut (L)			36	435	8.3
Crab			0	222	0
Shrimp trawl (S)			9	249	3.6
Groundfish trawl (T)			3	142	2.1
Cod (Z)			352	2,823	12.5
Pocking (D)			0	208	0

Source: Files, Native Brotherhood of BC, Prince Rupert Branch Office.
Note: Figures do not include Indian-owned vessels leased to non-Indians. A vessel usually had more than one type of licence, and so the sum total of licences over-represents the size of the fleet, Indian and other.

held halibut licences out of a total of 429 licences issued, or 8.3 per cent.[24] The lack of licences is resented by Indian groups such as the Haida, who live in the midst of the most productive halibut-fishing areas in the province, and for whom this activity was part of the traditional subsistence and trading economy.[25]

The Native Brotherhood's *Licensing Study* (1987) proposed that Indians should make up 30 per cent of this fishery rather than roughly 10 per cent. But this has not happened. To make matters worse, Indians operate mainly the mosquito fleet. So, although they held nearly 10 per cent of the halibut licences in 1992, they took in only about 2 per cent of the commercial catch. Should the 1992 trial with individual quotas become permanent policy, some Indian licence-owners will probably lose their licences. This is another case of economic forces and government regulations marginalizing Indians.

HERRING

Aboriginal Herring Fishery and Roe-on-Kelp Harvest, Then and Now

Schools of herring occupy inlets, bays, and kelp patches everywhere along the coast. For centuries, Indians caught herring principally in the spring, close to shore, just before the fish entered the small, sheltered coves and creeks to spawn. Women preserved the fish by roasting or drying it.

Indians travelled out in canoes to find schools of herring, which they caught using either dip nets or fish rakes. Small hand-held dip nets were the norm, but the nets used in Barkley Sound were observed to look like the 'scum net,' or beach seine, used in northeastern Scotland.[26] Made of woven strands of treated nettles, the nets could last decades. More common in herring-fishing (and harvesting smelts and eulachon), however, were rakes – long, comb-like instruments made of flat-sided poles armed with a dozen or so sharp bone splinters or hardwood barbs set close together to impale the fish. Their makers strengthened and waterproofed them by smoking and oiling them. So plentiful were schools of herring that Indians literally paddled through the shoals with this instrument, impaling herring as they went. The technique was deceptively simple, as Captain John Jewitt learned: 'It is astonishing to see how many are caught by those dextrous at this kind of fishing, as they seldom fail, when the shoals are numerous, of taking as many as ten or twelve at a stroke, and in a very short time will fill a canoe with them.'[27] This method was most effective at night, when the fish moved off the bottom. The Indians used flares to attract them to the surface, thus maximizing the return from their fishing effort.

Herring roe or spawn (fertilized eggs) deposited on kelp or other plant material was harvested on the coastal mainland and island chains. Herring lay eggs in thick layers that remain attached to seaweed or other matter. From aboriginal times, some Pacific Coast groups have set out special plant materials – branches or whole trees (cedar, spruce, or hemlock), or specially harvested kelp – in certain bays and coves, submerging them with stones. They suspended blades of kelp and branches from floating log frames.[28] They had to take great care to prevent the pre-set material from being grounded by the tides. Spawn-covered kelp growing naturally was collected as well, but Indians found that the pre-set material was easier to harvest.[29] A great delicacy on the order of caviar, spawn was eaten fresh or dried and stored to be eaten or traded later.

This fishery was such a curiosity to newcomers to the coast that scores of accounts appear in the historical and anthropological record. Captain James Cook commented in the 1770s that the Kyuquot 'make a very good caviare [sic], preserved dry on small pine branches and seaweed.'[30] Philip Drucker's ethnographic research revealed that for some Nootka groups living on the outer coast of Vancouver Island, the winter village proved to be the convenient centre for herring-fishing and collecting of herring eggs. But when groups owned grounds too far away from either summer or winter villages, they had camps where they erected permanent house frames.[31] Gilbert Sproat noted in the 1860s that in Barkley Sound immense quantities of spawn were deposited by herring each year and that the spawning ground was generally the rough, stony bottom of a bay that became shallow towards shore.[32] Roe harvested on branches or kelp was eaten fresh or, in most cases, hung for drying in the sun on trees or spread on mats to dry in the sun or wind. The crisp, dried egg masses were tied in bundles and stored in covered wooden boxes.

Herring spawn was not solely for consumption by family members, of course. It was also a trade item. As discussed in a previous chapter, groups specialized in producing certain goods; with fish roe, quality and variety were important. For some people, dried herring spawn was a special treat not locally available. Late-eighteenth- and early-nineteenth-century accounts confirm that the Bella Bella routinely traded large quantities of preserved herring spawn to their Bella Coola, Kitamaat, Kwakiutl, and Tsimshian neighbours.[33] Masset people traditionally acquired dried herring spawn from their Skidegate neighbours; it was not found in Masset territory.[34] William Pierce, the missionary of Tsimshian ancestry who worked among the Nass and Skeena rivers people in the late nineteenth century, described how Coast Tsimshian harvested herring spawn from kelp, trading surpluses with other Indians in the Nass and Upper Skeena rivers areas.[35]

The traditional herring-spawn harvest has survived to this day. It has become usual, however, to salt down the eggs in brine and, since the Second World War, to freeze them, to extend their shelf life. The head of the fisheries department in 1907, E.E. Prince, reported that coastal Indians collected herring spawn which they dried and used for food called 'skoe.'[36] He described their placing of cedar boughs on the spawning grounds to facilitate harvesting. He did not identify the groups involved, but others have. Franz Boas noted that the Kwakiutl of Vancouver Island early in this century harvested and dried herring spawn on branches and kelp; they stored dried spawn on kelp in boxes for winter use.[37] The same thing occurred in Clayoquot Sound. Reverend Charles Moser recorded in his diary for 10 February 1906 that the herring had begun to come in to spawn: 'This is always an interesting time, the little bays near Opitsat and Kakawis were thick with masses of herring ... The Indians too went down and collected canoe loads [of spawn].'[38] Diary entries by Reverend W.H. Gibson, for March and April in the years 1929–35, reveal that the annual harvest of herring spawn continued to be a village-wide activity for the Bella Bella during the Depression.[39] In 1939, Chief Charles Nowell of Alert Bay attended a feast at Bella Bella that featured herring eggs. He remarked to his biographer: 'Those Indians don't eat much of white man's food.'[40]

Herring spawn also remained an item of local commerce for Indians. Emily Carr wrote about 1912 concerning an Indian friend in the Queen Charlottes whom she found one day preparing her harvest of dried fish roe on kelp: 'Mrs. Green knew where the fish put their eggs in the beds of kelp, and she went out in her canoe and got them ... After she had dried them she sent them to the store in Prince Rupert and the store shipped them to Japan, giving Mrs. Green value in goods.'[41] Carr helped Green to select her goods from a catalogue. Likewise, the Bella Bella routinely traded dried herring spawn with Japanese Canadians for supplies of soya sauce, and they still do. Field workers for Hawthorn, Belshaw, and Jamieson observed in the mid-1950s how the Indians of Kitamaat supplied eulachon to the Skidegate in exchange for herring eggs, and Bella Coola people sent eulachon and eulachon grease to Bella Bella people in exchange for herring eggs and seaweed.[42] A 1955 amendment to the British Columbia Fishery Regulations banned harvests of herring eggs except by Indians fishing for food for their families.[43]

The aboriginal practice of harvesting, processing, and using herring spawn continued in many areas even alongside the new, heavily regulated industrial herring spawn–on-kelp fishery that started up about 1974. Visitors to coastal Indian villages where spawn on kelp is still harvested witness a sight similar to what Hilary Stewart observed in the Queen Charlotte Islands in the early spring of 1975, when there was an exceptionally heavy run of herring. From the dock at Skidegate Landing, she watched a small row boat arriving, laden with piled-up lengths of spawn-covered kelp draped over the seats and in the bow: 'In the Village of Skidegate long lengths of seaweed, creamy amber with spawn, hung from nearly every porch and sun deck; racks and clothes lines in gardens and carports were festooned with it. Some of the kelp was draped over the lines, but much of it hung down full length, held at the top with clothes pins, blowing freely in the breeze. The owner of the large hardware store in [Queen] Charlotte City said he hadn't a clothes pin left in the place.'[44]

Around the same time, a CBC radio documentary on fishing practices in the Queen Charlottes noted that the government still 'allowed' the Haida a few of their ancient fishing rights – including gathering of herring roe deposited on broad kelp leaves: 'In early June the women were spreading them out on the beach to dry.'[45] The Kyuquot people of the west coast of Vancouver Island still gathered herring eggs and spawn each February and March in the 1970s: 'Clanninick Bay and places "up west" are the best spots for this, and twigs and branches are laid on the water for the herring to spawn on as soon as the water turns milky from the roe.'[46] There, children ate dried herring spawn as a snack. I witnessed a similar phenomenon in April 1992 at the Southern Tsimshian village of Kitkatla, where herring spawn is collected naturally and on every conceivable form of pre-set material and is preserved in a variety of ways. One older woman in the village still knows how to prepare herring spawn by the traditional methods.

With introduction of the industrial herring 'roe-on-kelp' fishery in the mid-1970s, the government restricted the Indian food harvest of spawn to a pailful per household. Furthermore, Indians owning roe-on-kelp licences (J) are prohibited from using any of the product of their spawning ponds at home. So far, however, local fisheries officials have never shown much concern with enforcing these rules.

The Industrial Herring Fishery

Herring, like halibut, is a schooling fish and is particularly vulnerable to depletion from an intensive net fishery. The main industrial use for Pacific Coast herring until the First World War was as bait for the halibut fishery – usually it was frozen in cold-storage units – and a small amount was processed for oil and fertilizer or dry-salted by

Japanese producers for Oriental markets. Although catching of any fish in Canada for use as fertilizer was prohibited by the fisheries department in 1894, the enactment was evaded in the BC herring fishery by classifying fertilizer as a by-product of the reduction of fish into oil, which was permitted.[47] But following the Prince Commission's investigation (1905–07) of production of herring oil for use as lubricants and fertilizers, the department prohibited herring-reduction in 1910.[48] The idea was both to ensure adequate supplies of herring bait for the more lucrative halibut fishery and to see that fish would be used only for food purposes.

White, Japanese-Canadian, and Indian fishers caught herring industrially in shallow bays and inlets with drag or beach seines and gillnets. But the best herring had to be caught in deeper waters with purse seines (which were useless in shallow water); besides this, the inshore areas quickly suffered depletion. As herring is a schooling fish, purse seining would have been the ideal harvesting method. However, in the interests of conservation, the Department of Fisheries banned purse seines for herring-fishing, not lifting that ban until 1913.[49] Once purse seining for herring became legal, the department also imposed a closed season for the spawning period and soon brought all aspects of the herring fishery under regulation in the name of conservation.

Under pressure from processors during the open-door fishery regime in the 1920s, the department gave up its earlier stand and in 1925 sanctioned a 'reduction' fishery to produce fish meal and oil. Fish meal and fish solubles are protein concentrates that are taken from raw, oily fish by means of cooking, pressing, and drying. They are used mainly as additives for poultry and swine feeds. Since the Second World War, fish oil has been employed for manufacturing margarine, soaps, paints, and so forth. Herring-reduction between the wars was concentrated in the relatively marginal herring-fishing areas of Prince Rupert and Vancouver and on the west coast of Vancouver Island. These highly mechanized operations required few workers.

A second herring fishery between the wars was conducted by Japanese Canadians, who had been operating small herring salteries since the turn of the century. Dozens of small plants dotted the coast: in the southern region, at Nanaimo, Vancouver, and New Westminster; along the west coast of Vancouver Island, in the Strait of Georgia (on Galiano Island alone there were five owned by Japanese Canadians around the First World War); in the Fraser River estuary; and at the mouth of the Skeena River.[50] These plants cured herring and chum salmon for the Japanese market by dry-salting. The fish were soaked in brine, dried, and packed in large cases for shipping. The owners employed some local Indians, but mostly Japanese did the fishing and processing. In the mid-1920s, federal regulations required a minimum percentage of 'white' (including Indian) employees in the salteries owned by 'orientals,' with the intention of eliminating Japanese Canadians in these plants by 1930.[51] These salteries closed for good when international diplomacy eliminated Canadian access to the Japanese market in the late 1930s, before the outbreak of war.

Other processing methods included canning. Experiments with herring-canning took place at salmon canneries in the off-season for salmon. The first attempt, in 1903, involved use of left-over cans or experiments to extend the operating season for the salmon canneries. Canned Pacific herring is a considerably inferior product (it is too oily) compared to canned Atlantic herring. Only when international demand outstripped available supplies of BC canned salmon during the Second World War was herring canned extensively, in as many as 16 plants.[52] Even then, it had to be packed in tomato sauce to be palatable.

The only industrial method for processing herring that persisted after 1945 was reduction for fish oil, meal, and solubles, which grew quickly. The quantity of herring caught primarily for this purpose in British Columbia jumped steadily from 1.5 million tonnes live weight in 1948 to 11.9 million in 1962 – a gain of roughly 700 per cent.[53] The boom in herring-reduction was world-wide, and British Columbia was a major supplier.

Large-scale use of seines in the herring-reduction fishery was a holdover from wartime herring-canning. Keeping up with demand and cashing in on the high prices in the reduction fishery required even larger, more modern boats, fully equipped with the latest fish-finding technology and artificial fibre nets. By the 1950s, this meant a sizeable investment in seine boats – as much as $125,000 – with most of the equipment being owned or financed by the processing companies.[54]

An uncertain future for world markets for fish meal and oil and heavy declines in herring supply on Canada's west coast from over-fishing caused Ottawa to end the Pacific herring fishery in the 1960s. Reduction still occurs, but only as a by-product of the new herring-roe industry that preceded it. Also, a small herring food fishery developed during the mid-1970s. The main market is Japan, where dried herring is sold as migaki. A bit of that catch is frozen as bait for fishers of halibut, sablefish, prawn, and crab. The small herring food-and-bait fishery takes place at a few designated spots along the coast.[55]

Birth of the Industrial Herring-Roe Fisheries

The fisheries department created industrial roe-herring and herring roe–on-kelp fisheries in the early 1970s. These depended completely on Japanese markets and Japanese investment capital. In the roe-herring fishery, herring is harvested over a six-week period in the spring, when the roe is at its most mature pre-spawning stage, by the traditional purse-seine method or with gillnets strung from small, open, aluminum skiffs.[56] This is when the roe in the females is ripe and the fish are about to spawn. The catch is quick-frozen at dockside. Plant workers ('egg pullers') snap off the head and extract, or 'pop,' the roe from the females. The roe skeins are graded, rinsed in a weak brine solution, stored overnight in a stronger brine solution, drained, and skilfully packed in salt in pails. The product is shipped to Japanese markets, as barako, via Vancouver. Meanwhile, the male herring and gutted female herring carcasses are taken to a reduction plant. There, they are dewatered to remove water and salt, cooked, pressed, and processed further to yield meal (sold as animal feed) and oil. In the early 1970s, many of the old plants were reopened or converted to process herring (and salmon) roe, meal, and oil.[57]

Licence-limitation policies and regulations developed for the roe-herring fishery in the late 1970s resulted in over-capacity and increased competition in fishing, just as it had in the salmon fishery. From the start, anyone could obtain a licence (H). However, to hold down numbers in this 'open access' fishery, the department had deliberately set extremely high licence fees ($2,000 for seines and $200 for gillnets, although Indians paid less). The government assists Indians in this fishery in order to compensate them for loss of halibut and salmon licences. Unlike for salmon or halibut, H licences are issued to persons, not vessels. And there was no vessel-size or minimum-catch requirement for obtaining or renewing them. This turned out to be a surprisingly lucrative fishery and attracted many vessels. How the government dealt with demand for licences would be crucial for Indians.

Because of unexpectedly large profits from harvests, the number of seine boats operating in British Columbia jumped 29.5 per cent between 1968 and 1977, and average vessel capacity rose.[58] The fisheries department apparently expected to issue about 150 seine and 450 gillnet licences for the herring-roe fishery; instead, it issued 270 seine and 1,400 gillnet licences. The Pearse Commission warned that this was 'far in excess of the capacity required to harvest the available catch.'[59] Although licences were technically non-transferable, holders have ways of legally getting around this rule.

As for the salmon fishery, the department patched in ad hoc restrictions to control fleet size. It limited net length for the gillnet fleet and introduced area licensing and annual harvest quotas. Also, it declared a moratorium on issuing additional licences to non-Indians in 1974, then to Indian fishers in 1978. This move simply inflated the value of a herring-roe seine licence from the official price of $2,000 to between $600,000 and $700,000, although the fishers say that finding one for sale today even at those prices is difficult.[60] Added to the high price of the licence is the cost of a modern steel seiner, which runs at around $1 million plus about $250,000 for gear. It quickly became virtually impossible for anyone, let alone young Indians, to enter this fishery.

Excess capacity in the herring-seine fishery worked against the department's policy of limiting the size of the salmon fleet. Pearse warned Ottawa in 1982 that seine vessels that fish for roe-herring typically do so for salmon as well; high earnings in the roe-herring fishery in the 1970s had stimulated heavy investments in vessels used in both.[61] As with salmon licences, the commission recommended that the Department of Fisheries wipe the slate clean and begin again.

A different situation exists in the harvesting of herring roe on kelp, which is produced for a Japanese market as Kazunoko-konbu. This small but profitable fishery started up in an experimental way about the same time as the herring-roe fishery, in the early 1970s. It came under licence in 1974. It is the only BC fishery in which individual Indians and Indian communities hold the majority of licences.

As I discovered during my own experience with harvesting of roe on kelp out of Kitkatla in the spring of 1992, this commercial fishery and processing activity are shaped by requirements laid down by buyers in Japan.[62] The Japanese began importing roe on kelp from Alaska in the 1960s. Unlike Alaska, which markets naturally deposited roe, notes the Pearse Report, 'the Canadian permits authorize fishermen to impound spawning herring in ponds containing fronds of [giant] kelp strung on lines ... This produces a superior product and in the quality-sensitive Japanese market, it fetches much higher prices.'[63] Because of its special taste, soft texture, ideal configuration, and abundance, giant kelp (*Macrocystis integrifolia*) is the only plant material permitted in the regulation harvest. It is found in the very salty outer channels. In contrast, spawning ponds must be set in protected inshore bays and coves, in calm areas where there is the least chance of sand, dirt, or debris joining with the layers of eggs to reduce the purity, hence marketability, of the product.

Spawning ponds are anchored, rough-built timber frames that float on the surface of the ocean close to shore. The frame supports lines from which hundreds of metre-long, flat, tear-shaped leaves of kelp are hung. In the closed-pond method, herring must be captured and taken unharmed to the ponds, which are enclosed in a net. This is a delicate undertaking. A seine boat sets a net around a ball of herring about to spawn and then closes the net. The seiner and net are then towed slowly, sideways, by a power skiff, to the net ponds. The herring are gently released into the ponds to spawn on the kelp and later freed to return to the wild. Rough handling or over-crowding destroys the herring. Properly treated, most of the herring will survive to continue their cycle and to spawn again.

Since the 1980s, open ponds of the ancient type are also permitted, and it was this phase of the harvest that I witnessed with Cecil Hill and his crew on the *Western Spirit*. Open ponds are set without nets in areas where herring are ready to spawn. The herring are free to spawn on the blades of kelp at their pleasure, and so no fishing is involved and no herring are lost. But it takes an experienced eye to know where and when herring will spawn and thus to target the right spots at which to set the ponds.

With either method, the kelp harvest is a major consideration and concern: giant kelp will rot within about six days of being harvested, and it could take that long or longer for a harvestable amount of roe to form on it in the ponds. Thus kelp harvests must be skilfully coordinated with the ever-changing migratory and spawning habits of the locally available herring. All this of course assumes good weather. Since harvests take place mainly in March and April, coastal storms often wreak havoc with harvesting of kelp and roe on kelp. In 1991, the herring runs in the Kitkatla harvesting area were poor; it took three months for the *Western Spirit* to fill its quota. In 1992, it took only three weeks.

The fisheries department manages this fishery through restricted allocation of licences for 'roe on kelp' (J licences) to persons or Indian bands, and through division of an allowable catch among licensees. The annual licence specifies the maximum quantity (packaged weight) of product; timing of the fishery; location of the fishery, kelp harvest, and spawning enclosures; and other operating requirements. The annual allowable harvest per licence normally is 16,000 lb (7,264 kg). Licences are renewed at no charge and are non-transferable. This fishery is entirely subordinate to the roe-herring fishery, however. Herring roe–on-kelp licence-owners (and their crew members) are excluded from the latter, although the reverse is not true. And government regulations prohibit harvesting of roe on kelp during the roe-herring–fishing season.

The future of this small but profitable enterprise seems fairly secure. Unlike in the other fisheries, fish conservation is not a problem. In fact, the supply of kelp probably is under more threat than the supply of herring, for Victoria has issued private licences to harvest vast quantities of it for commerical purposes. In principle, a large production of roe on kelp is possible, subject to availability of herring and kelp, but in the spirit of keeping prices high, the Department of Fisheries worried that the small Japanese market could be flooded, and so it issued no additional licences between 1978 and 1990.[64]

Indians in the Industrial Herring and Herring-Roe Fisheries

Only after the cannery operators became interested in herring during the Second World War did fisheries officials question the Indian practice of harvesting large quantities of herring spawn for their own use and for trade.[65] It was of course well known that the long-standing Indian trade in herring spawn had never ended.

Given the historic monopoly of white fishers and the high cost of outfitting for the herring fishery relative to the salmon fishery, it was difficult for Indians to find boats or buyers for their catch before the Second World War. In the 1950s, the Native Brotherhood of BC convinced some operators of reduction plants to let Indians form a fleet of their own. A small pool of Indian-owned salmon seine vessels from Alert Bay, Bella Bella, and Masset operated successfully until the late 1960s, when the Department of Fisheries ended the commercial herring fishery.[66] Most cannery and cold-storage operations included a division reducing herring or fish offal, and in northern and central coast plants a hundred or so Indian men, usually no Indian women, were employed thus each season.[67]

Indians worried that the sheer expense involved in the roe-herring fishery that replaced the herring fishery in the 1970s would make it difficult for them to participate. They convinced the fisheries department to make special arrangements for them in terms of entry and licence fees. Special reduced-fee Indian licences (H-I), coupled with open access, have brought many Indians into this fishery, relative to other fisheries (except for roe-on-kelp harvesting).[68] Participation grew in the early years of the program. In 1973, Indians owned 19 licences for the seine-net roe fishery and 40 for the gillnet roe fishery; by 1976, they had 26 seine-net and 348 gillnet roe licences, comprising 24.5 and 12.1 per cent, respectively, of the roe-herring fleet.[69] By 1985, Indians owned 40 per cent of the gillnet licences (1,334) and 60 per cent of the seine licences (149) for the roe fishery.[70] Some groups, for example the Heiltsuk, held a sizeable number of them.[71]

There was a problem, however. Although licences could not be sold, they could be leased. So, in reality, because of the indebtedness of Indian fishers and the risks and high cost of this fishery, 84 per cent of the special Indian gillnet and 88 per cent of the special Indian seine licences for roe-herring fishing were under lease agreements with fishing companies or non-Indian fishers for from one to ninety-nine years and were therefore not controlled by Indian fishers.

A further complication arose from a controversial change in government policy in the late 1980s. A new policy made it possible for 99-year leased-licence–holders, mostly processing companies, to acquire the licences. Between 1988 and 1992, roe-herring licences numbering 1,327, Indian-owned gillnet licensees dropped from 414 to 357, and Indian-owned seine licensees from 68 to 57.[72] Unless there is a change in the policy, the proportion of roe licences held by Indians will continue to fall in the 1990s.

Unlike with herring-roe licenses, most herring roe–on-kelp licences (J) have always been in the hands of Indians. These licences are non-transferable. Indians both initiated and improved this industrial fishery. The Skidegate Band conducted the early experiments after Ottawa ended the Pacific Coast herring fishery in the late 1960s. Indian licence-holders such as Cecil Hill have continued to improve harvesting techniques and even convinced the government to accept some of the traditional harvesting methods, such as open ponds, for the licensed fishery. Permitting holders of J licenses the flexibility to harvest in both the aboriginal type of open ponds in the marginal herring-fishing areas and the enclosed ponds has made it easier for them to fill the annual quotas.

Although coastal Indians had been harvesting herring spawn in open ponds and on branches for thousands of years, most of the early licences went to individual non-Indian fishers. Indians campaigned successfully for change to this policy. The government stopped issuing new J licences in the late 1970s, by which time only 28 were available and renewed each year: with 18 to Indians (5 to bands and 13 to individuals), for an unprecedented 64.2 per cent of the total, and 10 to non-Indians.[73] No band had more than one licence, although some – for example, the Kitkatla – had one or more members holding individual licences in addition to there being a community licence. Having a J licence has allowed a number of Indian communities to operate their own custom roe-on-kelp–processing plants employing village band members. These include the villages of Bella Bella, Kitasoo, and Skidegate. Other communities, such as Kitkatla, prefer for marketing reasons to have their product custom graded, processed, and packed by fish-processing plants in major centres.

Although the fisheries department assured the Pearse Commission in 1981 that Indian bands would have priority for any new J licences issued, and some bands requested new licences for community economic development, the department refused to issue additional licences. A change of heart came in 1989, when the Heiltsuk Band filed its suit against the department for five commercial licences to harvest roe on kelp, for which it claimed an aboriginal right. Though eventually dismissed by the Federal Court, the case (*Heiltsuk Indian Band et al. v. Canada [Minister of Fisheries and Oceans]*, 1993) brought to a head the entire issue of federal policy on Indian licensing in the Pacific Coast commercial fisheries and the pressing need for Indian representatives to be fully involved in the process.

Heiltsuk Indian Band v. Canada

The Heiltsuk Band (successor to the Bella Bella Band) received annually one of the five J licences issued to BC Indian bands. No member of the Heiltsuk Band held an individual licence, and no one else had a license to harvest roe on kelp from the traditional Heiltsuk roe-harvesting areas (officially, statistical area no. 7). The Band Council applied for its licence in 1975 and eventually received it in 1977. This band had always depended more heavily on the industrial fishery than most other bands on the coast – there were and are few other commercially exploitable resources available to its members. As already discussed, the Bella Bella community had remained in the industrial salmon fishery before enactment of the Davis Plan in the late 1960s, after which it had found it increasingly difficult to do so. Its attempt to launch an Indian-owned salmon-canning operation at Bella Bella in the mid-1970s had convinced it to expand its roe-on-kelp operation. This was a new industrial fishery already dominated by Indians, so the band expected that it would be easier to succeed in it than to regain lost ground in the more established, white-dominated industrial fisheries, such as salmon or halibut.

Every year from 1980 to 1988, the Band Council applied for additional J licences to harvest in its traditional harvesting areas. The band prepared biology reports to show government officials that the scheme was conservationally sound. It prepared comprehensive business plans and undertook marketing studies. These show how the additional licences could transform the community, especially by providing local employment for young people. In 1988, the band went ahead and built a custom processing plant for dressing fresh salmon, freezing salmon and roe herring (which is then shipped to Vancouver for popping), and grading and packing roe on kelp. In 1992, a second plant doubled processing capacity and allowed the band to can salmon and fully to process herring roe and other products, such as geoduck (*Panopea generosa*).[74] The fisheries department neglected or ignored requests for more licences. Early in 1981, the council had also filed a comprehensive claim based on the aboriginal rights and title of the Heiltsuk; Ottawa accepted it for negotiation in 1983. Since 1984, the band has tried to negotiate the comprehensive claim and proposed that harvesting of roe on kelp be negotiated as an initial item within the claim. Ottawa ignored or refused to negotiate either the comprehensive claim or roe-on-kelp–harvesting.

Finally, in 1989 the Heiltsuk took the licensing issue to the Federal Court as a matter of aboriginal rights. Within months, the fisheries minister publicly announced his willingness to issue ten additional J licences, all to Indian bands. The Heiltsuk would not drop the suit, however. The minister appointed an all-Indian Indian Licence Advisory Board (ILAB) to generate proposals for allocation of the additional J licences.

Heiltsuk Indian Band et al. v. Canada (Minister of Fisheries and Oceans) did not go to trial until October 1990, in the Trial Division of the Federal Court of Canada in Vancouver. The plaintiffs, who represented members of the Heiltsuk Band, claimed existing aboriginal rights, pursuant to section 35(1) of the Constitution Act, 1982, and that these included a first-priority right to harvest from the band's roe-harvesting areas that quantity of herring spawn deposited on bough or kelp that they could reasonably process and use in any given year.[75] This would be for their own consumption or commercial purposes, subject only to resource conservation. They claimed that the licences were needed for the Band Council to take care of urgent social and economic needs.

In defence, the crown denied the existence then or ever of the plaintiffs' aboriginal rights to harvest herring, herring roe, or herring spawn commercially. While not admitting that roe-harvesting of any nature was ever conducted by the Heiltsuk, and while specifically denying that such harvest was ever traded or sold, the crown contended that if the plaintiffs ever had commercially harvested these resources, that activity was abandoned or alternatively, vastly curtailed prior to enactment of section 35(1) and so had ceased to be an existing and exercisable right. Or, if the plaintiffs ever possessed and exercised an aboriginal right to harvest these resources commercially, such a right was inconsistent with the Fisheries Act and regulations; as such, it was extinguished before it could have been protected by the Constitution Act, 1982. The trial took place five months after the Supreme Court of Canada had established in *Sparrow* that aboriginal rights cannot be extinguished except by legislation manifesting a clear and plain intention to do so. The plaintiffs relied on *Sparrow* in their arguments.

On the final day of closing arguments, 29 November 1990, Mr Justice Frank Collier handed down his decision. He dismissed the case against the crown, saying that the plaintiffs had not established an aboriginal right to harvest commercially herring roe or spawn on kelp or bough. He rendered his decision so quickly, he said, and would provide reasons later, because of the urgency of the matter: allocation by the Department of Fisheries in respect of the 1991 herring season was pending. And, he pointed out, the minister had promised to issue ten new licences, all to Indians. Perhaps Mr Justice Collier expected that the Heiltsuk's request for more licences would be met by the minister. A few days later, the minister did indeed award the additional J licences, all to Indian bands. But none went to the Heiltsuk. Mr Justice Collier delayed giving the reasons for judgment for 27 months. Then, in a short, two-page statement on 28 February 1993, he accepted the argument of the crown and the industry that the Heiltsuk's traditional harvesting of roe was for food consumption and not part of a 'market economy.' The Heiltsuk then negotiated an additional (special) J licence.

The story does not end there. The fisheries department did not strictly follow the advice of ILAB in awarding the additional J licences. Moreover, the government required new licence-owners to retire one seine or six gillnet herring-roe licences in order to use the J licence. Because the new licences went to financially troubled bands, the high start-up costs of leasing and retiring licences have made it virtually impossible for them to be used. The Native Brotherhood of BC has told Fisheries Minister John Crosbie that the new J licence requirements are unacceptable and has asked him to 'have those "guaranteed to fail" restrictions removed.'[76]

MISCELLANEOUS FISHERIES

Technological changes in processing and opening of markets for frozen-fish products, such as fish sticks, fillets, and 'TV dinners,' after 1945 boosted the province's small groundfish industry.[77] Although Indians had trolled the deep waters for cod and other groundfish for hundreds of years, they received almost no benefit from these new developments.[78] Similarly, the harvesting of intertidal resources, for which the tidal cycles of the coast set limits and offered opportunities, had long been important to coastal peoples. Several species of crab could be taken at low tide by wading, and many species of clam were available at low tide but required digging. Indian women and, to a lesser extent, Indian men did most of the supplying and processing of crab and clams for the handful of plants that specialized in these products in the mid-1950s – Masset (Queen Charlotte Canners Ltd), Nelson Bros. (Prince Rupert), Great Northern (F. Millerd and Co., West Vancouver), and Rupert Cold Storage.[79] Since introduction of licence-limitation for groundfish (excluding halibut) and shellfish in the 1970s, Indians have involuntarily deserted these fisheries –

they had only 2 per cent of the licences in 1991.[80] The figures for licence entitlements for groundfish and shellfish gathered by the Pearse Commission show how few Indians were active in these fisheries after the 1970s.[81]

The same low rates for Indians are there for harvesting of abalone. Until recently, abalone, which lay exposed on rocks and beaches at low tide, was found in the traditional fishing grounds of Indian communities along the entire Pacific Coast of North and South America. Men and women harvested it aboriginally and then industrially in the 1940s and 1950s for processors. The Queen Charlotte Islands have been an unusually productive habitat for this type of seafood. One-third of the industrial harvest in BC waters in the period 1953–83 came from this area.[82] For many coastal Indian groups, the abalone harvest has always been part of their seasonal round. And for some groups – the Kyuquot peoples, for example – abalone has until recently been an important source of food.[83]

Regulation of this fishery quickly moved from uncontrolled access in the 1950s, through limited entry in the 1970s, to the quota license system in the 1980s. In 1950, Indian harvesters held 20 of the 24 licences granted that year.[84] The abalone (E) licence was introduced in 1977 to limit entry to vessel operators who could pay the $200 licence fee, who had landed more than $2,000 worth of abalone in the previous year, and who had earned more than half their fishing income from abalone in either of the previous two years.[85] Overall quotas and vessel quotas are also attached to the licence. As with halibut, Indians harvested abalone on a seasonal basis, mostly not for sale, and so did not meet the requirements for licences. No Indians qualified for licences to harvest abalone industrially, and accordingly it was taken almost exclusively by non-Indian divers operating from licensed vessels.

Declining stocks and government regulations after 1979 slashed the annual catch in the main harvesting area, the Queen Charlottes, by 75 per cent. No Haida individual or community ever benefited from this small but profitable fishery after it came under licence-limitation.[86] Haida peoples feel that the fisheries department did not consider their special position when limiting licences in this fishery.[87] A crisis exists in the 1990s. Licensed sea-urchin (*Strongylocentrotus*) divers apparently have been harvesting abalone 'on the side.' Indians on the north-central coast recently revealed the locations of their traditional abalone grounds to fisheries officials on the understanding that the department would protect the grounds for the Indian food fishery. The information must have spread quickly, however, for soon afterwards abalone disappeared from these areas, too, and recovery of stocks is not expected. Abalone fisheries in BC were closed in 1990. Yet again, an important Indian fishery has been for ever lost because, in this instance, of poor federal management of fisheries.

CONCLUSION

The story of Indian participation in these and other alternative industrial fisheries is but a variation on the sorry tale of the salmon fishery. In every significant industrial fishery, despite occasional special deals for Indians, the regulations and policies under the Davis Plan either kept most Indians at the margins or simply forced them out completely. For coastal Indian communities, fishing traditionally had consisted of five or more fisheries, each of which became less accessible to Indians after British Columbia joined Canada. As in the industrial salmon fisheries, Indians left the other industrial fisheries at the end of a long line of local adaptations and adjustments to the vagaries of industry-based changes and increasingly restrictive state policies. The single exception is the new, small, brief, heavily regulated herring roe–on-kelp harvest, for which there are too few licences for it to be of much help to Indian communities.

Indians continue to resist all efforts of the state to marginalize them. They want more licences for Indians and more local control over fishing. They want their own aboriginal appeal board. They worry that soon there will be no resource to manage or harvest. They therefore want to be equal partners in all planning and policy-making that affect aboriginal fishing communities.

9 Conclusion:
Indians versus Conservation?

At one time, BC salmon-cannery camps depended completely on Indian families for their labour and general skills in fishing, fish-processing, boat-building, and net-making and for their local knowledge of navigation, fishing grounds, and fish. These families developed special arrangements and relationships with cannery operators, governed less by market incentives than by personal relations, bonds of mutual obligation, government policy, and the law. As the industry spread and mechanized in the twentieth century, changes in labour supply, in markets for fish, in technology, and in government regulations rendered Indians less central to fishing and, eventually, to fish-processing. These developments also affected the traditional and all-important Indian salmon fishery, further along the harvesting chain, on freshwater fishing grounds. Processors and officials attempted to restrict and eventually to outlaw that fishery as wasteful and unnecessary. Nonetheless, well into the present century Indian families and villages maintained their diversified fish-based economies through a mixture of fishing and fish-processing for domestic and commercial purposes.

Indians demonstrated impressive adaptability and cooperation as this seasonal industry evolved. Industrial fishing and fish-processing differed essentially from traditional Indian fishing and fish management and preservation. For Indians, industrial fisheries meant racially segregated work for strangers and use of foreign technology. These activities often took place away from home territories, and production was geared for open-ended, long-distance markets. Also, management of the resource was separated from harvesting and use of it.

Indians had traditionally conducted a communal and family-based enterprise in tribal territories. They had adapted hand-crafted technology to local environments, and produced items for the immediate benefit of the local group and for inter-village and inter-regional trade. Reciprocal use and other ancient rites and customs governed access to fish, and people made no distinction between harvesting for subsistence and harvesting for exchange or other purposes.

As the industry evolved, industrial fishing and fish-processing differed more and more from traditional ways, and the technology generally became less accessible to Indians. Even so, thousands of Indian men and women and their children mastered the new techniques and worked within new regulatory and management schemes and systems of industrial production. In so doing, Indians throughout the coast and along the major salmon rivers maintained a strong presence in the salmon-fishing and -processing sectors until just after the Second World War. Often, however, they stayed at the expense of Japanese Canadians. Simultaneously, they vigorously defended and exercised their traditional fisheries and maintained the fish-sharing networks necessary for their cultural and physical survival. Because of federal laws and policies, however, this often meant 'stealing' fish and illegally trading, potlatching, or selling some of it.

By the 1950s, tremendous changes in technology and markets drastically increased the range, mobility, and efficiency of the fishing fleet, accelerated centralization (including plant closures) and diversification of processing facilities, and helped reduce the quality and quantity of fish stocks in all the rivers and streams along the coast. Fisheries regulations now focused on reducing the areas and times for fishing and did little to prevent excessive numbers of high-priced vessels and equipment from chasing fewer fish. Indian indebtedness to fish-packing companies grew rapidly, and many Indians lost control, if not actual ownership, of their fishing vessels. Most of the 'out-of-town' canneries, where Indian families had always dominated the work-force, shut down for good. Indians left the industrial sector to an unprecedented degree.

With Indian economies in trouble after the war, Indians still depended on aquatic resources for food but found food harvesting increasingly difficult. Regulations under the Fisheries Act and the setting aside of some ancient fishing sites as Indian reserves in the nineteenth century had originally protected many subsistence fishing sites. Between the wars, federal regulations controlled and restricted the Indian food fishery, provincial policy denied Indians an adequate territorial base, and federal and provincial policies tended to secure resources for non-Native industrial use and development. These actions rendered the original fishing reserves woefully inadequate.

In the era following the Second World War, only in the Northern district did Indians have a sizeable presence in fishing and plant crews. And only in the north would summer 'Indian villages' continue in cannery camps. But even there, new federal and provincial regulations for fish and wildlife and the essentially unchecked spread of logging, mining, and hydro-electric projects, which extensively damaged tribal territories and fish habitats alike, were taking their toll on Indian economies. Maintenance of viable Indian communities in British Columbia became a real challenge. The new centralist federal policies that encouraged rural Indians to move to urban centres reinforced the trend.

Despite the host of problems facing them after the war, some Indians retained enough manoeuvrability in the industrial fishery to keep going – for a while. Many of those who persisted had no alternate sources of income. They either formed small-boat fleets or borrowed more money from processing companies in order to operate grander, more 'modern' vessels. Whatever their strategies for using resources, technology, and labour, however, these Indians faced an uphill struggle. Most of them simply lacked capital needed to succeed over the long term.

But none of these developments foretold the dramatic changes of the 1970s and 1980s. In 1968, the federal government introduced a rigid, limited-entry licensing policy based on an entirely new, wrongheaded, explicitly market-driven approach to fishery management. Created by a growing group of influential policy advisers – resource economists – the Davis Plan sanctioned and encouraged more use of costly harvesting and processing technology to maximize the economic yield from a declining catch. A drastically smaller, more expensive, privately owned, coast-wide fishing fleet took more of the harvest, and fewer, larger, more centralized, 'combination' plants in Vancouver and Prince Rupert processed the catch year-round.

These extraordinary shifts in policy and changes in the industry cost many fishers and shoreworkers their jobs – as intended. Yet they were predicated on the assumption that all groups of users had the same claim on the fish. Their perpetrators did not prepare for the damage that Indians would suffer, especially in the remote, isolated regions where fishing had always been the mainstay and few other economic opportunities were available. The processing companies shut down the out-of-town plants that once had provided so much employment for Indian families and withdrew the small-boat rental fleets that mostly Indian fishers had operated. In urban places, lack of free, temporary housing at fish plants made it uneconomical for Indians to go into town for plant work. The end of piece rates and new emphasis on year-round work strengthened the tendency. When unemployed Indian fishers found jobs in fish plants, they often replaced Indian women. Indian women, whose labour at one time had been even more crucial for coast plants than that of their male kin, now had little if any role to play. The latest practice – shipping fish caught in northern waters to Vancouver for processing – destroyed even more jobs in remaining northern plants.

Government departments and agencies set up special programs of financial aid to help fishers, boat-builders, and plant owners. They did this for Indians, too, ostensibly to increase or at least stabilize their participation. These attempts to 'paper over the cracks' in the Davis Plan usually involved assistance to individual Indian fishers, not to Indian communities as a whole. One unforeseen consequence of 'special deals' for Indians was to deepen hostility against Indian fishers. Besides, like the Davis Plan itself, the deals favoured 'haves' over 'have nots,' causing conflict within already divided and economically weakened BC Indian societies.

The new federal regulations intentionally ignored the geographical and gear-related distribution of income and the role of food-fish catches within the Indian fleet, emphasizing instead average commercial production by individual vessels. In the end, financial assistance for Indians upgraded the Indian fleet in efficiency and mobility. Yet it did not help the smaller, less productive vessels or the fishing communities that really needed backing in their efforts to support themselves in the ways they choose.

Similarly, the few experiments with Indian-owned canneries in communities such as Port Simpson got little cooperation from Victoria or Ottawa, unions, or the Native Brotherhood and generated tremendous opposition from the processing industry and non-Indian fishers. This lack of support helped defeat these initiatives and created further political divisions.

In a sense, the Davis Plan only completed what a century of government policies had started. Many of these policies had affected

Indians only indirectly. Others were specifically designed to limit, change, or even strengthen particular forms of Indian participation as required by major processors or by other areas and levels of government. Nevertheless, Indians were marginalized in relation to BC fisheries and specifically within their traditional territories. They have always refused to accept this predicament, as shown by their petitions, protests, testimonials to fisheries commissions, and arguments in the courts, as in *Derriksan, Jack, Heiltsuk Indian Band,* and *Sparrow.* The historic record is clear: Indians want to maintain their precontact position as the people with the first right to use the marine resources in their territories. They have been willing usually to share their fish and other resources in their aboriginal territories but not to surrender all control over management and use of them. They recognize that their own fate is tied to the fate of those resources.

Over the years, the Pacific Coast fisheries were the subject of dozens of studies and commissions, and the most important fisheries – salmon and halibut – came under international control. But virtually none of these investigations – except for Hawthorn, Belshaw, and Jamieson's study of Indian economies in the 1950s and the Pearse Commission in 1981 – took into account the needs or opinions of Indians. The fisheries commission headed by Sol Sinclair in 1959–60 was especially negligent. Ottawa launched this inquiry – to recommend transformation of the Pacific Coast industrial fishery – at a time when politicians and government officials knew that Indians were leaving fishing and fish-processing in droves. Yet Sinclair's report contains no analysis of the possible effect of licence-limitation on Indian people. It ignored Indians. Not until the 1970s, after the damage had been done, did the government examine the impact of its policies and programs on Indian participation in the Pacific Coast fisheries. These studies, however, inevitably focused on a narrow range of economic issues for Indians, using conventional indicators such as higher unemployment levels or percentages of the catch. Economic self-sufficiency, pride in heritage, and social goals are broader and deeper issues that Indians have repeatedly discussed but government and industry reports seldom have.

The history of the industry shows that protection and conservation of fish stocks have been only one goal of regulatory policy. Policy and regulations on licensing have been aimed primarily at managing the industry itself. This approach in itself is not unreasonable. Governments do and should promote economic development. But the historical record provides three major insights. First, although regulatory policy was clearly designed to achieve a broad range of management objectives, protection and conservation of fisheries have usually been the crown's public and judicial justification for most regulations. Second, managing the fisheries has meant principally assisting the processing sector. Third, laws and policies, and enforcement of them, have intentionally affected separate groups of 'users,' including Indians, differently.

The historic ties between the fish-processing industry and government regulations and policies have been as complex and shifting as the industry itself. The fishing industry changed greatly, as it evolved through distinct historical periods, before emerging in its present form. Not surprising, government policy also altered and developed to reflect those changes. Salmon-canning operations were the dominant influence in each period, effectively defining the technology and structure of the evolving industrial fishery. Consequently, they have shaped government regulatory policies for the Pacific Coast.

Examples of government assistance to the fish-packing industry are found in the regulations, programs, and practices designed to increase supplies of fish in key processing districts, such as the Fraser and Skeena rivers. This policy included prohibiting many Indian harvesting techniques and destroying inland fishing sites thousands of years old. Fishery regulations periodically banned certain processing methods, such as production of oil and fertilizer from pilchard and herring before 1925 and during the Second World War. The federal government sought thereby not to protect specific types of fish but to promote other forms of fishing or processing or to protect specific foreign markets for Pacific Coast fish products. Indeed, government actions allowed the herring-reduction branch of the industry to destroy herring stocks after the war. Government regulations and policies such as boat rating in the north early in this century eliminated competition in the processing sector. Fish conservation was of only secondary importance.

Other policies have provided for a secure supply of Indian labour – mostly women and children – for fish plants. These also had nothing to do with protecting fish. The fishing-licensing regulations of the 1890s, for example, favoured cannery (attached) licences over independent licences; cannery operators counted on Indians fishing under cannery licences to bring their families to work in the plants.

Regulations limiting use of purse seiners on the coast and (until the 1920s) banning gas-powered fishboats in the Northern district protected the Indian monopoly in addition to conserving fish.

The Department of Fisheries has always considered Indians one of several distinct interest groups whose participation in the fishing industry must be regulated. Some officials in the early days of salmon-canning, in the 1870s, talked of Indians as if they had special aboriginal or treaty rights. The Fisheries Act and federal regulatory policy, however, have treated Indians as an interest group whose needs stood to be addressed on the same legal basis as those of any other user and whose claims to traditional rights to fish competed with the interests of other 'users.' This is why the department has strictly regulated most aspects of Indian participation, including both subsistence and commercial activities. It began by inventing an 'Indian fishery' as a strictly subsistence activity. The regulations have always treated the official Indian food fishery as a privilege, and most government officials came to see it as nothing more than a welfare measure, to be permitted only when Indians were starving. Government policies have been in effect for so long that some BC Indians even today seem to accept the fisheries department's definition of the Indian fishery.

Whether fishing for food or for ceremonial or commercial purposes, Indians faced policies and practices that evolved over time and varied from region to region. Such changes and regional variations reflected alterations in the industry and markets for fish products, problems with supplies of labour or raw fish, evolution of government policy vis-à-vis settling the northern coast or promoting industry and tourism, and even shifts in attitudes towards Indians. Fisheries officials obviously hoped that industrial jobs would force Indians completely into the wage economy and so eventually eliminate their need to fish for their own needs. On many occasions, the government threatened to ban the Indian food fishery altogether. What we see instead is subjection of the Indian fishery to the massive regulatory scheme put together to manage the industrial salmon fishery. Other aspects of federal management of fisheries – such as blasting out canyons and rapids on the spawning rivers, from the 1890s to the 1950s, and closing specific inland fishing grounds, beginning after 1918 – did away with Indian fishing at economically and culturally significant ancestral fishing sites. Always, Indians were expected to cooperate with the established industrial processing sector, usually in the name of conservation.

Despite inconsistent application of Indian food fishing regulations over the years, policy has assumed a single regulatory regime for everyone in the industrial fishery. We have seen, however, that enforcement practices, special rules, and assistance programs for one group or another often altered application of policies and laws to whites, Indians, Japanese, and others. This has always been the case for Indians in the salmon-canning industry.

Through the Fisheries Act and regulations for British Columbia, Ottawa slowly shifted salmon production away from the rivers (Indian control) to the coast (controlled by processing companies). The fisheries department has always been unwilling to promote Indian ownership of processing plants. As a matter of policy, it used to award white operators virtual monopolies over entire ocean-fishing grounds by granting seine leases that were not available to Indians. Likewise, the Northern district during the 1910s allowed no independent commercial fishing licences, except for white settlers, as a federal concession to Victoria. Anti-orientalism and changes in government policies towards Canada's Indians often figured into the equation. In the 1920s, Ottawa introduced an 'open-door' fishery but bowed to anti-oriental campaigns in British Columbia by attempting to phase people of Japanese ancestry out of the fishing industry by withholding fishing licences from them – yet another concession to the province. Whites (and Indians – as a concession to Indian Affairs and the fish processors) were to benefit from this extraordinary policy. Until the 1950s, fishing regulations favoured gillnet licences over others, helping to keep Indians in the industrial fishery. After the Second World War, especially under licence-limitation, government policies favoured seines and trollers over gillnetters, thereby aiding non-Indian fishers and hindering Indians. And on it goes, even today, when the fisheries department is attempting to achieve effective regulation in a new legal environment by negotiating commercial fisheries agreements with Indian communities.

Clearly, federal regulatory policy for fisheries has changed conditions and opportunities for Indians in fishing activities of all types. Despite occasional special actions, policies, and programs designed to make application of regulations to Indians less harmful, the cumulative result has been to erode Indians' opportunities throughout their fisheries. The fisheries department and other administrative agencies and levels of government have always known this.

In the case of salmon, changes in industry patterns and government regulations have indirectly reduced the species and runs of fish available in each locale and have decreased the amount of time when Indian industrial fishers can fish for food. Above all, they have almost eliminated Indian families from the processing sector.

In the latest period, from about the time of the Davis Plan of 1968, several factors have interacted to destroy opportunities for Indian people in salmon-fishing and -processing. The former flexibility in the system vanished under the Davis Plan. Rigid licence-limitation, under which usually vessels, not persons, are licensed, shrank the fleet. The plan permitted only the larger, most expensive vessels to remain in the salmon fishery, favoured full-time fishing over part-time efforts, and encouraged centralization of processing, including company mergers and takeovers and closure of all but the high-profit, urban operations.

The problems did not end with salmon. After salmon-fishing came under limited-entry licensing in 1968, almost every type of fish and shellfish that had once been part of the aboriginal economy eventually came under licence controls, too. The cumulative result for Indians has been disastrous. For the 1992 season, Indians held less than 20 per cent of the licences for salmon-fishing, none in many other categories of fishing, and a mere fraction of those in others. Although government policy gives Indians the majority of licences in the herring roe–on-kelp harvest, the fisheries department allocates these to Indian communities as a type of welfare rather than as recognition of rights.

Regulatory policy since introduction of the Davis Plan has been designed to 'rationalize' the industry on a coast-wide basis. The same approach was taken for Canada's Atlantic fisheries, with a similar pattern of ruin for individuals and their communities. The macroeconomic approach inherent in BC licence-limitation of the past two decades has seriously prejudiced fishery-based economies, which are locally and regionally based. Federal mismanagement forced long-term, sometimes permanent, closures of fishing grounds in large areas of the central coast and the west coast of Vancouver Island, where many Indian and mixed Indian and non-Indian fishing communities had survived. Soon Indian families and communities stopped making their annual trek to fishing grounds or fish plants.

It was at the dramatic low-point for the Pacific Coast fisheries, the early 1980s, that the Constitution Act, 1982, granted constitutional protection to existing aboriginal rights. Also *Sparrow* (1990) gave priority to aboriginal fishing rights in British Columbia. Now, BC Indians want to and must be consulted about fisheries regulations and policies, although they find it difficult to agree on specific remedies. Responses by BC Indian men and women and communities to the changing opportunities of industrial society have generally been varied and intricate, ranging from formal and informal resistance to active acceptance and even cooperation in reproducing the conditions that threatened their societies. Contemporary involvement in the Pacific fisheries is therefore highly variable – insignificant to some communities, everything to others.

The geographical dimension of the issue is clear. An imaginary vertical line along the coast separates two distinct groups. The inland people have their restricted, productive, traditional, low-cost riverine salmon fisheries, which some Indians can commercialize and others cannot. Indians who occupy the coast and offshore islands can participate in the industrial fishery at the start of the harvesting chain. Many of these people face heavy investments in ocean-going commercial vessels and a highly competitive, more diversified fishery. They understandably object to the commercialization of food-fish catches. An imaginary line drawn horizontally across the northern tip of Vancouver Island separates the more prolific ocean fisheries and the centre of processing operations of the south, dominated by the Fraser River salmon runs, from the less productive, more diversified northern fishing areas.

Within individual coastal Indian bands, the community-oriented outlooks of many reserve-based Indians often differ from those of off-reserve, urban-based band members. And even among and within reserve-based communities, ideas differ widely on such issues as band-held fishing licences, union membership, theories of fisheries management, schemes for fisheries co-management with Indian bands and the fisheries department, commercialization of Indian fisheries in the traditional waters, and Indian aquaculture projects. The 1992 efforts – to bring together all BC Indian communities in a fisheries framework agreement or even simply to develop a coordinated fishing plan for the Indian groups on the Fraser – failed miserably. Under the circumstances, consensus among BC Indian groups, after more than 100 years of having no say in decisions about the fisheries, is difficult to achieve.

Ottawa is seeking to negotiate fisheries policy with individual bands and tribal councils. The process will be difficult, contentious, and extraordinarily challenging from a fisheries management perspective. It will undermine the current role of the established negotiating organization – the Native Brotherhood of BC – as well as that of the Pacific branch of the fisheries department. It has already provoked further anger and frustration among non-Indian fishing and fish-processing interests, which usually misinterpret fishing agreements favourable to Indians as 'resource giveaways' and 'welfare measures.'

Managing Salmon in the Fraser, the report of the Pearse inquiry in 1992, was sensitive to this crucial issue of public relations, calling on commercial and sport-fishing groups to participate constructively in policy development and to inform their constituents about changes in the law and government policy, even if they dislike them. Easier said than done. Government itself has an obligation to make policy clear to those who are affected, warned Pearse. This would include informing members of field staff who must administer and enforce it, even if they, too, dislike it. Policies on Indian fisheries must also be reconciled with those from the federal departments of Indian Affairs, Justice, and Finance, the BC Commercial Fisheries Branch, and myriad coordinating bodies and with constitutional discussions, land claims, and court decisions.

However this situation sorts itself out, and even without the existence of section 35(1) of the Constitution Act, 1982, or of the Supreme Court of Canada's decision in *Sparrow*, this much is clear. A crucial, internationally valuable marine resource, Pacific salmon, moves through the traditional territory of every BC Indian band occupying the Pacific slope. The Indians show no signs of giving up their claims to rights to occupy those territories or their insistence on effective protection for their resources. On the contrary. So far, the state, the processing industry, and non-Indian fishers have usually confronted these claims, on the fishing grounds, in the media, and in the courts. No longer a mere backroom lobbying effort, the fishing industry's attempt to control all aspects of Indian fishing is a well-funded, integral part of contemporary litigation.

In the Pacific Coast fisheries, as in other Canadian regional industries from northern fur trading to prairie agriculture, the state's economic agenda for Indians has always been self-serving. It has promoted their economic self-sufficiency while restraining them as a group from competing with non-Indians. This historic policy has

repeatedly led politicians and government administrators to disregard the special rights and position of Indians, with or without treaties. As it applies to the Pacific Coast fisheries, the policy cannot
continue. Problems of conservation and management for the world's
ocean fisheries are enormous and will not be overcome on Canada's
Pacific Coast without the cooperation of Indian people. The history
of Indians' involvement and struggles in the Pacific Coast fisheries
suggests to me that the state will not gain their cooperation unless it
is willing to accept the legitimacy and primacy of their interests in
the fisheries – interests that, for all the stated policy towards Indians,
have always been treated as privileges, not rights.

The historical issues being analysed here are national in significance and vital. Canada's Pacific Coast fisheries are in varying de-
grees linked to the economic and cultural future of most BC Indian
bands, and the bands in the province account for one-third of the
country's total. These matters must also be understood in the context
of efforts by aboriginal peoples around the world to gain recognition
and respect.

In broad context, the history of Indians and the law in Canada's
Pacific fisheries shows how close and continual interplay among and
between the executive, legislative, and judicial powers of the state
affects a resource and the people who depend on it. In their struggles
to promote aboriginal fishing rights, BC Indians have adeptly tacked
back and forth among branches of the state and government departments, agencies, and programs, at both federal and provincial levels.
Indian Affairs has at critical times in the past acted to soften potential damage that new federal fisheries policies might cause to Indian
fisheries in traditional waters. On a few occasions, the provincial
government has assisted Indians. When, for example, federal departments and branches, including fisheries and Indian Affairs, closed
ranks against the proposal by North Coast Indians for their own
modest, cooperative fish-processing operation, the province, a sup-
porter of small-business interests, stepped in with financing. Many
times, Victoria and Ottawa have joined forces for or against the interests of Indians.

In the Supreme Court of Canada, BC Indians have won judicial
victories that will make it easier for them to get around federal fisheries policies by negotiating rights to land and resources. The court's
opinion in *Calder* (1973) established the possibility of unextinguished
aboriginal rights in Canada and therefore led to federal policy of

negotiating major modern treaties in the form of comprehensive claims agreements. Fishing rights were crucial underpinnings for most of the claims advanced in British Columbia. Victoria took federal authorities 'off the hook' by continuing to refuse to recognize aboriginal rights or negotiate, although it has recently changed its stance.

Before entrenchment of section 35(1) in the Constitution Act, 1982, for which Canadian Indians fought, the line of cases represented by *Derriksan* (1976) established that the aboriginal right to fish was subject to regulations under the Fisheries Act and therefore to legislative control or regulation. Later, the Supreme Court of Canada in *Sparrow* confirmed the priority of the Indian right to the food fishery, subject only to valid conservation measures, over the interests of other groups of users and held that historic policy (such as the Fisheries Act and fishery regulations) can neither extinguish the existing aboriginal right without clear intention nor, in itself, delineate that right. The ruling on regulating for conservation will have an impact beyond fishing and beyond Indians, as Peter Usher reminds us, for the pressure that *Sparrow* puts on federal authorities to justify regulations affecting Indian harvesting will open all government fisheries and wildlife management practices to more rigorous testing and public scrutiny.[1]

Thus section 35(1) of the patriated and amended Canadian constitution of 1982 conferred a new constitutional status on the aboriginal right to fish, and entrenchment of Indian fishing rights, in turn, has affected the law. *Sparrow* makes it clear that section 35(1) provides the same kind of constitutional protection for aboriginal and treaty rights as the Charter of Rights and Freedoms – made the supreme law of Canada by section 52 of the Constitution Act, 1982 – provides for other fundamental common law rights. The Charter has imposed new and larger responsibilities on the Supreme Court of Canada and the lower courts, which Philip Resnick suggests 'are likely to become increasingly political institutions in the American sense, playing their part in checking and balancing executive and legislative powers.'[2] But the Supreme Court cannot on its own bring about liberal social reform; it depends on politicians, office-holders, and the public to carry out its decisions. When that support is missing, liberal court victories amount to little. 'At the end of the day, will you wait for a court to impose [agreements with aboriginal groups for the right to sell their fish] and have total chaos?' asked a representative of the fisheries department. He was responding to angry critics of the new post-*Sparrow* Indian commercial fisheries policy. He suggested an alternative approach: 'Or will you forge ahead and try to work out the management of it?'[3]

The central theme in the Indian agenda is a demand for a just accommodation. It is quite reasonable to speculate that negotiated resolutions and self-government, self-regulation, or co-management with respect to land and natural resources will help aboriginal peoples to regain the effective power over their cultural and economic destinies that Canadian policies and law have until recently been unwilling or unable to consider.

NOTES

CHAPTER ONE: INTRODUCTION

1 Berger, *Fragile Freedoms*, 219.
2 Hansen, 'Treaty Fishing Rights,' 1.
3 For a fascinating discussion of this argument, see British Columbia Archives and Records Service (BCARS), GR 1439, BC Department of Recreation and Conservation, Fish and Wildlife Branch, 'Survey of Native Rights as They Relate to Fish and Wildlife Protection in British Columbia,' by K. Krag (law student) for C.E. Estlin (chief of enforcement, Fish and Wildlife Branch), 22 August 1975. Both British Columbia and Canada continue to use these arguments against Indians in the courts, despite *Sparrow*.
4 *Regina v. Sparrow* (1990), 4 *Western Weekly Reports* (WWR), 410 (Supreme Court of Canada).
5 Pearse, *Turning the Tide*, 175.
6 *Regina v. Sparrow* (1990), 4 *WWR*, 435–6.
7 Trebilcock, 'The Consumer Interest,' 94.
8 See Daly and Brady, 'Federal Regulation,' 180; and Andrew and Pelletier, 'The Regulators.'
9 Trebilcock, 'The Consumer Interest,' 94.
10 Wilen, 'Modelling Fishermen,' 154–5.
11 Mumford, *Technics and Civilization*, 6.
12 Slattery, 'Understanding Aboriginal Rights,' 727.
13 See discussion in Elliot, 'Aboriginal Title.'
14 See, example, Slattery, 'Understanding Aboriginal Rights'; and Clark, *Native Liberty*.

15 See judgment of the Supreme Court of Canada in *Regina v. Sparrow* (1990).
16 *Calder et al. v. Attorney-General of BC* (1973), *Supreme Court Reports (SCR)* 313 (Supreme Court of Canada), affirming (1970) 74 *WWR* 481 (BC Court of Appeal) and (1970) *Dominion Law Reports (DLR)* (3d) 59 (BC Supreme Court). Six of the seven judges who had heard the case acknowledged the existence of aborignal title in Canadian law, but they split evenly on whether aboriginal title continues in British Columbia. See Tennant, *Aboriginal Peoples*, 218–26; and Bush, 'See You in Court.' The Supreme Court of Canada became the final court of appeal in 1949.
17 Clark, *Native Liberty*, 159–60.
18 Ibid, 162. Except for the Mackenzie Valley, the pattern for modern treaties has now been settled for Canada north of 60°.
19 Storrow and Bryant, 'Litigating Aboriginal Rights Cases,' 179.
20 Constitution Act, 1867 (UK), c. 3; *Revised Statutes of Canada (RCS)*, 1970, app. II, No. 5. See discussion in Ellis, 'Perspectives.'
21 Fisheries Act, *Statutes of Canada (SC)*, 1868, c. 60; Fisheries Act, *RSC*, 1970, c. F-14. See Scott and Neher, 'Evolution.'
22 Pearse, *Turning the Tide*, 227.
23 BC Fisheries Act, Revised Statutes of British Columbia (RSBC), 1901, c. 25. The province created a separate Department of Fisheries in 1936, the function of which was taken over by a new department, Recreation and Conservation, in 1957.
24 *Attorney-General of Canada v. Attorney-General of BC* (1930), *Appeal Cases (AC)* 111 (Judicial Committee of the Privy Council). See the earlier ruling, 2 December 1913, in *Attorney-General of BC v. Attorney-General of Canada* (1914), *AC* 153 (Judical Committee of the Privy Council), affirming (1913) *SRC* 493 (Supreme Court of Canada).
25 See Waugh, *Fisheries Management*, chap. 5. The newest scientific reference on Pacific salmon is Groot and Margolis, eds., *Pacific Salmon Life Histories*.
26 Hilborn and Peterman, 'Changing Management Objectives,' 70.
27 The agency's boundaries are based roughly on cultural boundaries. The Indians of northeastern British Columbia, in the Peace River District, who came under Treaty 8, are administered from Alberta.
28 See Frideres, Natives, *Natives Peoples*, chap. 2; and Weaver, *Making Indian Policy*, chap. 1. The Inuit came to be included under the Indian Act.
29 See Jarvenpa's comprehensive discussion, 'Political Economy.'

30 Scholarship on this question continues to change; I use Hawthorn, Belshaw, and Jamieson, *The Indians of British Columbia*, 19–20. See also Thompson and Kinkade, 'Languages.'
31 See Boyd, 'Demographic History,' 135.
32 See Tennant, *Aboriginal Peoples*.
33 Indian Act, *RSC* 1970, c. 1–6, s. 81.
34 As early as 1807. See Hansen, 'Treaty Fishing Rights,' 3. Fisheries Act, *SC*, 1868, c. 60.
35 Usher, 'Some Implications,' 20.
36 See Newell, 'Published Government Documents.'
37 See Slattery, 'The Hidden Constitution.'
38 Knight, *Indians at Work*.
39 Fisher, *Contact and Conflict*.
40 Tennant, *Aboriginal Peoples*, ix; LaViolette, *Struggle for Survival*.
41 Cohen, *Treaties on Trial*; Boxberger, *To Fish in Common*.
42 McEvoy, *The Fisherman's Problem*; Marchak, Guppy, and McMullan, eds., *Uncommon Property*.
43 Meggs, *Salmon*.
44 McEvoy, *The Fisherman's Problem*, 257.
45 Pearse, *Turning the Tide*, 174.

CHAPTER TWO: THE ABORIGINAL SALMON FISHERY

1 At least in the last several thousand years. See Suttles, ed., *Northwest Coast*; and Stewart, *Indian Fishing*.
2 Suttles, 'Coping with Abundance,' 47. Suttles writes of the Coast Salish, but there is no reason to think, given the biological habits of salmon, that his insights would not apply to other coastal groups. See also Prichard, 'Economic Development,' chap. 3.
3 Hewes, 'Aboriginal Use,' 47, 126–7. On the pre-contact fishery in Alaska, see Cooley, *Politics and Conservation*, chap. 2. Cooley, as was typical for the day, regards the aboriginal fishery as a mere opening phase that finished with the arrival of the commercial fishery. For California, see McEvoy's more sophiscated account, *The Fisherman's Problem*, 19–62. In the economies of aboriginal California, salmon was of subsistence value almost exclusively.
4 Sproat, *The Nootka*, 145.
5 Boyd, 'Demographic History,' 135–6.
6 Pearse, *Turning the Tide*, 174, citing Hewes, 'Indian Fisheries' (see Table 1, p. 136); Suttles, 'Environment,' 25. For a review of the methods for

obtaining data on subsistence harvests and for obtaining total subsistence volumes for fish, including use of recall surveys to reconstruct historical harvests, see Usher, 'Estimating Historical Sturgeon Harvests.'

7 Carrothers, *The British Columbia Fisheries*, 5. This assumes an average family of four and the lightest salmon at the time of spawning – humpback – which weighed 1.8 kg, and so this is a modest estimate.

8 See Ray, 'Early Economic History.'

9 Ibid.

10 Sproat, *The Nootka*, 58.

11 BCARS, Peter Skene Odgen, 'Notes on Western Caledonia,' 2. I am grateful to Arthur Ray for this information.

12 Canada, Department of Marine and Fisheries (title varies) (hereafter DOF), *Annual Report*, 1905 (1906), 210–11.

13 Ibid, 30. A type of small shark, valued for its oil.

14 Ibid, 18.

15 Kenyon, *The Kyuquot Way*, 41.

16 Berringer, 'Northwest Coast,' ii.

17 Ibid, 202, 212.

18 Ames, 'Stable and Resilient Systems,' 227.

19 Sproat, *The Nootka*, 148–50; Stewart, *Indian Fishing*.

20 See Berringer, 'Northwest Coast,' 37–44 and app. I, Table XII.

21 Stewart, *Indian Fishing*, 65–74.

22 See Berringer, 'Northwest Coast,' 22–7.

23 Stewart, *Indian Fishing*, 41.

24 Drucker, *Cultures*, 13.

25 Berringer, 'Northwest Coast,' 28, 33, and app. I, Table XI.

26 Ibid, 49–51 and app. I, Table XIII.

27 Lamb, ed., *Journals*, 371 ('dragnet'), 385 ('seining').

28 Berringer, 'Northwest Coast,' 60–6 and app. I, Table XV.

29 Ibid, 112–28 and app. I, Table XX.

30 Suttles, *Coast Salish Essays*, 10.

31 Berringer, 'Northwest Coast,' 85–111 and app. I, Tables XVI, XVIII, XIX. This is essential reading.

32 See Gitksan-Carrier Tribal Council, 'Submission to the Pearse Commission,' 14.

33 Hamori-Torok, 'Haisla,' 306–8.

34 Suttles, 'Central Coast Salish,' 457.

35 Sproat, *The Nootka*, 149–50.

36 Cited in Stewart, *Indian Fishing*, 111. She suggests that 'pine' surely

ought to read 'cedar.' This tendency to confuse cedar for pine is common in the early accounts.

37 Detailed in Berringer, 'Northwest Coast,' 101–11 and app. I, Table XIX.
38 Ibid, 106.
39 Lamb, ed., *Journals*, 358.
40 Ibid.
41 Ibid, 371–2.
42 Barbeau, 'An Indian Paradise Lost,' *Canadian Geographical Journal* 1 no. 2 (June 1930) 132–48, cited in Berringer, 'Northwest Coast,' 101–4.
43 Drucker, 'Cultural Element Distributions 26: Northwest Coast,' *Anthropological Records* 9 no. 3 (1950), cited in Berringer, 'Northwest Coast,' 107–8.
44 Suttles, 'Coping with Abundance,' 64.
45 Hicks, ed., *From Potlatch to Pulpit*, 110.
46 Stewart, *Indian Fishing*, 135.
47 Lamb, ed., *Journals*, 361.
48 Ibid, 390.
49 Usher, 'Aboriginal Property Systems,' 40. See also Usher, 'Property'; and Usher and Banks, *Property*.
50 Usher, 'Aboriginal Property Systems,' 39.
51 Prichard, 'Economic Development,' 49.
52 Ray, 'Fur Trade History,' 303.
53 See Lamb, ed., *Journals*, 393–4. This describes for the Bella Coola area the chief's power over fishing weirs.
54 Suttles, 'Affinal Ties,' 20–1.
55 Berringer, 'Northwest Coast,' 80.
56 Drucker, *Northern and Central Nootkan Tribes*, 250.
57 Berringer, 'Northwest Coast,' 110.
58 Ray, 'Fur Trade History,' 301–15.
59 Sproat, *The Nootka*, 30.
60 Halpin and Seguin, 'Tsimshian Peoples,' 269; Fladmark, ed., 'Fragments.'
61 MacDonald, Coupland, and Archer, 'The Coast Tsimshian,' Plate 13.
62 Halpin and Seguin, 'Tsimshian Peoples,' 281.
63 Ibid, 274, 269–71.
64 Spradley, with Sewid, *Guests*, 8.
65 Kenyon, *The Kyuquot Way*, 39.
66 Drucker, *Northern and Central Nootkan Tribes*, 36–7. This system of residential flexibility probably was unique to the Nootka (Prichard, 'Economic Development,' 44–5).

67 Drucker, *Cultures*, 145.
68 Marshall and Moon, 'Fieldwork.'
69 See Ray, 'Fur Trade History,' 312.
70 McEvoy, *The Fisherman's Problem*, 22–3.

CHAPTER THREE: INDIAN FISHERY INVENTED, 1871–1888

1 BCARS, Peter Skene Odgen, 'Notes on Western Caledonia,' 4.
2 Gibson, *Otter Skins*, 143, 210–11.
3 See Forester and Forester, *Fishing*, 53.
4 British Columbia, *Papers connected with the Indian Land Question*, 5–11.
5 DOF, *Annual Report*, 1871–72 (1873), 177.
6 Scott and Neher, 'Evolution,' 9. The province of Canada passed the first comprehensive fisheries bill for British North America in 1857.
7 See Hansen, 'Treaty Fishing Rights.'
8 *SC*, 1874, c. 28.
9 See *Canada Gazette*, vol. 9, 1483.
10 This section draws on Newell, 'Dispersal and Concentration.'
11 Newell, 'Rationality.'
12 DOF, *Annual Report*, 1893 (1894); Order in Council, 30 May 1878, *SC*, 1878.
13 DOF, *Annual Report*, 1873-74 (1875), lxxiii.
14 Ibid.
15 BCARS, GR 213, testimony of J.A. Russell, canner, before the Canada Commission on the Salmon Fishing Industry of British Columbia (1902), typescript evidence, sessions 8–12, 10th session, pp. 4–6.
16 DOF, *Annual Report*, 1871–72 (1873), appendices, 184.
17 Chittenden, *Official Report*, 57, cited in Stearns, *Haida Culture*, 43.
18 Canada, Department of Indian Affairs (titles varies) (hereafter DIA), *Annual Report*, 1872–73 (1874), appendices, 205.
19 Ibid, 1881 (1882), 220.
20 Knight, *Indians at Work*, 11.
21 Ibid.
22 DIA, *Annual Report*, 1881 (1882), xlv, xiv, 160, 166.
23 Ibid, 1882 (1883), 113. In the 1904 season, the Bella Bella worked for the canneries at Rivers Inlet and the one at Namu; ibid, 1904 (1906), 259. In 1912, it was reported that the Bella Bella, like so many Indians of the Bella Coola Agency, went down to Rivers Inlet in summer to fish for, or to work at, the canneries; ibid, 1912 (1913), 205.
24 Ibid, 1882 (1883), 117.

25 Ibid, 121.
26 National Archives of Canada (hereafter NAC), Records of the Office of the Indian Superintendent for British Columbia, Incoming Correspondence, RG 10, vol. 1329, Indian Agent's Incoming Correspondence, 26 August 1882, Cowichan Agency, New Westminster, 95–6, University of British Columbia Library (hereafter UBC), microfilm.
27 Drucker, *The Native Brotherhoods*, 123–6.
28 See Lyons, *Salmon*, 174–8.
29 Ray, 'Early Economic History.'
30 See, for example, Chief Commissioner of Lands and Works Robert Beavan to Superintendent of Indian Affairs I.W. Powell, 14 December 1873; I.W. Powell to Robert Beavan, 15 December 1873, BC Attorney-General George A. Walkem to I.W. Powell, 26 February 1874; and A. Dods (settler) to George A. Walkem, 11 June 1874, all reprinted in BC, *Papers Connected with the Indian Land Question*, 122, 128; DOF, *Annual Report*, 1878 (1879), 293, 304 (letter from Deputy Minister of Fisheries E.A. Meredith to Minister of Fisheries Hon. A. Smith, 23 October 1877).
31 See Johnston, *The Taking of Indian Lands*, 8.
32 See BC, *Report of the Government of British Columbia on the Subject of Indian Reserves, 17 August 1875*, 1, reprinted in BC, *Papers Connected with the Indian Land Question*; Kew, 'History,' 160.
33 See Kew, 'History,' 160; and Tennant, *Aboriginal Peoples*.
34 Memo, 'British Columbia Reserves,' 1 March 1874, cited in BC, *Papers Connected with the Indian Land Question*, 131.
35 BC, *Report on Indian Reserves*, 7.
36 Ibid.
37 Ibid, 8-9. This also applied to Indian 'labourers,' who should be encouraged to live in centres of labour, where they would also have access to missionaries and school teachers.
38 Ibid, app. C, 15.
39 Ibid, 7–8
40 Ibid, 16.
41 Memo, R.W. Scott, acting minister of the interior, 5 November 1875, cited in BC, *Papers Connected with the Indian Land Question*, 162.
42 DIA, *Annual Report*, 1901 (1902), part II, Tabular Statements, 'Schedule of Indian Reserves in the Dominion.'
43 BC, *Papers Relating to ... Indians of the North-West Coast*, 449.
44 DIA, *Annual Report*, 1882 (1883), 103–10.
45 Ibid.
46 Ibid, 94–6.

47 BC, *Papers Relating to ... Indians of the North-West Coast*, 418–23.
48 Ibid, 423, 425–59.
49 Ibid, 423.
50 Ibid, 427, for this quotation and the one that follows.
51 DIA, *Annual Report*, 1901 (1902), 'Schedule of Indian Reserves in the Dominion,' 122.
52 BC, *Papers Relating to ... Indians of the North-West Coast*, 422.
53 Ibid, 429.
54 Ibid, 449.
55 Ibid, 456.
56 DIA, *Annual Report*, 1901 (1902), 'Schedule of Indian Reserves in the Dominion,' 125.
57 Order in Council, 26 November 1888, *Canada Gazette*, vol. xxii, 956.
58 Hansen, 'Treaty Fishing Rights,' 7.
59 DOF, *Annual Report*, 1876 (1877), 343.
60 Ibid, 291.
61 Ibid, 1878 (1879), 293.
62 Ibid.
63 Ibid, 290.
64 Ibid, 1881 (1882), 209.
65 Ibid, 1878 (1879), 305; McFarland, 'Indian Reserve Cut-offs,' 37.
66 McDonald, 'Images,' 51.
67 DOF, *Annual Report*, 1878 (1879), 293.
68 Ibid, 299.
69 Ibid, 1886 (1887), 248.
70 BC, *Papers Relating to ... Indians of the North-West Coast*, 459.

CHAPTER FOUR: INDIAN LABOUR CAPTURED, 1889–1918

 1 Ward, *White Canada Forever*, 170–1.
 2 See Newell, 'Dispersal and Concentration.'
 3 DOF, *Annual Report*, 1888 (1889), xiv.
 4 Order in Council, 14 March 1890, *Canada Gazette*, vol. xxiii, 1903.
 5 Canada, *British Columbia Fishery Commission Report*, 1892 (hereafter Wilmot Report), vii.
 6 Ibid, 56.
 7 Fraser, *License Limitation*, 2.
 8 Order in Council, 3 March 1894, *Canada Gazette*, vol. xxvii, 1579.
 9 Scott and Neher, 'Evolution,' 10.
10 DOF, *Annual Report*, 1901 (1902), 'Special Reports by Professor E.E. Prince, 1901,' Supp. No. 4, iii, 30.

11 Scott and Neher, 'Evolution,' 11.
12 DOF, *Annual Report*, 1897 (1898), xxviii; ibid, 1895 (1896), 192. The canned-salmon pack for 1897 stood at 1,015,477 cases, virtually double that of the previous next-best year, 1896.
13 Carrothers, *The British Columbia Fisheries*, 18.
14 See Ralston, 'The 1900 Strike.'
15 See Newell, ed., *Development*, based on records left by Henry Doyle, founder and first general manager of BC Packers Association, 1902.
16 DOF, *Annual Report*, 1900 (1901), xxxvii.
17 Ibid, 1897 (1898), 321.
18 See Newell, 'Rationality.'
19 Order in Council, 30 March 1917, *SC*, 1917.
20 See Canada, Dominion–British Columbia Fisheries Commission, 1905–07, *Report and Recommendations*.
21 Order in Council, 8 June 1908, *SC*, 1908.
22 BCARS, GR 435, box 71, file 670, BC Department of Fisheries, Fishery Overseers' Reports, 1912, V.H. Abley, provincial constable, Port Essington, 26 December 1912, to D.N. McIntyre, deputy commissioner of fisheries, Victoria.
23 The new provincial fishery overseer for the Nass, C.P. Hickman, reported in 1908 that in that region ' "The canneries supply the boats and nets and licences for each boat and pay for the fish accordingly" so there being practically no independent fishermen'; BCARS, GR 435, box 70, file 654, BC Fisheries, Fishery Overseers' Reports, 1908, Hickman to J.P. Babock, Nass Harbour P.O., 23 May 1908.
24 Order in Council, 22 December 1910, *SC*, 1911. The report by the Economic Committee of the Fisheries Association of British Columbia (FABC) – 'Raw Fish Pricing and Licence Limitation,' 18 December 1961 (UBC, FABC, box 27, 'Licence Limitation – 1961') – assumes incorrectly that the 1917 report of the commission headed by Sanford Evans was the first to propose limiting the number of canneries.
25 Order in Council, 14 March 1911, *SC*, 1911; amended by Order in Council, 19 November 1912, *SC*, 1913, to apply only to gillnet or drift-net operations; rescinded by Order in Council, 14 April 1923, *SC*, 1923. A similar prohibition existed for the lucrative Alaska sockeye district Bristol Bay; remarkably, American officials did not eliminate this ban until 1951; Cooley, *Politics*, 200.
26 DOF, *Annual Report*, 1913–14 (1915), 294.
27 BC, *Annual Report of the Commissioner of Fisheries*, 1912 (1913), 1–7; Lyons, *Salmon*, 286–7.
28 BCARS, GR 435, box 71, files 680 (1914) and 681 (1915), correspondence

between Kenneth Birchall, fishery overseer, Port Essington, and D.N. McIntyre, deputy commissioner of fisheries, Victoria.

29 See app. F of Order in Council, 9 February 1915, *SC*, 1915, and Order in Council, 30 March 1917, *SC*, 1917. Order in Council, 28 February 1918, *SC*, 1918, re-enacted subsection 12 of section 13, Special Fishery Regulations, BC (1915), rescinded in 1917. Fraser, 'License Limitation,' 6; Canada, Royal Commission on the Salmon Fisheries and Canning Industry in British Columbia (Evans Commission), *Report*.

30 This certainly applied to the Indian fishers of the Skeena watershed; Wilmot Report, 310.

31 DOF, *Annual Report*, 1893 (1894), 285.

32 Hawthorn, Belshaw, and Jamieson, *The Indians of British Columbia*.

33 See, example, DOF, *Annual Report*, 1887 (1888), app. 7; ibid, 1888 (1889), 243; ibid, 1889 (1890), 257. See also testimony, Canada, Royal Commission on Chinese and Japanese Immigration, *Report*, *Sessional Papers* (1902), No. 54.

34 Wilmot Report, 117, 121.

35 Ibid. 142.

36 Order in Council, 1 May 1900, *SC*, 1900.

37 Wilmot Report, 46–7 (testimony of P. McTiernan, Indian agent for New Westminster).

38 NAC, Canada, Department of Indian Affairs, RG 10, AW1, R6405:1, Indian Agent's Incoming Correspondence, vol. 1337, Cowichan Agency, 22 March 1890, Ewen & Co. Canners, 4; 29 February 1892, Fisheries Inspector McNab (microfilm, UBC).

39 Wilmot Report, 46.

40 Ibid, 142.

41 DIA, *Annual Report*, 1891 (1892), 203, 131.

42 BCARS, GR 213, Canada Commission on the Salmon Fishing Industry in British Columbia, 1902, Evidence for sessions 13–16, testimony of John Elliot, Cowichan Indian, 16th session, p. 10.

43 DIA, *Annual Report*, 1897 (1898), 120, 189.

44 Ibid, 236, 247.

45 NAC, RG 10, AW1, R6405:32, Field Office Correspondence and Miscellaneous, vol. 1461, Indian Agent's Letterbook, New Westminster Agency, 31 August 1904, 468.

46 See BCARS, Debeck Family Papers, Three Seasons Work, Manuscript by Edwin Keary Debeck, 20–1, 16–17.

47 See Assu with Inglis, *Assu of Cape Mudge*, 62–3.

48 Ford, *Smoke from Their Fires*, 208, 228.

49 See NAC, RG 10 AW1, Field Office Correspondence and Miscellaneous, Indian Agent's Letterbooks for various years and agencies, especially the Cowichan Agency.
50 Prichard, 'Economic Development,' 85.
51 Campbell, 'Hartley Bay,' 15.
52 Assu, *Assu of Cape Mudge*, 62–3.
53 NAC, RG 10, AW1, R6405:44, Monthly Report, Kwakeweth Agency, August 1899.
54 '50 Years of Cannery Life,' taped interview with Agnes Alfred, by Daisy Smith, English translation by Colleen Hemphill, for D. Newell, 31 May 1984, in possession of author. See also Neel, *Our Chiefs and Elders*, 27–31, 171.
55 DIA, *Annual Report*, 1905–6 (1906), 238.
56 Blackman, *During My Times*, 74, 80–1, 57.
57 BCARS, Add. Ms. 870, Philip Drucker Field Notes, box 2, part 7, Biographical Notes on Alfred Adams, photocopied typescript, 47–8.
58 BCARS, Add. Ms. 364, Imbert Orchard Collection, box 4, file 7, People and Landscape IV – No. 12 – 'The Salmon Industry on the Skeena,' interview with Walter Wicks, 2–3.
59 BCARS, Add. Ms. 870, Biographical Notes on Alfred Adams, 48–9.
60 BCARS, Add. Ms. 879, Philip Drucker Field Notes, box 1, Part 2, vol. 5, BC, fall 1953, interview with William Matthews, December.
61 BCARS, Add Ms. 870, Biographical Notes on Alfred Adams, 48–9; Blackman, *During My Time*, 110.
62 DIA, *Annual Report*, 1907–08 (1908), 229. Probably Quashela or Quashella.
63 In 1902, Newell, ed., *Development*, 47–8.
64 Ibid, 47.
65 Ibid, 46.
66 North and Griffin, *A Ripple*, 2; Knight, *Indians at Work*, chap. 6; Ralston, 'The 1900 Strike.'
67 See Newell, ed., *Development*, 71, 119–24.
68 Ibid, 67–8, 99, citing letter from Henry Doyle to H. Bell-Irving & Co., 16 December 1902.
69 BCARS, GR 213, Commission on the Salmon Fishing Industry in British Columbia, 1902, Evidence, third session, evidence of Theodore Demes.
70 Ibid, evidence of John Wallace.
71 Ibid, fourteenth session, evidence of C.F. Todd.
72 Creese, 'Class, Ethnicity, and Conflict.'
73 BCARS, GR 213, Commission, 1902, Evidence, fifth session, evidence of E.P. Bremner.

74 BCARS, GR 435, BC Provincial Fisheries Department, box 71, file 676 (1913), 'Detail of Licenses Issued, No. 2' (by name and cannery), 16 July 1913, Kenneth Birchall, fishery overseer; Birchall to McIntyre, 28 August 1913. And there were 60 attached and 54 independent licences for whites, for a total of 895 licences; ibid, file 679, Arthur W. Stone, provincial constable, to C.P. Hickman, inspector of fisheries for BC, 30 January 1914.

75 Ibid, box 71, file 675, Arthur W. Stone to D.N. McIntyre, 3 July 1913.

76 BCARS, GR 213, Commission, 1902, Evidence, eighth session, evidence of John Scott, New Westminster.

77 BCARS, GR 435, box 70, file 657 (1909), 'The Skeena River Division,' n.d.

78 See Newell, 'Rationality.'

79 Assu, Assu of Cape Mudge, 68.

80 Hicks, ed., From Potlatch to Pulpit, 92.

81 Ibid, 93.

82 BCARS, GR 672, BC, Provincial Secretary, Correspondence Inward from the Royal Commission on Indian Affairs, 1913–1916, box 1, file 27, E.L. Wetmore to Louis Codere, Secretary of State, Ottawa, 29 November 1913.

83 McFarland, 'Indian Reserve Cut-offs,' 76–7 and Table 4.1.

84 Hawthorn, Belshaw, and Jamieson, The Indians of British Columbia, 55.

85 BC, Royal Commission on Indian Affairs for the Province of British Columbia (McKenna-McBride Commission), Report, vol. 1, 175.

86 BCARS, Union of BC Indian Chiefs, Evidence Submitted to the Royal Commission on Indian Affairs for the Province of British Columbia, 1913–24, evidence of Chief Michael, microfilm, reel 2.

87 DIA, 'Schedule of Indian Reserves in the Province of British Columbia,' attached to Dominion Order in Council 1265 (Ditchburn-Clark Report), 19 July 1924, cited and used as a data source in McFarland, 'Indian Reserve Cut-offs,' 68–9, Table 3.5.

88 Sterritt, 'Gitksan'; BC, Royal Commission on Indian Affairs, Report, vol. 3, 278.

89 McFarland, 'Indian Reserve Cut-offs,' 74–5.

90 See BC, Royal Commission on Indian Affairs, Report, vol. 3, 276.

91 DOF, Annual Report, 1891 (1892), 167.

92 NAC, Canada, Department of Fisheries, RG 23, Archives Materials on BC (microfilm), General Correspondence, file 583, fishery guardian to inspector of fisheries, New Westminster, 15 February 1894.

93 Order in Council, 3 March 1894, SC, 1894; Carrothers, British Columbia Fisheries, 38.

94 NAC, RG 23, file 2233, R.H. Pidock, Indian agent, to A.W. Vowell, Indian superintendent, 30 December 1897, 13 January 1898, and 4 November 1898.

95 BCARS, GR 213, Commission, 1902, sixteenth session, evidence of W.R. Robertson; Victoria *Colonist*, 6 Feburary 1902.

96 BCARS, GR 213, Commission, 1902, sixteenth session, evidence of Sweehelt.

97 See Burrows, 'A Much-Needed Class of Labour,' 37–8. Burrows carefully compiled and analysed the economic information in Indian Affairs records but does not provide an overall interpretation of the data.

98 *Vancouver Province*, 31 October and 14 July 1906.

99 DOF, *Annual Report*, 1904 (1905), introduction.

100 NAC, RG 23, Archives Materials on BC, General Correspondence, file 2233, F. Gourdeau, deputy minister of marine and fisheries, to deputy superintendent general of Indian Affairs, 16 June 1897; John T. Walbran, fishery and revenue officer, report, 6 July 1897. The fisheries belonged to the 'Koskumo' (Koskimo).

101 Ibid, Annual Report, J.T. Williams to E.E. Prince, dominion commissioner of fisheries, 6 December 1905.

102 DOF, *Annual Report*, 1904 (1905), xlv; *Vancouver Province*, 19 November 1904.

103 NAC, RG 23, Archives Materials on BC, General Correspondence, file 2235, Peter Wallace to Hon. William Sloan, Ottawa, 11 April 1905.

104 *Vancouver Province*, 19 November 1904.

105 DOF, *Annual Report*, 1904 (1905).

106 NAC, RG 23, Archives Materials on BC, General Correspondence, file 2235, Helgesen to Williams, 25 October 1905.

107 DOF, *Annual Report*, 1905 (1906), 207 (full account, 206–11).

108 Ibid, 1906 (1907), 214.

109 NAC, RG 23, Archives Materials on BC, General Correspondence, file 2235, Annual Report, Williams to Prince, 6 December 1905.

110 Ibid. See also Victoria *Daily Times*, 14 December 1906; *Vancouver Province*, 17 March 1909.

111 BCARS, GR 435, box 70, file 657 (1909), 'The Skeena River Division,' n.d.

112 NAC, RG 23, Archives Materials on BC, General Correspondence, file 583, L.P. Brodeur, minister of marine and fisheries, to Frank Oliver, minister of the interior, 14 January 1907.

113 Ibid, memo, F.H. Cunningham, chief inspector of fisheries for BC, to Department of Marine and Fisheries, Ottawa, 18 April 1912.

114 Ibid., J.C. McAllan, acting Indian agent, Stuart Lake Agency, Fraser

Lake, to J.D. McLean, assistant deputy minister, Department of Indian Affairs, Ottawa, 22 January 1911.
115 Ibid, W.A. Found, for superintendent of fisheries, to Cunningham, 21 March 1911; Father Cocoola, Fort St James, Stuart Lake, to H.P. Horton, fishery guardian, Clinton, 11 February 1911.
116 Confirmed by the McKenna-McBride Commission, BC, Royal Commission on Indian Affairs, *Report*, vol. 4, 907 (Ilthpaya Reserve No. 8, West Coast Agency).
117 BCARS, Add. Ms. 2172, Charles Ludwig Moser Papers, 'Thirty Years a Missionary on the West Coast of Vancouver Island,' by Dorothy Abraham, transcript based on the diary of Charles Ludwig Moser, 24.
118 NAC, RG 23, Archives Materials on BC, General Correspondence, file 583, Clayoquot, 10 January 1906.
119 Ibid, Nanaimo, to R.W. Venning, Ottawa, 24 June 1907.
120 See Hudson, 'Fraser River Fisheries,' 37; and Hudson, 'Traplines and Timber.'
121 DOF, *Annual Report*, 1915–16 (1916), 249.
122 Canada, Department of Naval Service, Fisheries Branch, *Annual Report*, 1916–17 (1918), 243.
123 Order in Council, 11 September, 1917, SC, 1918. Amendment to the special fishery regulations for the province of BC, adopted by Order in Council, 9 February 1915, SC, 1915.
124 By Order in Council, 4 May 1916, SC, 1917; Order in Council, 11 September 1917, SC, 1918.
125 See Lytwyn, 'Ojibwa and Ottawa Fisheries'; and Van West 'Ojibwa Fisheries.'
126 Carter, *Lost Harvests*; Elias, *The Dakota*.

CHAPTER FIVE: BATTLING A REVOLVING DOOR, 1919–1945

1 Canada, Commission to Investigate Fisheries Conditions in BC, 1922 (Duff Commission), *Report and Recommendations* (hereafter Duff Report); BCARS, GR 435, BC Department of Fisheries, box 160, 1922, 'Bell-Irving Statement to Ottawa Committee of the House,' 28 April 1922. The Bell-Irvings (ABC Packing) were major figures in BC salmon-canning. Henry P. Bell-Irving was lieutenant-governor of the province from 1978 to 1983.
2 See Newell, 'Politics of Food.'
3 See Orders in Council, 5 and 19 March 1919, SC, 1919–20.
4 Duff Report, 11.
5 See Creese, 'Class,' 66–8.

6 Order in Council, 14 April 1923, *SC*, 1923.
7 DOF, *Annual Report*, 1925–26 (1926), 51.
8 Ibid, 1927–28 (1928), 72.
9 (1927) 39 *British Columbia Law Reports (BCLR)* (1st) 103 (BC Supreme Court). This court did not rule on the issue of fishing licensing.
10 *Attorney-General of Canada v. Attorney-General of British Columbia, et al.* (1930), *Appeal Court* (AC) 111 (Judicial Committee of the Privy Council), affirming (1928) *Supreme Court Reports (SCR)* 457 (Supreme Court of Canada). *Vancouver Sun*, 5 November 1929.
11 *Vancouver Province*, 6 December 1929.
12 Deutsch, Jamieson, Matuszewski, Scott, and Will, 'Economics,' 65–6.
13 Hawthorn, Belshaw, and Jamieson, *The Indians of British Columbia*, 110–11.
14 See Newell, 'Politics of Food.'
15 See BCARS, GR 435, BC Department of Fisheries, box 50, file 449, 1941, various correspondence; file 451, 1942, Notice re: Salmon Seining, Area No. 17 (Johnstone Strait), J.A. Motherwell, 1 September 1942.
16 Newell, 'Politics of Food.'
17 North and Griffin, *A Ripple*, 17–19.
18 Order in Council, 4 March 1942, PC 1665, created the BC Security Commission, which conducted the evacuation.
19 DOF, *Annual Report*, 1923–24 (1924), 52.
20 BC, *Report on Oriental Activities*, 18–21.
21 Ibid; Newell, ed., *Development*, 165; and see testimony on the issue of gas boats by Indian fishers to the hearings of the Parliamentary Fisheries Commission, 1922, UBC, Henry Doyle Papers, box 11, file 17.
22 Summarized in Meggs, *Salmon*, 109–10.
23 DOF, *Annual Report*, 1923–24 (1924), 54.
24 Prichard, 'Economic Development,' Table XII, p. 114.
25 See Knight, *Indians at Work*, 84ff; Assu with Inglis, *Assu of Cape Mudge*, 65; and BC, *Report on Oriental Activities*, 18–21.
26 Spradley with Sewid, *Guests*; Assu, *Assu of Cape Mudge*.
27 BCARS, Add. Ms. 870, Philip Drucker Field Notes, Notebooks, box 1, part 2, vol. 1, BC fall 1953, interview with William D. Scow, 7 October, n.p.
28 Spradley, *Guests*, 19.
29 Ibid, 64–5.
30 Ibid, 79–80.
31 Ibid, 96–106.
32 Ibid, 113–18.
33 Ibid, 118.

34 Ibid, 125.
35 Ibid, 127.
36 Ibid, 166, 193–4.
37 Assu, *Assu of Cape Mudge*, 64; Neel, *Our Chiefs and Elders*, 35.
38 Carr, *Klee Wyck*, 46–8.
39 Assu, *Assu of Cape Mudge*, 66–7.
40 See Newell, 'Rationality.'
41 Newell, 'Politics of Food,' 190, and Table 2, 191.
42 'Working in Bones Bay Cannery,' taped interview with Lucy Smith, by
    Colleen Hemphill for Dianne Newell, 20 August 1984, in possession of
    author.
43 'Experiences at Bones Bay Cannery,' taped interview with Ann Brochie,
    by Colleen Hemphill for Dianne Newell, 8 September 1984, in
    possession of author.
44 '50 Years of Cannery Life,' taped interview with Agnes Alfred, by
    Daisy Smith, English translation by Colleen Hemphill, for Dianne
    Newell, 31 May 1984, in possession of author.
45 BCARS, Add. Ms. 870, Philip Drucker Field Notes, box 6, part 48,
    'Research Problems and Conditions on the Northwest Coast,'
    photocopied typescript, 5, 7.
46 Assu, *Assu of Cape Mudge*, 62–3.
47 Kenyon, *The Kyuquot Way*, 52.
48 Ibid, 40, 52–3; BCARS, Add. Ms. 2172, Charles Ludwig Moser Papers,
    'Thirty Years a Missionary on the West Coast of Vancouver Island,' by
    Dorothy Abraham, transcript based on the diary of Charles Ludwig
    Moser, 110–11, 126.
49 Arima and Dewhirst, 'Nootkans,' 410.
50 Shoop, 'Participation,' 50.
51 Ibid, 52.
52 Ibid, 54.
53 Richmond, BC, Richmond Arts Centre Collection, taped interview with
    Buck Suzuki, by David Stevenson, 15 January 1976.
54 Drucker, *Native Brotherhoods*, 95–101.
55 Alan Morley's biography of Kelly, *Roar of the Breakers*, is an uncritical
    source without much solid information. Kelly, too, experienced cannery
    work. He supplemented his income as a minister at Hartley Bay by
    acting as foreman at a local cannery (p. 79) – probably the small clam
    cannery run by Charles Robinson (who also owned a large store in
    Hartley Bay) in Lachljeets or Clamstown, an ancient camp site on Fin
    Island. See Campbell, 'Hartley Bay,' 19.

56 Canada, *Report and Evidence of Special Joint Committee Appointed to Enquire into the Claims of the Allied Indian Tribes of British Columbia* (hereafter *Claims*), 108.
57 Ibid, 110.
58 Ibid, 109.
59 Ibid, 109.
60 Ibid, 109–10, 194–6, 200–1. Stevens was, however, not at all sympathetic on the issue of Indian title.
61 Ibid, 194, 200ff.
62 *Attorney-General of BC v. Attorney-General of Canada* (1914), *AC* 153 (Judicial Committee of the Privy Council), affirming (1913) *SCR* 493 (Supreme Court of Canada).
63 *Claims*, 204–5.
64 For some original accounts and correspondence on the Rivers Inlet strike, see BCARS, GR 435, BC Fisheries Department, 1935–6, box 98, file 964; also North and Griffin, *A Ripple*, 10–11.
65 See Drucker, *Native Brotherhoods*, and BCARS, Add. Ms. 870, Philip Drucker Field Notes, box 2, part 7, typescript, 13–14.
66 See BCARS, GR 435, BC Department of Fisheries, box 97, file 956, 1939–43, 'Fishermen's Union in British Columbia,' reporting 30 March 1939. Indians belonged to the locals of either the Native Brotherhood of BC or the Pacific Coast Fishermen's Union.
67 Kew, 'History,' 164.
68 See Skogan, *Skeena*, interviews with Hazel Stewart, Dorothy Young, Emma Nyce, and John Atchison; taped interview with Ann Brochie and Lucy Smith, Campbell River, by Colleen Hemphill for Dianne Newell, 8 September 1984 (in possession of author); BCARS, GR 435, BC Department of Fisheries, box 97, file 956, 1939–43, various memos dated 20 August 1941.
69 BCARS, Add. Ms. 870, Philip Drucker Field Notes, box 2, part 7, interviews with William D. Scow, 7 October 1953, and Charley Nowell, 14 October 1953, n.p.
70 Patterson, 'Andrew Paull,' 51.
71 Muszynski, 'Shoreworkers,' 274.
72 See Drucker, *Native Brotherhoods*; and Gladstone, 'Native Indians,' 32.
73 DOF, *Annual Report*, 1918 (1919), 12.
74 Ibid, 1921–22 (1922), 52–3.
75 Victoria *Daily Times*, 16 August 1922.
76 'Parlimentary Fisheries Commission, 1922,' 'Evidence: William Collison, Prince Rupert, 14 August, UBC, Doyle Papers, box 11, file 17, 27–28B.

77 Ibid, 28B.
78 Victoria *Daily Times*, 6 September 1922.
79 'Parlimentary Fisheries Commission, 1922,' Evidence: various testimony, East Bella Bella and Kimsquit, BC, 23 August.
80 *Claims*, 190.
81 Ibid, 197–8.
82 Ibid.
83 Ibid, 199–200.
84 Drucker, *Native Brotherhoods*, 101.
85 *Vancouver Province*, 18 December 1927.
86 Ibid, 22 September 1929.
87 DOF, *Annual Report*, 1929–30 (1930), 105.
88 *Vancouver Province*, 22 September 1929.
89 DOF, *Annual Report*, 1930–31 (1931), 103.
90 Ibid, 1931–32 (1932), 57–8.

CHAPTER SIX: CAST ADRIFT, 1946–1968

1 Bradley, 'Some Seasonal Models,' 33; and see Gordon, 'Economic Theory'; Christy, Jr, and Scott, *The Common Wealth*, 215–30; and Crutchfield and Pontecorvo, *Pacific Salmon Fisheries*. See also the discussion in Fraser, *License Limitation*, 7–18.
2 Canada, Department of Fisheries and the Fisheries Research Board, *The Commercial Fisheries of Canada*, 12.
3 Ibid, 8.
4 UBC, FABC, box 27, file: 'West Coast Salmon Fleet Development Committee – Phase IV – License Limitation 1972,' 'Salmon Gear Conflicts: A Discussion Paper, by R. Roberts,' n.d., 6.
5 See Ricker, Bilton, and Aro, *Causes*. Use of synthetic fibres in gillnetting also contributed.
6 UBC, FABC, box 27, file: 'West Coast Salmon Fleet Development,' 'Salmon Gear Conflicts, by R. Roberts,' n.d., 1–4.
7 Newell, ed., *Development*, 236.
8 Meggs, *Salmon*, chap. 21.
9 Muszynski, 'Class Formation,' 107–8, 110. See also UBC, United Fishermen and Allied Workers' Union Collection, box 310.
10 Hawthorn, Belshaw, and Jamieson, *The Indians of British Columbia*, 91–2.
11 Sinclair, *Licence Limitation*, 90, 228.
12 Crutchfield and Pontecorvo, *Pacific Salmon Fisheries*; Hardin, 'Tragedy.'
13 Hardin, 'Tragedy,' 1247.

14 See, for example, Commoner, *The Closing Circle*; Wadley, 'Common Lands'; Spry, 'Tragedy'; Berkes, 'Common Property'; Tough, 'Fisheries Economics'; and Feeny, Berkes, McCay, and Acheson, 'Tragedy.' For critical studies on ocean fisheries, see McEvoy, *The Fisherman's Problem*, especially chap. 1; and Marchak, Guppy, and McMullan, eds., *Uncommon Property*.

15 Buchanan and Campbell, *Economics*.

16 Sinclair, *Licence Limitation*, 222–3.

17 Knight, *Indians at Work*, 202–3; Doeman, *Indians*. This transformation of reserve societies occurred in both Canada and the United States. See Jarvenpa, 'Political Economy.'

18 Canada, Department of Indian Affairs, *Statement of the Government of Canada on Indian Policy* (White Paper, 1969).

19 See Weaver, *Making Canadian Indian Policy*. Weaver says that she hoped that her study would contribute to a 'corporate memory in government about Indian policy' (xiii).

20 The literature is summarized in Shetlings, 'Death of a Community?,' 52–60.

21 Ibid. Shetlings gives examples and provides a case study of the attempts to relocate the Tanakteuk Band, a Kwakiutl tribal group located on the northwest coast of Vancouver Island. Illustrating the policy for Canada's Indians are two booklets published by Indian Affairs in the 1960s: *The Indian in Transition: The Indian Today* (1962) and *The Indian in Industry: Road to Independence* (1965).

22 See Suttles, ed., *Northwest Coast*, tables on reserve/off-reserve population.

23 Gladstone, 'Native Indians,' 20.

24 Hawthorn, Belshaw, and Jamieson, *The Indians of British Columbia*, 107 and Tables VIII (75–6) and XII (114). The statistics that follow are taken from chapter 7, 72–83.

25 Ibid, Table IX (77).

26 Ibid, 72.

27 Ibid, 107; Drucker, *Native Brotherhoods*, 123–4.

28 Hawthorn, Belshaw, and Jamieson, *The Indians of British Columbia*, 117.

29 Spradley with Sewid, *Guests*, 193.

30 Assu with Inglis, *Assu of Cape Mudge*, 59.

31 Gladstone, 'Native Indians,' 24–5.

32 James, *Historic and Present Native Participation*, 2.

33 Hawthorn, Belshaw, and Jamieson, *The Indians of British Columbia*, 113.

34 Ibid, 113, 115, Table XII (114), citing special reports submitted January

1954 by the Indian superintendents of all BC agencies, for the Income Tax Division, Department of National Revenue.

35 Glenbow-Alberta Institute, tape RCT-127-1, Tatsuzo Yamashita, taped interview with Mr Yamashita and his daughter-in-law, Ruriko (Mrs Yas) Yamashita, Vauxhall, Alberta, 'Recollections of Japanese Experience in Western Canada, 1908–1973,' 3 May 1973; tape RCT-125-1, Tono Ohama, taped interview with Mr and Mrs Tono Ohama, Rainier, Alberta, 'Some Comments on Japenese Experiences in Western Canada, 1912–1973,' 20 April 1973.

36 Richmond, BC, Richmond Art Centre Collection, taped interview with Buck Suzuki, 15 January 1976.

37 See Muszynski, 'Organization,' which illuminates the labour situation in the 1940s.

38 The complex, fishery-related work history of the Sparrow family of the Musqueam Indian Reserve (Central Coast Salish), which soon became known through the celebrated *Sparrow* judgment, is a good example of this custom. See Sparrow, 'Work Histories.'

39 Shoop, 'Participation,' 50–4.

40 Hawthorn, Belshaw, and Jamieson, *The Indians of British Columbia*, 114–16.

41 *Native Voice*, February 1949, February 1950.

42 Hawthorn, Belshaw, and Jamieson, *The Indians of British Columbia*, 116.

43 Ibid, 117.

44 Prichard, 'Economic Development,' 108.

45 Ibid, 82.

46 Hamori-Torok, 'Haisla,' 310.

47 Ray, *The Canadian Fur Trade*.

48 See Phidd and Doern, *Politics and Management*, chap. 9.

49 See discussion in Hawthorn, Belshaw, and Jamieson, *The Indians of British Columbia*, 190–4.

50 Ibid, 194.

51 Gladstone, 'Native Indians,' 34.

52 BCARS, Add. Ms. 870, Philip Drucker Field Notes, Notebooks, box 1, part 2, vol. 6, BC fall 1953, interview with William Matthews, n.d.

53 Ibid.

54 Ibid. The company originally asked for $800, but the engines were so worn that the trollers negotiated a lower price.

55 BCARS, Add. Ms. Philip Drucker, 'Research Problems and Conditions on the Northwest Coast,' 9.

56 Stearns, *Haida Culture*, 95, and the information that immediately follows, 96–101, and 93, Table 4.

57 Hawthorn, Belshaw, and Jamieson, *The Indians of British Columbia*, 107–8.
58 Ibid, 84.
59 Ibid, 124.
60 Victoria *Daily Times*, 24 August 1960.
61 See Rohner and Rohner, *The Kwakiutl Indians*, 30-6.
62 Rohner, *The People of Gilford*, 53.
63 Stearns, *Haida Culture*, 102.
64 BCARS, Add. Ms. 364, Imbert Orchard Collection, box 4, file 4, People in Landscape Series II, 1968–72, typed script no. 22, 'Fishermen of the Queen Charlotte Islands,' interviews conducted 1969–70, 2.
65 Stearns, *Haida Culture*, 96.
66 Ibid, 43–4.
67 Ibid, 102ff.
68 Ibid, 106–9.
69 Ibid, 88–91, including Table 1 (89).
70 Ibid, 116.
71 McKay and Ouellette, *Review*, 4–14.
72 Spradley, *Guests*, 221–2.
73 *Vancouver Province*, 7 May 1968.
74 McKay and Ouellette, *Review*, 14. The IFAP's budget was approximately $4.6 million.
75 *Vancouver Province*, 7 May 1968.
76 Hawthorn, Belshaw, and Jamieson, *The Indians of British Columbia*, 96.
77 Ibid, 44.
78 BCARS, Add. Ms. 364, Imbert Orchard Collection, 'Fishermen of the Queen Charlottes,' 3.
79 Blackman, *During My Time*, 57.
80 Hawthorn, Belshaw, and Jamieson, *The Indians of British Columbia*, 210–11.
81 Spradley, *Guests*, 158.
82 Hawthorn, Belshaw, and Jamieson, *The Indians of British Columbia*, 213.
83 Gitksan-Carrier Tribal Council, 'Submission,' 14–15.
84 See Sanders, 'Case Law Digest.' Most appellate and supreme court decisions are reported in law report volumes.
85 *Regina v. Cooper* (1968), 1 *Dominion Law Reports* (*DLR*) (3d) 113 (BC Supreme Court).
86 See Sanders, 'Case Law Digest'; Victoria *Daily Times*, 30 May 1968; and *Vancouver Sun*, 4 June 1968.
87 See Friedlaender, *Economic Status*, 74–7.
88 *Vancouver Province*, 20 July 1967.
89 Ibid, 15, 29 August 1967.

90 Ibid, 24 October 1967.
91 *Vancouver Sun*, 29 November 1967.
92 *Vancouver Province*, 16 April 1868; *Vancouver Sun*, 3 May 1968.
93 *Vancouver Province*, 16 April 1968.
94 UBC, FABC, box 27, file: 'Licence Limitation – 1961,' Report of the Fisheries Association of BC on 'Licence Limitation – British Columbia: A Method of Economic Fisheries Management, by Sol Sinclair,' 1 May 1961.

CHAPTER SEVEN: RIGHTS RECONSIDERED, 1969–1993

1 Fraser, *License Limitation*, 24ff.
2 Ibid, 54–5; Native Brotherhood of BC, *Licence Study 1987*, 53.
3 Landale, *Harvest*, 119–220. The price of A licences dropped temporarily to $1,500 a ton largely because of low fish prices in 1974 and an 'off year' for salmon in 1975.
4 Warriner and Guppy, 'From Urban Centre,' 139.
5 The government-operated buyback gave one fishing family $2,700 for its old troller in 1971. Any vessel that interested the family was either undergoing or waiting for government appraisal under the buyback scheme. The family combed Vancouver Island and the lower mainland searching for a boat for sale and eventually found an old 25-m 'junker,' with a $20,000 price tag. Landale, *Harvest*, 69, 76.
6 Mitchell, 'Hindsight Reviews,' 178.
7 Shoop, 'Participation,' 31.
8 Hayward, 'The Co-op Strategy,' 60, 57.
9 Shoop, 'Participation,' 15.
10 UBC, FABC, box 9, file: 'Indian Employment – 1972,' draft re: Indian Employment in North Coast Fish Plants, K.M. Campbell, Fisheries Association of BC, 7 March 1972.
11 See Newell, 'Report.' The North Pacific plant operated for only one other year, on an emergency basis, in 1972, when (Old) Oceanside cannery accidentally burned down just as the salmon-canning season was about to begin. It was later purchased by BC Packers and then acquired in the early 1980s by the North Coast Marine Museum Society and redeveloped as a fishery museum with the status of national historic site. BC Packers burned down the Sunnyside camp in the 1980s.
12 Pinkerton, 'The Fishing Dependent Community,' 303. This prompted the growth of small, local, diversified stations and plants in the 1970s and 1980s (see 306–10).
13 See Hill, *Tides of Change*; and Hayward, 'The Co-op Strategy.'

14 For details, see also Blyth, *Salmon Canneries*, 109–10.
15 Mitchell, 'Hindsight Reviews,' 151–3.
16 See, for example, interview with Professor Carl Walters, University of British Columbia, *Globe and Mail*, 1 August 1992. Spring and cohoe seem to be in the worst difficulty.
17 See Meggs, *Salmon*, 216–18.
18 Ellis, 'Perspectives,' 63.
19 Blyth, *Salmon Canneries*, 103.
20 Pearse was an influential member of the West Coast Fleet Development Committee and in 1973 chaired a subcommittee on fleet rationalization that guided future development of the industry. See Doucet and Pearse, *Fisheries Policy*, prepared in response to the minister's request for assessment of the state of the Pacific Coast fisheries and recommendations on policy.
21 For a list of programs, see Elsey, 'Government Intervention,' 93; and Pearse, *Turning the Tide*, 160ff.
22 Thomas Berger, then NDP MLA for Vancouver-Burrard and later a justice of the BC Supreme Court, warned that since the new regulations licensed the vessel and not the fisher, they would eliminate from the industry Indians and any other fishers 'without boats, lots of capital, or credit' (*Vancouver Province*, 30 September 1968). The North Coast District Council (made up of nine north coast villages) charged that the program favoured seine fishers (mostly Vancouver-based) over north coast and Indian gillnetters (ibid, 13 December 1969). See comments of Frank Howard, NDP MP for Skeena, in Canada, House of Commons, *Debates*, various vols., 1968–70.
23 Pinkerton, 'The Fishing Dependent Community,' 317.
24 James, *Historic and Present Native Participation*, 4.
25 Pearse, *Turning the Tide*, 152–3.
26 McKay, *Native Commercial Fisheries*, 19.
27 Canada, House of Commons, *Debates*, vol. 1, 1967, 1178–9; UBC, FABC, box 41, file: 'Health Committee.' See letters (M.H. McLean, manager, West Coast Packing, to FABC, 10 January 1969, and to Dr J.A. Taylor, BC Department of Health, 12 March) and memo: 'Meeting of Health Committee,' 6 February 1970, between representatives of Skeena River canneries and Namu and officials from the provincial health department.
28 Ibid, typescript, re: Department of Health, notes on the 'Harrison/ Campbell visit and discussion,' dated 30 January (probably 1969).
29 Ibid, memo headed 'Department of Health, notes on the Harrison/ Campbell visit and discussion, January 30.'

30 Ibid.
31 McKay, *Native Commercial Fisheries*, 19; Friedlaender, *Economic Status*, 4, and Table 5.2, 38. Friedlaender (70) attributes the layoff figures to the closure of only four of these plants; Namu is excluded. He cites Hall and Tsong, 'Report,' 4.
32 Friedlaender, *Economic Status*, 70.
33 Draper, 'Resource Management,' 181. On BC Indians' increasing dependency on government, see Fields and Stanbury, *Economic Impact*.
34 UBC, FABC, box 9, file: 'Indian Employment – 1972,' Internal document: 'Fisheries Association of B.C. – Survey of Numbers of Native Indians Employed by or Fishing for Member Companies North of Cape Caution,' 30 June 1972. This document cautions that the figures can be considered only as estimates, since compilation included some guesswork by plant managers and personnel.
35 Friedlaender, *Economic Status*, 72.
36 Ibid, 6 and Tables 1–4.
37 McKay, *Native Commercial Fisheries*, 3–4.
38 Production of pink and chum salmon, which became so critical to the processing industry after 1945, here provided a substantial proportion of the province's total landings of these species. Including 1967, when salmon landings in the district accounted for a mere 2 per cent of the total BC catch of pink salmon, the central district contributed an annual average of 36 per cent of coastal pink catches in the period 1951–69, reaching a high of 74 per cent in 1962. Similarly, of the coast's annual chum production, 27 per cent was caught in the central area in the same period. See Canada, Department of Fisheries and Oceans, *Report on the Status of the Odd-Year Pink Salmon Stocks ... and on the Prospects for 1969*, 2–5.
39 UBC, FABC, box 9, file: 'Indian Employment – 1972,' 'Draft re: Indian Employment in North Coast Fish Plants,' n.d., 3.
40 See Gislason, *Participation Levels*. Sol Sinclair chaired the licensing study.
41 Friedlaender, *Economic Status*, 12, 46 (in 1965, rental gillnetters could still be found in the south).
42 UBC, FABC, box 9, file: 'Indian Employment – 1972,' 'Draft re: Indian Employment in North Coast Fish Plants,' n.d., 3.
43 Gislason, *Participation Levels*, 19.
44 James, *Historic and Present Native Participation*, 7.
45 Friedlaender, *Economic Status*, 12.
46 Fraser, *License Limitation*, 3; Friedlaender, *Economic Status*, 14.

47 See Pearse, *Turning the Tide*, 153–5; Campbell, *Assessment*; McKay and Ouellette, *Review*; McKay, *The Indian Fishermen's Emergency Assistance Program*; and Cummins, Friedlaender, and Williams, *Impact*.
48 McKay and Ouelette, *Review*, 16, 17.
49 Port Simpson and Bella Bella received this kind of assistance, for example.
50 McKay and Ouellette, *Review*, 37.
51 McKay, *Native Commercial Fisheries*, 2.
52 McKay and Ouellette, *Review*, 39.
53 Ibid, 39–41.
54 McKay, *Native Commercial Fisheries*, 2.
55 Ibid, 6.
56 Ibid, 11 note 6.
57 Warriner and Guppy, 'From Urban Centre.'
58 Friedlaender, *Economic Status*, 13.
59 Assu with Inglis, *Assu of Cape Mudge*, 74.
60 McKay, *Native Commercial Fisheries*, 2.
61 Ibid, 2, 3.
62 *Prince Rupert Daily News*, 26 January 1971.
63 McMullan, 'State,' 144–7; Canada, Department of Fisheries and Oceans, *The Salmonid Enhancement Program*.
64 McKay, *Native Commercial Fisheries*, 25; McMullan, 'State,' 145–7.
65 Draper, 'Resource Management.'
66 Agriculture and Rural Development Agency (ARDA) was established in 1970, within the new federal Department of Regional Economic Expansion (DREE). The Agricultural Rehabilitation Development Act, passed in 1961, was broadened to include fisheries and tourism. The later programs emphasized both economic growth and social development. See Phidd and Doern, *Politics and Management*, chap. 9.
67 Draper, 'Resource Management,' 475; and see *Vancouver Sun*, 29 February 1972, and *Vancouver Province*, 1 March 1972, for further rationalizations; telegram, J. Marchand to C. Shelford, BC minister of agriculture, 25 February 1972, cited in Draper, 'Resource Management,' 252–3. Draper apparently had access to provincial government departmental files.
68 Letter, J. Marchand to C. Shelford, 8 March 1972, cited in Draper, 'Resource Management,' 259.
69 Letter, A.E. Macmillan to C. Shelford, 19 May 1971, cited in ibid, 228.
70 Letter, K.M. Campbell to J. Davis, 14 May 1971, cited in ibid, 228.
71 See UBC, FABC, box 9, file: 'Indian Employment – 1972.'

72 Hall and Tsong, 'Report,' 21–2, cited in Draper, 'Resource Management,' 186.

73 UBC, FABC, box 41, file: '"Indian Employment" – Oceanside.' Letter, K.M. Campbell, manager, FABC, to R.J. McInnes, director, British Columbia Indian Advisory Committee, 29 June 1972.

74 Ibid, Memo, 'Points for Discussion with Indian Advisory Committee: Employment of Indians North of Cape Caution,' 11 January 1973.

75 *Vancouver Sun*, 13 March 1972; *Native News*, April 1972; *Vancouver Sun*, 11 April 1972.

76 *Vancouver Sun*, 5 August 1972; *Prince Rupert Daily News*, 17 November 1972; *Vancouver Province*, 28 February 1973.

77 *Vancouver Province*, 2, 20 March 1972; *Vancouver Sun*, 6 December, 1973.

78 Draper, 'Resource Management,' 317.

79 See ibid, chapter 5.

80 Ibid, 433–4.

81 Hayward, 'The Co-op Strategy,' 63 note 24; Elsey, 'Government Intervention,' 74–5.

82 See Blyth, *Salmon Canneries*, 91.

83 Personal communication with Bob Hill, executive director, Tsimshian Tribal Council and business agent, Native Brotherhood of BC, Prince Rupert, 15 April 1992.

84 BCARS, GR 1118, BC Marine Resources Branch, box 6, file 5, 'Memorandum to the Honourable the Minister, Re: Central Native Fishermen's Co-Operative,' 16 June 1975, from Michael Coon, acting director, CNFC.

85 BCARS, GR 1118, BC Marine Resources Branch, box 6, file 5, S.L. Hardy and R.C. Atkinson, 'Bella Bella Marine Resource Development Study, Phase One, for the Bella Bella Band,' prepared by Edwin, Reid & Associates, Vancouver, May 1974; ibid, R.C. Atkinson, 'Addendum to the Bella Bella Marine Resources Development Study, Phase Two, for the Bella Bella Band,' Edwin, Reid & Associates, Vancouver, April 1975; ibid, 'Request for Financial Assistance Bella Bella Fish Plant, submitted to Province of British Columbia by Bella Bella Band Council, 29 May 1975.'

86 The arguments are taken from BCARS, GR 1118, BC Marine Resources Branch, box 6, file 5, 'memos,' Cecil Reid, chief councillor, Bella Bella Council, to E.H. Vernon, acting deputy minister, Department of Recreation and Conservation, Victoria, 'Re: Bella Bella Fish Plant Proposal,' 18 June 1975, and Reid to Frank Howard, consultant on Indian matters, Victoria, 'Re: L. Michael Coon Memorandum on Bella

Bella Proposal,' 25 June 1975.

87 BCARS, GR 1118, BC Marine Resources Branch, box 6, file 5, 'memo,' 'Request for Financial Assistance Bella Bella Fish Plant,' 11.

88 Ibid, E.H. Vernon, acting deputy minister, Department of Recreation and Conservation, Victoria, to Cecil Reid, 'Re: Bella Bella Fish Plant Proposal,' 30 June 1975; see also Vernon to Howard, Victoria, 23 June 1975.

89 Ibid, memo to file, copy to Coon, 'Re: Bella Bella Proposal,' 30 June 1975.

90 Elsey, 'Government Intervention,' 75–6, 57.

91 Hayward, 'The Co-op Strategy,' 59.

92 McKay and Healey, *Analysis*, 28.

93 Ibid, 23–4.

94 Ibid 28–9.

95 Pearse, *Turning the Tide*, 181.

96 Ibid, 173; see, for example, Gitksan-Carrier Tribal Council, 'Submission,' 2.

97 Pearse, *Turning the Tide*, 176–8.

98 Ibid, 178, 261, 181; for details, see 181–5.

99 Ellis, 'Perspectives,' 67–70, 72.

100 McMullan, 'State,' 139.

101 Personal communication with Bob Hill.

102 With 76 per cent of the fleet (compared to 52 per cent for the total coast-wide salmon fleet) in these categories. James, *Historic and Present Native Participation*, 30–3, and see Table 4.3 (31), for Heiltsuk.

103 Friedlaender, *Economic Status*, 12.

104 See Pinkerton, 'The Fishing Dependent Community,' 314–15.

105 Native Brotherhood of BC, Prince Rupert Office files, table: 'Licence Ownership in the Pacific Fishery, 1991.'

106 McMullan, 'State,' 141.

107 Native Brotherhood, *License Study*, 88–9.

108 Stearns, *Haida Culture*, 297.

109 Mirschitzka, 'Usage,' 14.

110 The extent of the Indian fishery on the coast is graphically illustrated for territory north of the lower mainland in Department of Fisheries and Oceans, Map No. 6, 'Native Food Fishery.'

111 See Friedlaender, *Economic Status*, 74–5, Tables 14, 15.

112 The 1974 decision reserved rights to 50 per cent for Indians, excluding on-reservation catches and fish taken by Indians for subsistence and

ceremonial purposes. In 1979, the US Supreme Court upheld the decision but modified it to include in the 50-per-cent allocation all fish caught by Indians anywhere and for any purpose.

113 See Cohen, *Treaties*. See also Boxberger, *To Fish in Common*, a case study of the history of the Indian group that was in the best position to benefit from the new fisheries policy.

114 See McEvoy, *The Fisherman's Problem*, 245–6, chap. 3.

115 Pearse, *Turning the Tide*, 178 (from Exhibit No. 133, 18).

116 *Vancouver Province*, 28 August 1970.

117 *Vancouver Sun*, 21 September 1970 (Peachland Creek, known as 'Deep Creek' to the Indians).

118 *Vancouver Province*, 22 September 1970.

119 Ibid.

120 *Vancouver Sun*, 1 October 1970; *Vancouver Province* 22 September, 10 November 1970.

121 *Regina v. Derriksan*, (1975) 52 *Dominion Law Reports* (*DLR*) (3d) 744 (BC Supreme Court).

122 *Regina v. Derriksan*, (1977) 71 *DLR*, (3d) 159 (Supreme Court of Canada), affirming (1976) 60 *DLR* 140 (BC Court of Appeal). See Sanders, 'Case Law Digest'; and BCARS, GR 1439, BC Department of Recreation and Conservation, Fish and Wildlife Branch, 'Survey of Native Rights as they Relate to Fish and Wildlife Protection in British Columbia,' by K. Krag (a law student) for C.E. Estlin (chief of enforcement, Fish and Wildlife Branch), 22 August 1975, 7–8.

123 Elliott, 'Aboriginal Title,' 118.

124 Sterritt, 'Gitksan,' 270–2.

125 On the ongoing struggle of these people to deal with the conflict between Indian law and the Fisheries Act through negotiations, see Morrell, 'Struggle,' 245–8.

126 'Manuel Says Fisheries "Enemy No. 1",' *Native News* (Ottawa) 19 no. 2 (June 1978).

127 'Chiefs Demand Rights,' ibid, 19 no. 4 (August 1978).

128 'Bootleg Salmon Big Business,' ibid, 20 no. 5 (September 1979).

129 Sterritt, 'Unflinching Resistance,' 268.

130 Ibid.

131 Constitution Act, 1982, s. 35(1). See Tennant, *Aboriginal Peoples*, 225–6. For influential discussions of the application of section 35(1) to unextinguished aboriginal rights in Canada, see Slattery, 'Understanding Aboriginal Rights,' and Sanders, 'Pre-Existing Rights' (both of which figured heavily in the Supreme Court of Canada's reasoning in *Sparrow*). See also Sanders, 'The Rights of the Aboriginal Peoples,' and Ash, *Home and Native Land*.

132 *Regina v. Sparrow* (1986), *BC Weekly Law Digest (BCWLD)* 599 (County Court).

133 *Regina v. Sparrow* (1987), 36 *DLR* (4th) 246 (BC Court of Appeal).

134 *Regina v. Sparrow* (1990), 4 *WWR* 410 (Supreme Court of Canada).

135 This approach was taken from judicial decisions in the U.S. Pacific Northwest (see *Boldt*), and argued by Douglas Sanders, who was then staff lawyer for the Union of BC Indian Chiefs. *Jack v. The Queen* (1980), 1 *Supreme Court Reports (SCR)* 294 (Supreme Court of Canada). Mr Justice Dickson agrees 'with the *general tenor* of this argument' but does not unequivocally endorse or adopt those priorities as part of his judgment (*Jack*, 313). The lower courts had convicted the appellants, Joseph Daniel Jack and others, all Indians, under the Fisheries Act for fishing during a prohibited period (September and October 1974); they were taking salmon for food, but without permits. The Supreme Court of Canada dismissed the appeals.

136 'The right to intervene,' write Franklin Gertler and Peter W. Hutchins, 'is an important and necessary corollary of the increasingly important role played by the Supreme Court in shaping Canadian society'; 'Introduction,' 118.

137 *Vancouver Sun*, 20 November 1990.

138 Ibid.

139 Judgment rendered 8 March 1991. *Delgamuukw et al. v. the Queen in Right of British Columbia and the Attorney General of Canada* (1991), 79 *DLR* (4th) 185. *Delgamuukw* is 455 pages long in the *Dominion Law Review* and one of the few reported judgments ever to include an index. See also Cassidy and Dale, *After Native Claims?* See also BC Court of Appeal, 'Reasons for Judgment,' Aboriginal Appeals, 25 June 1993, 2 vols.

140 *Globe and Mail*, 14 July 1992; *Vancouver Province*, 5 July 1992.

141 See, for example, Assu with Inglis, *Assu of Cape Mudge*, 79.

142 *Vancouver Sun*, 8 September 1992; 'Salmon Fishing Crisis: Hatred Doesn't Help,' *Vancouver Sun*, 29 August 1992.

143 Pearse, *Managing Salmon*; Larkin, *Analysis*.

144 *Vancouver Sun*, 17 November 1992.

145 *Globe and Mail*, 9 December 1992.

146 McLeod, 'Strategies,' 263.

CHAPTER EIGHT: VANISHING ALTERNATIVES

1 Stewart, *Indian Fishing*, 33–4.

2 Suttles, 'Coping,' 48–9.

3 Blackman,'Haida,' 244.

4 BCARS, Add. Ms. 2172, Charles Ludwig Moser Papers,'Thirty Years a Mis-

sionary on the West Coast of Vancouver Island,' by Dorothy Abraham, typescript based on the diary of Charles Ludwig Moser, 9–10, 16.

5 This account is taken from Blackman, *During My Time*, 55–6.
6 Stewart, *Indian Fishing*, 46–53.
7 Kenyon, *The Kyuquot Way*, 72; Stewart, *Indian Fishing*, 32; Boas with Hunt, *Kwakiutl Ethnology*, 32–3.
8 Sproat, *The Nootka*, 151–2.
9 Gladstone, 'Native Indians,' 25.
10 Thompson and Freeman, *History*, 25.
11 See Bell, *Pacific Halibut*, 233.
12 Canada, Department of Fisheries of Canada and the Fisheries Research Board, *The Commercial Fisheries of Canada*, 5.
13 Carrothers, *The British Columbia Fisheries*, 102–3.
14 Bell, *Pacific Halibut*, 20.
15 Thompson and Freeman, *History*, 17.
16 Gladstone,'Native Indians,' 25.
17 BCARS, Add. Ms. 870, Philip Drucker Field Notes, Notebooks, BC fall 1953, box 1, part 2, vol. 6, interview with Godfrey Kelly, n.d.
18 Native Brotherhood of BC, *License Study*, 74.; Pearse, *Turning the Tide*, 123; James, *Historic and Present Native Participation*, 39.
19 Native Brotherhood of BC, *License Study*, 75.
20 Pearse, *Turning the Tide*, 123.
21 Native Brotherhood of BC, *License Study*, 72.
22 James, *Historic and Present Native Participation*, 39. The licences applied to one owned and eight rental boats.
23 Native Brotherhood of BC, Prince Rupert Branch Office files, table: 'Native Licence Holdings in the Herring Fishery [1985–92],' table: 'License Ownership in the Pacific Fishery, 1991.'
24 Native Brotherhood of BC, *License Study*, 73; 1991 statistics on licence ownership in the Pacific Coast fishery supplied by the Prince Rupert Branch Office of the Native Brotherhood.
25 Richardson and Green, 'Fisheries,' 254.
26 Sproat, *The Nootka*, 150; Stewart, *Indian Fishing*, 87, 90.
27 Cited in Stewart, *Indian Fishing*, 76.
28 See ibid, 125, for a sketch of this arrangement.
29 Ibid, 124. See also Drucker, *Cultures*, 15.
30 Kenyon, *The Kyuquot Way*, 73, citing James Cook, *The Journals of His Voyages of Discovery: The Voyage of the Revolution and Discovery*, ed. by J.C. Beaglehole (Cambridge: Cambridge University Press), 319.
31 Drucker, *Cultures*, 150–1, 15.

32 Sproat, *The Nootka*, 150.
33 See Lane, 'Harvest,' 10–13; Lane cites, for example, Lamb, ed., *Journals*, 384; William Fraser Tolmie, *The Journals of William Fraser Tolmie: Physician and Fur Trader* (Vancouver: Mitchell Press, 1963), 275–6, 304; and also William Beynon, *Tsimshian Stories, Recorded by William Beynon*, vol. IV, reprint (Metlakatla, Alaska: Metlakatla Native Community, 1983), 106.
34 Blackman, *During My Time*, 134.
35 Hicks, ed. *From Potlatch to Pulpit*, 114. It is, however, not entirely clear to what period Pierce is referring.
36 E.E. Prince, 'The Pacific Fishing Industries of Canada,' in DOF, *Annual Report*, 1907 (1907), special appended reports, II, p. lxvii.
37 Boas, *Ethnology*, 242, 254–5, 426–8; see Lane, 'Harvest,' 6–7.
38 Abraham, 'Thirty Years a Missionary,' 26. I am speculating that 'Kakawis' is the same as 'Kyakis,' located in Barkley Sound, which became the 'Deekyakus' reservation. See Figure 1 in Arima and Dewhirst, 'Nootkans,' 391.
39 Cited in Lane, 'Harvest,' 14.
40 Ford, *Smoke from Their Fires*, 236.
41 Carr, *Klee Wyck*, 75.
42 Hawthorn, Belshaw, and Jamieson, *The Indians of British Columbia*, 219.
43 SOR/55–260 s. 3, new s. 21A.
44 Stewart, *Indian Fishing*, 147.
45 BCARS, Add. Ms. 364, Imbert Orchard Collection, box 4, file 4, People in Landscape Series II, 1968–72, no. 22, typescript, 'Fishermen of the Queen Charlotte Islands' (interviews conducted 1969–70), 3.
46 Kenyon, *The Kyuquot Way*, 73.
47 Fisheries Act of Canada, amendment, *SC*, 1894, c. 51, s. 5; Carrothers, *British Columbia Fisheries*, 110.
48 Carrothers, *British Columbia Fisheries*, 110–11; Fisheries Act of Canada, amendment, *SC*, 1910, c. 20, s. 10.
49 Order in Council, 4 February 1913, *SC*, 1913.
50 BCARS, Add. Ms. 364, Imbert Orchard Collection, transcript of tape 797, 'Mrs. Frances Brown, Porlier Pass Lighthouse 1902–1941,' interviewed by Imbert Orchard, October 1965, 1-1, pp. 6–9, 1-2, pp. 1–2.
51 See BCARS, GR 1118, BC Department of Fisheries, box 6, file 1.
52 Newell, 'Politics of Food.'
53 Christy, Jr, and Scott, *The Common Wealth*, 25.
54 Gladstone, 'Native Indians,' 26.
55 See UBC Library, Map Division, Map No. 10, 'Herring Resource and

Fishery' (Vancouver: Department of Fisheries and Oceans, Pacific Region, Habitat Management Division, February 1985).

56 SOR/55–260, s. 3, 21A (1), (2). McMullan, 'Organization,' 42.

57 See BCARS, GR 1118, BC Commercial Fisheries Branch, Department of Recreation and Conservation, Annual Returns of Salmon Canneries, Cold Storage, and Misc. Plants.

58 Hayward, 'The B.C. Salmon Fishery.'

59 Pearse, *Turning the Tide*, 104.

60 Pynn, 'Golden Egg Rush.'

61 Pearse, *Turning the Tide*, 105.

62 On the *Western Spirit*, 9–15 April 1992, harvesting commercially under licence and for food for the community, in the vicinity of Wilson Inlet. Pacific Herring Regulations s. 17 (a), (b), 1980.

63 Pearse, *Turning the Tide*, 136.

64 Ibid, 136.

65 DOF, *Annual Report*, 1915–16 (1916), 247.

66 Drucker, *Native Brotherhoods*, 125–6.

67 In the mid-1950s, the Namu, Port Edward, and BC Packers' Rupert Cold Storage plants had the greatest number of Indians employed in herring-reduction. See BCARS, GR 1378, BC Department of Fisheries, box 11, file 1, Returns of Record of Operation of Plants Other than Salmon Canneries, 1955–56, 1956–57.

68 Friedlaender, *Economic Status*, 70; James, *Historic and Present Native Participation*, 14–15.

69 McKay, *Native Commercial Fisheries*, 4.

70 Native Brotherhood of BC, Prince Rupert Branch Office files, table: 'Native License Holdings in the Herring Fishery [1985–92].' See also Native Brotherhood, *License Study*, 61, although there is a slight difference in the figures.

71 The Heiltsuk held 50 (of 374) gillnet licences and three (of 46) seine licences in 1983; James, *Historic and Present Native Participation*, 36, Table 5.1.

72 Native Brotherhood of BC, table: 'License Ownership in the Pacific Fishery, 1991'; Native Brotherhood, 'NBBC/ILAB Proposal,' Background paper prepared for the meeting of the Native Brotherhood and the minister of fisheries and oceans, Hon. John Crosbie, Four Seasons Hotel, Vancouver, 3 March 1992, 6.

73 Changes to the regulations in the 1970s provided for the concept of a band food-fishing licence. Under this arrangement, the band council assumes much of the responsibility for supervising the fishery.

74 Personal communication with Everett Pierce, Vancouver, May 1992; he manages the plant during salmon-fishing season. Geoduck, a large species of clam, is harvested commercially for the Japanese market. The fishery came under limited-entry licensing in 1981; see Pearse, *Turning the Tide*, 138–9.

75 In the Federal Court of Canada, Trial Division, Vancouver, Court File No. T1265-89, Statement of Claim, *Reid et al. v. The Queen et al.*, original filed 19 June 1989; Final Amended Statement of Claim, 17 July 1990. See also Further Amended Defense, filed 10 August 1990. Reasons for judgment submitted 28 February 1993. The roe-harvesting areas referred to involve the Heiltsuk Tribal Homeland, an area from the southern tip of Calvert Island in the south to Kynock Inlet in the north, and from the head of Dean Channel on the east to the Goose Island Banks area on the west.

76 Native Brotherhood of BC, 'NBBC/ILAB Proposal,' 6.

77 See Canada, Department of Fisheries of Canada and the Fisheries Research Board, *The Commercial Fisheries of Canada*, app. D.

78 Gladstone, 'Native Indians,' 24–5.

79 BCARS, GR 1378, box 11, file 1, Returns of Record of Operation of Plants Other than Salmon Canneries, 1955–56. BC Packers' Imperial plant processed clams and oysters but employed no Indians for the work, only 'whites' and 'orientals.'

80 See Native Brotherhood of BC, *License Study*, 102, and James, *Historic and Present Native Participation*, 40, for this and the statistics that follow.

81 Native Brotherhood of BC, table: 'License Ownership in the Pacific Fishery, 1991.'

82 Richardson and Green, 'Fisheries,' 251–2.

83 Kenyon, *The Kyuquot Way*, 74.

84 Native Brotherhood of BC, *License Study*, 93–4.

85 Pearse, *Turning the Tide*, 137.

86 Worth $250,000 annually after 1979. See Richardson and Green, 'Fisheries,' 252.

87 Native Brotherhood of BC, *License Study*, 95.

CHAPTER NINE: CONCLUSION

1 Usher, 'Implications,' 21.

2 Resnick, *The Masks of Proteus*, 85.

3 *Globe and Mail*, 9 December 1992.

4 British Columbia Court of Appeal, 'Reasons for Judgment,' Aboriginal

Appeals, 25 June 1993, vol I, *Delgamuukw et al. v. The Queen in Right of the Province of British Columbia and the Attorney-General of Canada*, 239.

BIBLIOGRAPHY

ARCHIVAL SOURCES

BRITISH COLUMBIA ARCHIVAL AND RECORDS SERVICE (BCARS), VICTORIA

BC Attorney General, Correspondence Inward
BC Commercial Fisheries Branch Records
BC Department of Fisheries Records
BC Department of Recreation and Conservation, Fish and Wildlife Branch
BC Executive Council, Minutes 'relative to the Indian Fishing Troubles on
    the Skeena River,' 1888
BC Marine Resources Branch Records
Provincial Police, Records
(BC) Provincial Secretary, Correspondence Inward
BC Royal Commission on Labour, Transcripts
Canada, Commission on the Salmon Fishing Industry in BC, 1902,
    Unpublished Reports
CBC Imbert Orchard Collection, Oral History Tapes and Transcripts
Charles Ludwig Moser Papers
Debeck Family Papers
Philip Drucker, Field Notes and 'Research Problems and Conditions
    on the Northwest Coast' (manuscript)
Union of BC Indian Chiefs, Vancouver, Transcripts of evidence taken by
    Royal Commission on Indian Affairs in British Columbia, 1914–15

GLENBOW-ALBERTA INSTITUTE, CALGARY

Tatsuzo Yamashita, taped interview with Mr Tatsuzo Yamashita and his
    daughter-in-law, Ruriko (Mrs Yas) Yamashita, Vauxhall, Alberta, 1973

Tono Ohama, taped interview with Mr and Mrs Tono Ohama, Rainier, Alberta, 1973

NATIONAL ARCHIVES OF CANADA, OTTAWA

Indian Affairs

Field Office Correspondence and Miscellaneous
Indian Agent's Incoming Correspondence
Records of British Columbia Indian Agents, 1881–1948
Records of the Chief Inspector of Indian Agencies/Office of the Indian Inspector for BC
Records of the Indian Reserve Commission (Joint Reserve Commission) relating to allotment and establishment of Indian Reserves in British Columbia, Journals and letterbooks
Records of the Royal Commission on Indian Affairs for British Columbia

NATIVE BROTHERHOOD OF BC, NORTHERN BRANCH, PRINCE RUPERT

Miscellaneous records

RICHMOND ARTS CENTRE COLLECTION, RICHMOND, BC

Taped interview with Buck Suzuki, Steveston, BC, 15 January 1976

UNIVERSITY OF BRITISH COLUMBIA, VANCOUVER

Department of History

Taped interviews, summer 1984, with Katie ('Ubumpa') Adams, Agnes ('Axu') Alfred, Ann Brochie, and Lucy Smith, Campbell River, BC

Library

Canada Department of Fisheries, Archives materials on BC (microfilm)
Fisheries Association of BC Collection
Henry Doyle Papers
United Fishermen and Allied Workers' Union Collection

CASES CITED

Attorney-General of BC v. Attorney-General of Canada (1914),
    AC 153 (Judicial Committee of the Privy Council), affirming (1913)
    SCR 493 (Supreme Court of Canada, reference re: powers of the

legislature of BC to authorize BC government to grant exclusive rights
to fish).

Attorney-General of Canada v. Attorney-General of BC (1930),
AC 111 (Judicial Committee of the Privy Council), affirming (1928)
SRC 457 (Supreme Court of Canada, reference re: the constitutional
validity of certain sections of the Fisheries Act, 1914).

British Columbia Court of Appeal, 'Reasons for Judgment,' Aboriginal
Appeals, 25 June 1993, vol I, *Delgamuukw et al. v. The Queen in Right of
the Province of British Columbia and the Attorney-General of Canada*, vol II,
*Regina v. William Alphonse; Regina v. Harry Thomas Dick; Regina v.
Dorothy Marie Van Der Peet; Regina v. William Gladstone and Donald
Gladstone; Regina v. N.T.C. Smokehouse Ltd; Regina v. Allen Jacob Lewis,
Allen Frances Lewis, Jacob Kenneth Lewis; Regina v. Jerry Benjamin Nikal.*

Calder et al. v. Attorney-General of BC (1973), SCR 313 (Supreme Court of
Canada), affirming (1970) 74 *WWR* 481 (BC Court of Appeal) and
(1970) 8 *DLR* (3d) 59 (BC Supreme Court).

*Delgamuukw et al. v. The Queen in Right of British Columbia and the Attorney
General of Canada* (1991), 79 *DLR* (4th) 185 (BC Supreme Court).

Jack v. The Queen (1980), 1 *SCR* 294 (Supreme Court of Canada).

Regina v. Cooper (1968), 1 *DLR* (3d) 113 (BC Supreme Court).

Regina v. Derriksan (1977), 71 *DLR* (3d) 159 (Supreme Court of Canada),
affirming (1976) 60 *DLR* 140 (BC Court of Appeal) and (1975) 52 *DLR*
(3d) 744 (BC Supreme Court).

Regina v. Sparrow (1990), 4 *WWR* 410 (Supreme Court of Canada), affirming
(1987) 36 *DLR* (4d) 246 (BC Court of Appeal), which reversed (1986)
BCWLD 599 (County Court).

Regina v. White and Bob (1966), 52 *DLR* (2d) 481 (Supreme Court of Canada),
affirming (1965) 50 *DLR* (2d) 613 (BC Court of Appeal).

*Reid et al. v. The Queen in Right of Canada and the Minister of Fisheries and
Oceans* (1993). In the Federal Court of Canada Trial Division at
Vancouver, Court File No. T1265-89. Unreported.

Rex v. Somerville Cannery Company Limited (1927), 39 *BCLR* (1st) 103
(BC Supreme Court).

United States v. State of Washington (Boldt Decision), 384 F. Supp. 312 (1974).

STATUTES AND REGULATIONS

British Columbia Fisheries Act. *Revised Statutes of British Columbia*, 1901, c. 25.
British Columbia Terms of Union. *Revised Statutes of Canada*, 1985, app. II,
No. 10.

Canneries Revenue Act. *Statutes of the Province of British Columbia*, 1908, c. 9.
Constitution Act, 1867 (UK) c. 3; *Revised Statutes of Canada*, 1970, app. II,
    No. 5 (formerly British North America Act, 1867).
Constitution Act, 1982. Enacted by the Canada Act, 1982 (UK), c. 11, Sched-
    ule B.
Fisheries Act. *Revised Statutes of Canada*, 1886, c. 95.
—   *Revised Statutes of Canada*, 1906, c. 45.
—   *Revised Statutes of Canada*, 1914, c. 45.
—   *Revised Statutes of Canada*, 1927, c. 73.
—   *Revised Statutes of Canada*, 1952, c. 119.
—   *Revised Statutes of Canada*, 1970, c. F-14.
—   *Revised Statutes of Canada*, 1985, c. F-14.
—   *Statutes of Canada*, 1868, c. 60.
Game Act. *Revised Statutes of British Columbia*, 1960, c. 160.
Indian Act. *Revised Statutes of Canada*, 1886, c. 43.
—   *Revised Statutes of Canada*, 1906, c. 81.
—   *Revised Statutes of Canada*, 1927, c. 98.
—   *Revised Statutes of Canada*, 1951, c. 29.
—   *Revised Statutes of Canada*, 1952, c. 149.
—   *Revised Statutes of Canada*, 1970, c. 1–6.
—   *Statutes of Canada*, 1868, c. 42.
—   *Statutes of Canada*, 1876, c. 18.
Migratory Birds Convention Act. *Revised Statutes of Canada*, 1952, c. 179.
Royal Proclamation of 1763. *Revised Statutes of Canada*, 1970, app., 123–9.
Wildlife Act. *Statutes of British Columbia*, 1966, c. 55.

PERSONAL COMMUNICATIONS

Hill, Cecil, Kitkatla, April 1992: president, Western Spirit Fishing Ltd,
    secretary-treasurer, Native Brotherhood of BC, holder of herring roe–
    on-kelp and salmon-seine licences.
Hill, Robert, Prince Rupert, April 1992: executive director, Tsimshian Tribal
    Council, and business agent, Native Brotherhood of BC, Northern
    Office.
Pierce, Everett, Vancouver, May 1992: 39 years in the Pacific Coast salmon
    fishery as collector-operator, filling-machine–operator, and plant
    manager (Canfisco's Butedale, Oceanside, and Vancouver plants),
    retired but currently managing summer salmon-processing by the
    Bella Bella Indian Band at Bella Bella.

ALL OTHER SOURCES

Abel, Kerry, and Friesen, Jean, eds. *Aboriginal Resource Use in Canada: Historical and Legal Aspects.* Winnipeg: University of Manitoba Press, 1991.

Abler, Thomas S., and Weaver, Sally M., comps. *A Canadian Indian Bibliography, 1960–1970.* Toronto: University of Toronto Press, 1974.

Ainsworth, Allan H. 'Conservation in the British Columbia Salmon Fishing Industry.' BA graduating essay, University of British Columbia, 1946.

Alexander, George J. *The Commercial Salmon Fisheries of British Columbia.* Victoria: Provincial Fisheries Department, 1938.

Ames, Kenneth. 'Stable and Resilient Systems along the Skeena River: The Gitksan/Carrier Boundary.' In Richard Inglis and George MacDonald, eds., *Skeena River Prehistory*, Archaeological Survey of Canada, Mercury Series, Paper No. 87, Ottawa: National Museum of Man, 1979, 219–43.

Andrew, Caroline, and Pelletier, Réjean. 'The Regulators.' In Doern, ed., *Regulatory Process*, 147–64.

Arima, Eugene, and Dewhirst, John. 'Nootkans of Vancouver Island.' In Suttles, ed., *Northwest Coast*, 391–411.

Asch, Michael. *Home and Native Land: Aboriginal Rights and the Canadian Constitution.* Toronto: Methuen, 1984.

Assu, Harry, with Inglis, Joy. *Assu of Cape Mudge: Recollections of a Coastal Indian Chief.* Vancouver: University of British Columbia Press, 1989.

Beddington, J.R., and Rettig, R.B. *Approaches to the Regulation of Fishing Effort.* FAO Fisheries Technical Paper No. 243. Rome: FAO, 1983.

Bell, F. Heward. *The Pacific Halibut: The Resource and the Fishery.* Anchorage, Alaska: Alaska Northwest Publishing, 1981.

Berger, Thomas R. *Fragile Freedoms: Human Rights and Dissent in Canada.* Rev. ed. Toronto: Irwin Publishing, 1982.

Berkes, Fikret. 'The Common Property Resource Problem and the Creation of Limited Property.' *Human Ecology* 13 no. 2 (1985) 187–208.

— 'Fishermen and "The Tragedy of the Commons".' *Environmental Conservation* 12 (1985) 199–206.

— ed., *Common Property Resources: Ecology and Community-Based Sustainable Development.* London: Belhaven Press, 1986.

Berringer, Patricia Ann. 'Northwest Coast Traditional Salmon Fisheries: Systems of Resource Utilization.' MA thesis, University of British Columbia, 1982.

Blackman, Margaret B. *During My Time: Florence Edenshaw Davidson, a Haida*

Woman. Seattle, Wash.: University of Washington Press, 1982.

— 'Haida: Traditional Culture.' In Suttles, ed., *Northwest Coast*, 240–60.

Blyth, Gladys Young. *Salmon Canneries: British Columbia North Coast*. Lantzville, BC: Oolichan Books, 1991.

Boas, Franz. *Ethnology of the Kwakiutl*. 35th Annual Report of the Bureau of Ethnology, Smithsonian Institution, 1913–14. Washington, DC: US Government Printing Office, 1921.

Boas, Franz, with Hunt, George. *Kwakiutl Ethnology*, ed. by Helen Codere. Chicago: University of Chicago Press, 1966.

Boxberger, Daniel L. 'Lummi Indians and the Commercial Salmon Fishery of North Puget Sound, 1880–1900.' *Ethnohistory* 35 no. 2 (1988) 161–90.

— *To Fish in Common: The Ethnohistory of Lummi Indian Salmon Fishing*. Lincoln, Neb., and London: University of Nebraska Press, 1989.

Boyd, Robert 'Demographic History, 1774–1874.' In Suttles, ed., *Northwest Coast*, 135–48.

Bradley, Paul G. 'Some Seasonal Models of the Fishing Industry.' In Scott, ed., *Economics of Fisheries Management*, 33–46.

British Columbia. *British Columbia Regulations*.

— *Memorandum Respecting Salmon Fishery Regulations for the Province of British Columbia*. Victoria: Provincial Fisheries Department, 1919.

— *Mid-Coast Report*. Victoria: Department of Economic Development, 1974.

— *Papers Connected with the Indian Land Question, 1850–1875*. Reprinted in 1987. Queen's Printer, 1875.

— *Papers Relating to the Commission Appointed to Enquire into the State and Conditions of the Indians of the North-West Coast*. Victoria: Government Printer, 1888.

— *Papers Respecting the Number of Chinese and Japanese Landed in the Province from Foreign Parts during the Years 1897 and 1898*. Victoria: Department of the Provincial Secretary, 1899.

— *Report of the Government of British Columbia on the Subject of Indian Reserves*. Victoria: Government Printer, 1875.

— *Report on Oriental Activities within the Province*. Victoria: King's Printer, 1927.

— *Statutes of British Columbia*.

— Department of Labour. *Annual Report*, 1940–45.

— Fisheries Department (title varies). *Report of the Commissioner of Fisheries* (title varies). Victoria, 1902– .

— Royal Commission on Indian Affairs for the Province of British Columbia (McKenna-McBride Commission). *Report*. 4 vols. Victoria: Acme Press, 1916.

Brown, Anja, and Martin, Clarence. 'Heiltsuk Herring Roe Harvest: A
    Living History.' Typescript report, Heiltsuk Cultural Education
    Centre, Waglisla, BC, July 1985.
Bryant, Michael. 'Canada and the U.S. Public Policy on Aboriginal Land
    Claims, 1969–1988: Alaska and British Columbia Compared.' MA
    thesis, University of British Columbia, 1989.
Buchanan, D.R., and Campbell, Blake A. *The Economics of Salmon Fishermen
    in British Columbia*. Ottawa: Economic Service, Department of
    Fisheries, 1957.
Burrows, James K. '"A Much-Needed Class of Labour": The Economy and
    Income of the Southern Interior Plateau Indians, 1897–1910.' *BC
    Studies* 71 (1986) 27–46.
Bush, Pamela J. 'See You in Court: Native Indians and the Law in British
    Columbia, 1969–1985.' MA thesis, University of British Columbia, 1987.
Campbell, Blake A. *An Assessment of the Salmon Vessel Licence Control
    Program, 1968–1973*. Vancouver: Department of the Environment,
    1974.
Campbell, Ken. 'Hartley Bay, B.C.: A History.' In Seguin, ed., *The Tsimshian*,
    3–26.
Canada. *British Columbia Fishery Commission Report, 1892* (Wilmot
    Commission). Ottawa: Queen's Printer, 1893.
—   *British Columbia: Report of the Hon. H.L. Langevin, Minister of Public
    Works*. Ottawa: Queen's Printer, 1872.
—   *Canada Gazette*.
—   *The Indian in Industry: Road to Independence*. Ottawa: Indian Affairs
    Branch, 1965.
—   *The Indian in Transition: The Indian Today*. Ottawa: Indian Affairs
    Branch, 1962.
—   *Report and Evidence of Special Joint Committee Appointed to Enquire into
    the Claims of the Allied Indian Tribes of British Columbia, as Set Forth in
    their Petition Submitted to Parliament in June 1926*. Ottawa: King's
    Printer, 1927.
—   *Report of the Dominion–British Columbia Boat Rating Commission, 1910*.
    Ottawa: King's Printer, 1911.
—   *Revised Statutes of Canada (RSC)*.
—   *Statutes of Canada (SC)*.
—   *Statutory Orders and Regulations (SOR)*.
—   Commission to Investigate Fisheries Conditions in British Columbia,
    1922 (Duff Commission). *Report and Recommendations*. Ottawa: King's
    Printer, 1923.
—   Department of Fisheries (title varies). *Annual Report*. Ottawa, 1868– .

— Department of Fisheries and Oceans (DFO). *A New Policy for Canada's Pacific Fishery.* Vancouver, 1984.

— *New Regulations for B.C. Salmon Fishing Industry.* Vancouver: Department of Fisheries and Oceans, 1968.

— *Report on the Status of the Odd-Year Pink Salmon Stocks in the Butedale, Bella Bella and Bella Coola Sub-districts and on the Prospects for 1969.* Vancouver: Conservation and Protection Branch, 1968.

— *The Road to 1995 – a Blueprint for Western Fisheries Development.* Vancouver, 1980.

— *The Salmonid Enhancement Program.* Vancouver: Fisheries and Environment Canada, Fisheries and Marine Service, Information Branch, 1978.

— DFO. Pacific Region. 'Herring Resource and Fishery.' Map 10. 1985.

— 'Native Food Fishery.' Map 6. 1985.

— Department of Fisheries and the Fisheries Research Board. *The Commercial Fisheries of Canada: A Study Prepared for the Royal Commission on Canada's Economic Prospects.* Ottawa: Queen's Printer, 1956.

— Department of Indian Affairs (title varies). *Annual Report.* Ottawa, 1870–1925.

— *Annual Report, 1902.* Part II, Tabular Statements. 'Schedule of Indian Reserves in the Dominion.' Ottawa: King's Printer, 1902.

— *Statement of the Government of Canada on Indian Policy* (White Paper). Ottawa: Queen's Printer, 1969.

— Department of Indian and Northern Affairs. *An Indian Aquaculture Development Program.* Ottawa: Indian Aquaculture Task Force, 1983.

— *A Review of the British Columbia Indian Fishermen's Emergency Assistance Program.* Vancouver: Regional Indian Fishermen's Assistance Board, 1982.

— Department of Marine and Fisheries. *Annual Report,* App. No. 4. *Special Report on the Salmon Fishery and Fishery Regulations of Fraser River, B.C. Sessional Papers,* No. 8. 1891.

— *Annual Report,* Supplement No. 1. *Special Reports: III, The Aim and Method of Fishery Legislation, by Professor E.E. Prince, 1901.* Ottawa: King's Printer, 1902.

— Department of the Environment. *Policy for Canada's Commercial Fisheries.* Ottawa: Fisheries and Marine Service, 1976.

— *West Coast Salmon Fleet Development Committee Report.* Vancouver: Fisheries and Marine Service, 1973.

— Dominion–British Columbia Fisheries Commission, 1905–07. *Report and Recommendations.* Ottawa: King's Printer, 1908.

—   House of Commons. *Debates.*
—   Royal Commission on Chinese and Japanese Immigration. *Report. Sessional Papers,* No. 54. 1902.
—   Royal Commission on the Salmon Fisheries and Canning Industry in British Columbia (Evans Commission). *Report of the Special Fishery Commission, 1917.* Ottawa: King's Printer, 1918.
Cant, Garth, Overton, John, and Pawson, Eric, eds. *Indigenous Land Rights in Commonwealth Countries: Dispossession, Negotiation and Community Action: Proceedings of a Commonwealth Geographical Bureau Workshop, Christchurch, February 1992.* Christchurch, New Zealand: Department of Geography, University of Canterbury, and the Ngai Tahu Maori Trust Board for the Commonwealth Geographical Bureau, 1993.
Carr, Emily. *Klee Wyck.* First published in 1941. Toronto: Irwin Publishing, 1965.
Carrothers, W.A. *The British Columbia Fisheries.* Toronto: University of Toronto Press, 1941.
Carter, Sarah. *Lost Harvests: Prairie Indian Reserve Farmers and Government Policy.* Montreal and Kingston: McGill-Queen's University Press, 1990.
Cassidy, Frank, ed. *Aboriginal Title in British Columbia*: Delgamuukw v. The Queen. *Proceedings of a Conference Held September 10 & 11, 1991.* Lantzville, BC, and Montreal: Oolichan Books and Institute for Research on Public Policy, 1992.
Cassidy, Frank, and Dale, Norman. *After Native Claims? The Implications of Comprehensive Claims Settlement for Natural Resources in British Columbia.* Lantzville, BC, and Halifax, NS: Oolichan Books and Institute for Research on Public Policy, 1988.
Chittenden, Newton H. *Official Report of the Exploration of the Queen Charlotte Islands for the Government of British Columbia.* Victoria: Government Printer, 1884.
Christy, Francis T., Jr. *Territorial Use Rights in Marine Fisheries: Definitions and Conditions.* FAO Fisheries Technical Paper No. 227. Rome: FAO, 1982.
Christy, Francis T., Jr, and Scott, Anthony. *The Common Wealth in Ocean Fisheries: Some Problems of Growth and Economic Allocation.* Baltimore, Md.: Johns Hopkins University Press, 1965.
Clark, Bruce. *Native Liberty, Crown Sovereignty: The Existing Aboriginal Right of Self-Government in Canada.* Montreal and Kingston: McGill-Queen's University Press, 1990.
Cohen, Fay G. *Treaties on Trial: The Continuing Controversy over Northwest Indian Fishing Rights.* Seattle, Wash.: University of Washington Press, 1986.

Commoner, Barry. *The Closing Circle: Nature, Man and Technology.* New York: Alfred A. Knopf, 1971.

Cooley, Richard A. *Politics and Conservation: The Decline of the Alaska Salmon.* New York: Harper & Row, 1963.

Copes, Parzival. 'The Evolution of Marine Fisheries Policy in Canada.' *Journal of Business Administration* 11 nos. 1 and 2 (1979–80) 125–48.

Creese, Gillian. 'Class, Ethnicity, and Conflict: The Case of Chinese and Japanese Immigrants, 1880–1923.' In Rennie Warburton and David Coburn, eds., *Workers, Capital, and the State in British Columbia: Selected Papers,* Vancouver: University of British Columbia Press, 1988, 55–85.

Crosby, Thomas. *Up and Down the Pacific Coast by Canoe and Mission Ship.* Toronto: Ryerson Press, 1914.

Crutchfield, James A. *The Pacific Halibut Fishery.* The Public Regulation of Commercial Fisheries in Canada, Case Study No. 2. Ottawa: Economic Council of Canada, 1981.

Crutchfield, James A., ed. *The Fisheries: Problems in Resource Management.* Seattle, Wash.: University of Washington Press, 1965.

Crutchfield, J.A., and Pontecorvo, G. 'Economic and Social Implications of the Main Policy Alternatives for Controlling Fishing Effort.' *Journal of the Fisheries Research Board of Canada* 36 no. 7 (1969) 742–52.

— *The Pacific Salmon Fisheries: A Study of Irrational Conservation.* Baltimore, Md.: Johns Hopkins University Press, 1969.

Cummins, C., Friedlaender, M., and Williams, D. *Impact of the Salmonid Enhancement Program on Native People.* Vancouver: Environment Canada, Fisheries and Marine Service, Pacific Region, 1978.

Daly, George, and Brady, David W. 'Federal Regulation of Economic Activity: Failure and Reforms.' In James E. Anderson, ed., *Economic Regulatory Policy,* Carbondale and Edwardsville, Ill.: University of Illinois Press, 1977, 171–86.

Darling, John D. 'The Effects of Culture Contact on the Tsimshian System of Land Tenure during the Nineteenth Century.' MA thesis, University of British Columbia, 1955.

Deutsch, J.J., Jamieson, S.M., Matuszewski, T.I., Scott, A.D., and Will, R.M. 'Economics of Primary Production in British Columbia,' Vol. 3, 'The Fishing Industry of British Columbia.' Typescript, University of British Columbia Library, 1959.

Doern, G. Bruce, ed. *The Regulatory Process in Canada.* Toronto: Macmillan of Canada, 1978.

Dosman, Edgar J. *Indians: The Urban Dilemma.* Toronto: McClelland and Stewart, 1972.

Doucet, Fernand J., and Pearse, Peter H. *Fisheries Policy for the Pacific Coast:*

Issues and Advice. A Report to the Hon. Roméo LeBlanc, Minister of Fisheries and Oceans. Vancouver: Department of Fisheries and Oceans, 1980.

Draper, Dianne Louise. 'Resource Management, Socio-Economic Development, and the Pacific North Coast Native Cooperative: A Case Study.' PhD dissertation, University of Waterloo, 1977.

Drucker, Philip. *Cultures of the North Pacific Coast.* San Francisco: Chandler Publishing, 1965.

— *The Native Brotherhoods: Modern Intertribal Organizations on the Northwest Coast.* Smithsonian Institution, Bureau of American Enthnology, Bulletin 60. Washington, DC: US Government Printing Office, 1958.

— *The Northern and Central Nootkan Tribes.* Smithsonian Institution, Bureau of American Ethnology Contributions to Ethnology, Bulletin No. 144. Washington, DC: US Government Printing Office, 1951.

Durrenberger, E.P., and Palsson, G. 'Ownership at Sea: Fishing Territories and Access to Sea Fisheries.'*American Ethnologist* 14 no. 3 (1987) 508–19.

Dyck, Noel. 'The Politics of Special Status: Indian Associations and the Administration of Indian Affairs.' In J. Dahlie and T. Fernando, eds., *Ethnicity, Power and Politics in Canada,* Toronto: Methuen, 1981, 279–91.

Elias, Peter Douglas. *The Dakota of the Canadian Northwest: Lessons for Survival.* Winnipeg: University of Manitoba Press, 1988.

Elliot, G.H. 'Problems Confronting Fishing Industries Relative to Management Policies Adopted by Governments.' *Journal of the Fisheries Research Board of Canada* 30 no. 12, part 2 (1973) 2486–9.

Elliott, David W. 'Aboriginal Title.' In Morse, ed., *Aboriginal Peoples and the Law,* 48–121.

Ellis, David W. 'Perspectives on Policy in the British Columbia Salmon Fisheries.' MSc thesis, University of British Columbia, 1988.

Ellis, Derek V., ed. *Pacific Salmon: Management for People.* Western Geographical Series, Vol. 13. Victoria: University of Victoria, Department of Geography, 1977.

Elsey, Janet C. 'Government Intervention in the British Columbia Salmon and Herring Industries (1969–1982).' MA thesis, Simon Fraser University, 1984.

Feeny, David, Berkes, Fikret, McCay, Bonnie J., and Acheson, James M. 'The Tragedy of the Commons: Twenty-Two Years Later.' *Human Ecology* 18 no. 1 (1990) 1–19.

Fields, D.B., and Stanbury, W.T. *The Economic Impact of the Public Sector upon the Indians of British Columbia.* Vancouver: University of British Columbia Press, 1970.

Fisher, Robin. *Contact and Conflict: Indian-European Relations in British*

Columbia, 1774–1890. First published in 1977. 2nd. ed. Vancouver: University of British Columbia Press, 1992.

Fladmark, K.R., ed. 'Fragments of the Past: British Columbia Archaeology in the 1970s.' Special issue. *BC Studies* 48 (Winter 1980–81).

Ford, Clellan S. *Smoke from Their Fires: The Life of a Kwakiutl Chief*. First published in 1941. Hamden, Conn.: Archon Books, 1968.

Forester, Joseph E., and Forester, Anne D. *Fishing: British Columbia's Commercial Fishing History*. Sannichton, BC: Hancock House, 1975.

Fraser, G.A. *License Limitation in the British Columbia Salmon Fishery*. Technical Report Series No. PAC/T-77-13. Vancouver: Department of the Environment, Economics and Special Industry Services Directorate, Pacific Region, 1977.

— 'Limited Entry: Experience of the British Columbia Salmon Fishery.' *Journal of the Fisheries Research Board of Canada* 36 no. 7 (1979) 754–63.

Fraser, G.A., and Friedlaender, M.J. *Social Impacts and Economic Efficiency in Resource Development Planning: The Case of Salmonid Enhancement on Canada's Pacific Coast*. Fisheries and Marine Service, Technical Report No. 923. Vancouver: Department of Fisheries and Oceans, Planning and Evaluation Branch, Salmonid Enhancement Program, 1980.

Frideres, James S. *Native Peoples in Canada: Contemporary Conflicts*. 3rd ed. Toronto: Prentice-Hall Canada, 1988.

Friedlaender, M.J. *Economic Status of Native Indians in British Columbia Fisheries, 1964-1973*. Technical Report Series PAC/R-75-25. Vancouver: Fisheries Operations Branch, Pacific Region, 1975.

Garrod, S. 'The Production and Distribution of B.C. Salmon in the World Context.' In Marchak, Guppy, and McMullan, eds., *Uncommon Property*, 92–106.

Gertler, Franklin S., and Hutchins, Peter W. 'Introduction: The Marriage of History and Law in *R. v. Sioui*.' *Native Studies Review* 6 no. 2 (1990) 115–30.

Gibson, James R. *Otter Skins, Boston Ships, and China Goods: The Maritime Fur Trade of the Northwest Coast, 1785–1841*. Montreal and Kingston: McGill-Queen's University Press, 1992.

Gislason, G.S. *Participation Levels and Performance of the Fish Processing Company–Owned Fishing Fleet in British Columbia*. Background Report No. 4. Vancouver: British Columbia Coastal Fisheries Licensing Study, 1979.

— *Participation Levels and Performance of the Indian-Operated Fishing Fleet in British Columbia*. Background Report No. 5. Vancouver: British Columbia Coastal Fisheries Licensing Study, 1979.

Gitksan-Carrier Tribal Council. 'Submission to the Pearse Commission on
Pacific Fisheries Policy.' Kispiox, BC, 23 May 1981.
Gladstone, Percy H. 'Industrial Disputes in the Commercial
Fisheries of BC.' MA thesis, University of British Columbia, 1959.
—   'Native Indians and the Fishing Industry of British Columbia.'
Canadian Journal of Economics and Political Science 19 (February 1953)
20–34.
Globe and Mail.
Gordon, H. Scott.'The Economic Theory of a Common-Property Resource:
The Fishery.' *Journal of Political Economy* 62 (1954) 124–42.
Griffin, Harold. 'Native Indians Played Important Part in Early Labor
Struggles.' *Fisherman* 25 no. 40 (14 December 1962) 9, 16.
Groot, C., and Margolis, L., eds. *Pacific Salmon Life Histories.* Vancouver:
University of British Columbia Press, 1991.
Halpin, Marjorie M., and Seguin, Margaret. 'Tsimshian Peoples: Southern
Tsimshian, Coast Tsimshian, Nishga, and Gitksan.' In Suttles, ed.,
Northwest Coast, 267–84.
Hamori-Torok, Charles. 'Haisla.' In Suttles, ed., *Northwest Coast*, 306–11.
Hansen, Lise C. 'Treaty Fishing Rights and the Development of Fisheries
Legislation in Ontario: A Primer.' *Native Studies Review* 7 no. 1 (1991)
1–21.
Hardin, Garrett. 'The Tragedy of the Commons.' *Science* 162 (1968) 1243–8.
Hawthorn, Harry B., ed. *A Survey of the Contemporary Indians of Canada:
Economic, Political, Educational Needs and Policies.* 2 vols. Ottawa:
Department of Indian and Northern Affairs, Indian Affairs Branch,
1966 and 1967.
Hawthorn, Harry B., Belshaw, C.S., and Jamieson, S.M. *The Indians of British
Columbia: A Study of Contemporary Social Adjustment.* First published in
1958. 2nd ed. Toronto: University of Toronto Press and University of
British Columbia, 1960.
Hayward, Brian. 'The B.C. Salmon Fishery: A Consideration of the Effects of
Licensing.' *B.C. Studies* 50 (Summer 1981) 39–51.
—   'The Co-op Strategy.' *Journal of Canadian Studies* 19 no. 1 (1984) 48–64.
—   'The Development of Relations of Production in the British Columbia
Salmon Fishery.' MA thesis, University of British Columbia, 1981.
Healey, M.C. 'Facts, Values, Interests and Resource Management Gamble.'
Canadian Fishing Report 4 no. 11 (November 1982) 5.
Helm, June, ed. *Subarctic.* Vol. 6 of *Handbook of North American Indians.*
Washington, DC: Smithsonian Institution Press, 1981.
Hewes, Gordon W. 'Aboriginal Use of Fishery Resources in Northwestern

North America.' PhD dissertation, University of California, Berkeley,
1947.

— 'Indian Fisheries Productivity in Pre-contact Times in the Pacific Salmon
Area.' *Northwest Anthropological Research Notes* 7 no. 1 (1973) 133–55.

Hicks, Rev. J.P., ed. *From Potlatch to Pulpit: Being the Autobiography of the Rev.
William Henry Pierce, Native Missionary to the Native Tribes of the Northwest Coast of British Columbia*. Vancouver: Vancouver Bindery, 1933.

Hilborn, Ray. *Fleet Dynamics and Individual Variation: Why Some People Catch
More Fish than Others*. Report No. 15. Vancouver: University of British
Columbia, Institute of Animal Resource Ecology, 1984.

Hilborn, Ray, and Peterman, Randall M. 'Changing Management
Objectives.' In D.V. Ellis, ed., *Pacific Salmon*, 68–94.

Hill, A.V. *Tides of Change: A Story of Fishermen's Co-Operatives in British
Columbia*. Prince Rupert: Prince Rupert Fishermen's Co-Operative
Association, 1967.

Hoar, W.S. *The Chum and Pink Salmon Fisheries, 1917–1947*. Bulletin No. 90.
Ottawa: Fisheries Research Board of Canada, 1951.

Hudson, Douglas R. 'Fraser River Fisheries: Anthropology, the State and
First Nations.' *Native Studies Review* 6 no. 2 (1990) 31–41.

— 'Traplines and Timber: Social and Economic Change among the
Carrier Indians of Northern British Columbia.' PhD dissertation,
University of Alberta, 1983.

Hutchins, Peter W. 'Commentary, Supreme Court of Canada, *Ronald Edward
Sparrow v. Her Majesty the Queen, and The National Indian Brotherhood/
Assembly of First Nations, et al.*, Intervenors. Judgment Rendered: May 31,
1990.' Typescript, Hutchins, Soroka & Dionne, Montreal, June 1990.

International North Pacific Fisheries Commission. *Historical Catch Statistics
for Salmon of the North Pacific Ocean*. Bulletin No. 39. Vancouver:
Commission, 1979.

James, M.D. *Historic and Present Native Participation in the Pacific Coast
Commercial Fisheries*. Vancouver: Department of Fisheries and Oceans,
Planning and Economics Branch, 1984.

Jamieson, Stuart, and Gladstone, Percy H. 'Unionism in the Fishing
Industry of B.C.' *Canadian Journal of Economics and Political Science* 16
no. 1 (February 1950) 1–11 and no. 2 (May 1950) 143–71.

Jarvenpa, Robert. 'The Political Economy and Political Ethnicity of
American Indian Adaptations and Identities.' *Ethnic and Racial Studies*
8 no. 1 (1985) 29–48.

Johnston, Darlene. *The Taking of Indian Lands in Canada: Consent or Coercion?*.
Saskatoon: University of Saskatoon, Native Law Centre, 1989.

Kenyon, Susan M. *The Kyuquot Way: A Study of a West Coast (Nootkan) Community.* Canadian Ethnology Service, Paper No. 61. Ottawa: National Museums of Canada, 1980.

Kew, J.E. Michael. 'History of Coastal British Columbia since 1846.' In Suttles, ed., *Northwest Coast*, 159–79.

Klee, G.A., ed. *World Systems of Traditional Resource Management.* Winston, NY: Wiley, 1980.

Knafta, L., ed. *Law and Justice in a New Land: Essays in Western Canadian Legal History.* Toronto: Carswell, 1986.

Knight, Rolf. *Indians at Work: An Informal History of Native Indian Labour in British Columbia, 1858–1930.* Vancouver: New Star Books, 1978.

Kopas, Leslie. 'Political Action of the Indians of British Columbia.' MA thesis, University of British Columbia, 1972.

Kroeber, Alfred L. *Cultural and Natural Areas of Native North America.* First published in 1939. University of California Publications in American Archaeology and Ethnology No. 38. Berkeley, Calif.: University of California Press, 1956.

Lamb, W. Kaye, ed. *The Journals and Letters of Sir Alexander Mackenzie.* Cambridge: University Press, 1970.

Landale, Zoe. *Harvest of Salmon: Adventures in Fishing the B.C. Coast.* Sannichton, BC: Hancock House, 1977.

Lane, Barbara. 'Harvest of Herring Spawn and Commerce in Herring Spawn by the Heiltsuk (Bella Bella) Indians of Central British Columbia from Aboriginal Times to the Present.' Unpublished paper, April 1990, in possession of author.

Larkin, Peter A. *Analysis of Possible Causes of the Shortfall in Sockeye Spawners in the Fraser River. A Technical Appendix to 'Managing Salmon on the Fraser' by Peter H. Pearse.* Vancouver: Department of Fisheries and Oceans, November 1992.

— 'An Epitaph for the Concept of Maximum Sustained Yield.' *Transactions of the American Fisheries Society* 106 no. 1 (1977) 1–11.

— 'The Future of Fisheries Management: Managing the Fisherman.' *Fisheries* 13 no. 1 (1988) 3–9.

— 'The Invisible Hand: Commerce As a Factor in Fisheries Management.' In P.N. Nemetz, ed., *Resource Policy: International Perspectives,* Montreal: Institute for Research on Public Policy, 1980, 211–20.

— 'Maybe You Can't Get There From Here: A Foreshortened History of Research in Relation to Management of Pacific Salmon.' *Journal of the Fisheries Research Board of Canada* 36 (1979) 98–106.

— 'Natural Laws Governing the Management of Sport and Commercial

Fisheries.' In R.H. Shroud, ed., *Proceedings of the Seventh Annual Marine Recreational Symposium, Fort Lauderdale, Florida*, Washington, DC: Sport Fishing Institute, 1982, 33–9.

LaViolette, Forrest E. *The Struggle for Survival: Indian Cultures and the Protestant Ethic in British Columbia*. First published in 1961. Reprinted with additions. Toronto: University of Toronto Press, 1973.

Lyons, Cicely. *Salmon: Our Heritage, the Story of a Province and an Industry*. Vancouver: BC Packers, 1969.

Lytwyn, Victor P. 'Ojibwa and Ottawa Fisheries around Manitoulin Island: Historical and Geographical Perspectives on Aboriginal and Treaty Fishing Rights.' *Native Studies Review* 6 no. 1 (1990) 1–30.

MacDonald, George F., Coupland, Gary, and Archer, David. 'The Coast Tsimshian, ca 1750.' In R. Cole Harris, ed., Geoffrey J. Matthews, cart., *The Historical Atlas of Canada*, Vol. 1, Toronto: University of Toronto Press, 1987, Plate 13.

McDonald, James A. 'Images of the Nineteenth-Century Economy of the Tsimshian.' In Seguin, ed., *The Tsimshian*, 40–54.

McEvoy, Arthur F. *The Fisherman's Problem: Ecology and Law in the California Fisheries, 1850–1980*. Cambridge: Cambridge University Press, 1986.

—   'Law, Public Policy, and Industrialization in the California Fisheries, 1900–1925.' *Business History Review* 57 no. 2 (1983) 494–521.

McFarland, Dana. 'Indian Reserve Cut-offs in British Columbia, 1912–1924: An Examination of Federal-Provincial Negotiations and Consultation with Indians.' MA thesis, University of British Columbia, 1990.

McFeat, Tom, ed. *Indians of the North Pacific Coast*. Toronto: McClelland and Stewart, 1969.

McIlwraith, Thomas F. *The Bella Coola Indians*. Toronto: University of Toronto Press, 1948.

McKay, Will. *The Indian Fishermen's Emergency Assistance Program*. Research Document No. R-2. Vancouver: For the Commission on Pacific Fisheries Policy, 1981.

—   *The Native Commercial Fisheries and the Potential Impacts of Oil Spills on or En Route to Kitimat, Port Angeles and Cherry Point*. Regional Program Report 78–82. Vancouver: For the West Coast Oil Ports Inquiry, 1978.

McKay, Will, and Healey, Julie. *Analysis of Attrition from the Indian Owned Salmon Fleet, 1977 to 1979*. Vancouver: For the Native Brotherhood of British Columbia and the Department of Fisheries and Oceans, 1981.

McKay, Will, and Ouellette, Ken. *A Review of the British Columbia Indian Fishermen's Assistance Program, 1968/69–1977/78*. Vancouver: For the

Department of Indian and Northern Affairs, 1978.

McKervill, Hugh W. *The Salmon People: The Story of Canada's West Coast Salmon Fishing Industry.* Vancouver: Gray's Publishing, 1967.

McLeod, J.R. 'Strategies and Possibilities for Indian Leadership in Co-Management Initiatives in British Columbia.' In Pinkerton, ed., *Co-operative Management*, 262–72.

McMullan, John. 'The Organization of the Fisheries: An Introduction.' In Marchak, Guppy, and McMullan, eds., *Uncommon Property*, 35–45.

— 'State, Capital, and the B.C. Salmon-Fishing Industry.' In Marchak, Guppy, and McMullan, eds., *Uncommon Property*, 107–52.

Mann, K.H. *Ecology of Coastal Waters: A Systems Approach.* Studies in Ecology, Vol. 9. Berkeley and Los Angeles: University of California Press, 1982.

Marchak, Patricia. 'Uncommon Property.' In Marchak, Guppy, and McMullan, eds., *Uncommon Property*, 3–31.

— 'What Happens When Common Property Becomes Uncommon?' *B.C. Studies* 80 (Winter 1988–89) 3–23.

Marchak, Patricia, Guppy, Neil, and McMullan, John, eds. *Uncommon Property: The Fishing and Fish-Processing Industries in British Columbia.* Toronto: Methuen, 1987.

Marshall, Yvonne, and Moon, Heather. 'Fieldwork in Nootka Sound.' *The Midden* 21 no. 5 (1989) 6–9.

May, Edwin. 'The Nishga Land Claim, 1873–1973.' MA thesis, University of British Columbia, 1979.

Meggs, Geoff. *Salmon: The Decline of the British Columbia Fishery.* Vancouver: Douglas & McIntyre, 1991.

Miller, Perry C. 'A British Columbia Fishing Village.' PhD dissertation, University of British Columbia, 1978.

Mirschitzka, Susanne. 'Usage and Management of Marine Resources on the Northwest Coast.' *European Review of Native American Studies* 6 no. 1 (1992) 9–16.

Mitchell, Bruce. 'Hindsight Reviews: The B.C. Licence Programme.' In D.V. Ellis, ed., *Pacific Salmon*, 148–86.

Mitchell, Darcy. 'The Allied Indian Tribes of British Columbia: A Study in Pressure Group Behaviour.' MA thesis, University of British Columbia, 1977.

Morely, Alan. *The Roar of the Breakers: A Biography of Peter Kelly.* Toronto: Ryerson Press, 1967.

Morrell, M. 'The Struggle to Integrate Traditional Indian Systems and State Management in the Salmon Fisheries of the Skeena River, British

Columbia.' In Pinkerton, ed., *Co-operative Management*, 231–48.

Morse, Bradford W. 'Aboriginal Peoples and the Law.' In Morse, ed., *Aboriginal Peoples and the Law*, 1–15.

—   ed. *Aboriginal Peoples and the Law: Indian, Metis and Inuit Rights in Canada*. Carleton Library Series, No. 131. Ottawa: Carleton University Press, 1985.

Mumford, Lewis. *Technics and Civilization*. First published in 1934. New York: Harcourt, Brace, Jovanovich, 1963.

Muszynski, Alicja. 'Class Formation and Class Consciousness: The Making of Shoreworkers in the B.C. Fishing Industry.' *Studies in Political Economy* 20 (1986) 85–116.

—   'The Creation and Organization of Cheap Wage Labour in the British Columbia Fishing Industry.' PhD dissertation, University of British Columbia, 1986.

—   'Major Processors to 1940 and Early Labour Force: Historical Notes.' In Marchak, Guppy, and McMullan, eds., *Uncommon Property*, 46–65.

—   'The Organization of Women and Ethnic Minorities in a Resource Industry: A Case Study of the Unionization of Shoreworkers in the B.C. Fishing Industry, 1937–1982.' *Journal of Canadian Studies* 19 no. 1 (1984) 89–107.

—   'Shoreworkers and AFAWU Organization: Struggles between Fishers and Plant Workers within the Union.' In Marchak, Guppy, and McMullan, eds., *Uncommon Property*, 270–90.

Native Brotherhood of British Columbia. *License Study 1987: A Proposal for Restitution*. Prepared by Peter Scow. Vancouver: Brotherhood, 1987.

Native News.

Native Voice.

Needler, A.W.H. 'Evolution of Canadian Fisheries Management towards Economic Rationalization.' *Journal of the Fisheries Research Board of Canada* 36 no. 7 (1979) 716–24.

Neel, David. *Our Chiefs and Elders: Words and Photographs of Native Elders*. Vancouver, BC, and Seattle, Wash.: University of British Columbia Press and University of Washington Press, 1992.

Netboy, Anthony. *The Salmon: Their Fight for Survival*. Boston: Houghton Mifflin, 1973.

Newell, Dianne. 'Dispersal and Concentration: The Slowly Changing Spatial Pattern of the British Columbia Salmon Canning Industry.' *Journal of Historical Geography* 14 no. 1 (1988) 22–36.

—   'A Dynamic Tradition: Canada's Pacific Coast Commercial Salmon Fishery and Aboriginal Rights.' In Cant, Overton, and Pawson, eds., *Indigenous Land Rights*, 51–62.

—   'The Industrial Archaeology of the Organization of Work: A Half Century of Women and Racial Minorities in B.C. Fish-Packing Plants.' *Material History Review* 33 (Spring 1991) 25–36.

—   'The Politics of Food in World War II: Great Britain's Grip on Canada's Pacific Fishery.' *Journal of the Canadian Historical Association* (1988) 178–97.

—   'Published Government Documents as a Source for Interdisciplinary History: A Canadian Case Study.' *Government Publications Review, An International Journal of Issues and Information Resources* 5 (1981) 381–93.

—   'The Rationality of Mechanization in the Pacific Salmon-Canning Industry Before the Second World War.' *Business History Review* 62 no. 4 (1988) 626–55.

—   'Report on the North Pacific Cannery for the BC Heritage Conservation Branch.' Victoria, 1989.

—   ed. *The Development of the Pacific Salmon-Canning Industry: A Grown Man's Game*. Montreal and Kingston: McGill-Queen's University Press, 1989.

North, George, and Griffin, Harold. *A Ripple, a Wave: The Story of Union Organization in the B.C. Fishing Industry*. Vancouver: Fisherman Publishing Society, 1974.

O'Donnell, Jacqueline. 'The Native Brotherhood of British Columbia, 1931–1950: A New Phase in Native Political Organization.' MA thesis, University of British Columbia, 1985.

Parman, Donald L. 'Inconsistent Advocacy: The Erosion of Indian Fishing Rights in the Pacific Northwest.' *Pacific Historical Review* 53 (1983) 163–89.

Patterson, E. Palmer, III. 'Andrew Paull and Canadian Indian Resurgence.' PhD dissertation, University of Washington, Seattle, 1962.

—   'Andrew Paull and the Early History of British Columbia Indian Organizations.' In Ian A.L. Getty and Donald B. Smith, eds., *One Century Later: Western Canadian Reserve Indians since Treaty 7*, Vancouver: University of British Columbia Press, 1978, 43–54.

Pearse, Peter H. *Exhibits 1–200 of the Commission on Pacific Fisheries Policy*. Ottawa: Minister of Supply and Services Canada, 1981.

—   *Managing Salmon in the Fraser: Report to the Minister of Fisheries and Oceans on the Fraser River Salmon Investigation, with Scientific and Technical Advice from Peter A. Larkin*. Vancouver: Department of Fisheries and Oceans, November 1992.

—   *Proceedings of the Commission on Pacific Fisheries Policy*, vols. 1–69. Ottawa: Minister of Supply and Services Canada, 1981.

—   'Rationalization of Canada's West Coast Salmon Fishery: An Economic Evaluation.' In *Economic Aspects of Fish Production*, Paris: OECD, 1972, 171–202.

—   *Regulation of Fishing Effort*. FAO Fisheries Technical Paper No. 197. Rome: FAO, 1980.

—   *Turning the Tide: A New Policy for Canada's Pacific Fisheries*. Final Report of the Commission on Pacific Fisheries Policy (Pearse Commission), 1981. Ottawa: Minister of Supply and Services Canada, 1982.

Petty, Kenneth E. 'Accommodation of Indian Treaty Rights in an International Fishery: An International Problem Begging for an International Solution.' *Washington Law Review* 54 (1979) 403–58.

Phidd, Richard W., and Doern, G. Bruce. *The Politics and Management of Canadian Economic Policy*. Toronto: Macmillan, 1978.

Pinkerton, Evelyn. 'Competition among B.C. Fish-Processing Firms.' In Marchak, Guppy, and McMullan, eds., *Uncommon Property*, 66–91.

—   'The Fishing-Dependent Community.' In Marchak, Guppy, and McMullan, eds., *Uncommon Property*, 293–325.

—   'Indians in the Fishing Industry.' In Marchak, Guppy, and McMullan, eds., *Uncommon Property*, 249–69.

—   ed. *Co-operative Management of Local Fisheries: New Directions for Improved Management and Community Development*. Vancouver: University of British Columbia Press, 1989.

Prichard, A.L. 'The Skeena River Salmon Investigation.' *Canadian Geographical Journal* (August 1949) 60–7.

Prichard, John C. 'Economic Development and the Disintegration of Traditional Culture among the Haisla.' PhD dissertation, University of British Columbia, 1977.

Prince Rupert Daily News.

Pynn, Larry. 'The Golden Egg Rush: The Frantic Race for B.C. Herring Roe.' *Canadian Geographic* (October–November 1991) 79–84.

Ralston, H. Keith. 'The 1900 Strike of Fraser River Sockeye Salmon Fishermen.' MA thesis, University of British Columbia, 1965.

Ray, Arthur J. *The Canadian Fur Trade in the Industrial Age*. Toronto: University of Toronto Press, 1990.

—   'The Early Economic History of the Gitksan-Wet'suwet'en-Babine Tribal Territories, 1822–1915.' Report prepared for the Gitksan-Wet'suwet'en Tribal Council, Hazelton, BC, 1985.

—   'Fur Trade History and the Gitksan-Wet'suwet'en Comprehensive Claim: Men of Property and the Exercise of Title.' In Abel and Friesen, eds., *Aboriginal Resource Use*, 301–15.

Resnick, Philip. *The Masks of Proteus: Canadian Reflections on the State.*
    Montreal and Kingston: McGill-Queen's University Press, 1990.
Rettig, R.B. 'License Limitation in the United States and Canada: An
    Assessment.' *North American Journal of Fisheries Management* 4 no. 3
    (1984) 231–48.
Richardson, Miles, and Green, Bill. 'Fisheries Co-Management Initiative in
    Haida Gwaii.' In Pinkerton, ed., *Co-Operative Management*, 241–61.
Ricker, W.E., Bilton, H.T., and Aro, K.V. *Causes of the Decrease in Size of Pink
    Salmon (Orcorhynchus gorbuscha).* Fisheries and Marine Service Tech-
    nical Report No. 820. Nanaimo, BC: Pacific Biological Station, 1978.
Rohner, Ronald P. *The Ethnography of Franz Boas: Letters and Diaries of
    Franz Boas Written on the Northwest Coast from 1886–1931.* Chicago:
    University of Chicago Press, 1969.
—   *The People of Gilford: A Contemporary Kwakiutl Village.* Bulletin No. 225.
    Ottawa: National Museum of Man, 1967.
Rohner, Ronald P., and Rohner, Evelyn C. *The Kwakiutl Indians of British
    Columbia.* New York: Holt, Rinehart, and Winston, 1970.
Rounsefell, G.A., and Kelez, G.B. *The Salmon and Salmon Fisheries of Swiftsure
    Bank, Puget Sound, and the Fraser River.* Bulletin of the Bureau of Fish-
    eries, Vol. 49. Washington, DC: US Government Printing Office, 1938.
Sanders, Douglas E. 'Aboriginal Peoples and the Constitution.' *Alberta Law
    Review* 19 no. 3 (1981) 410–35.
—   'Case Law Digest.' In Abler and Weaver, comps., *A Canadian Indian
    Bibliography*, 306–61.
—   'The Nishga Case.' *B.C. Studies* 19 (Spring 1973) 3–20.
—   'Pre-Existing Rights: The Aboriginal Peoples of Canada.' In Gerald A.
    Beaudoin and Ed Ratushny, eds., *The Canadian Charter of Rights and
    Freedoms: A Commentary*, 2nd ed., Toronto: Carswell, 1989, 707–38.
—   'The Rights of the Aboriginal Peoples in Canada.' *Canadian Bar Review*
    61 (1983) 313–38.
Scott, Anthony D. 'The Fishery: The Objectives of Sole Ownership.' *Journal
    of Political Economy* 63 (1955) 116–24.
—   ed. *Economics of Fisheries Management: A Symposium.* H.R. MacMillan
    Lectures in Fisheries, Institute of Animal Resource Ecology, Univer-
    sity of British Columbia, Vancouver, 1970.
—   ed. *Progress in Natural Resource Economics: Essays in Resource Analysis
    by Members of the Programme in Natural Resource Economics at the
    University of British Columbia.* Oxford: Clarendon Press, 1985.
Scott, Anthony, and Neher, Philip A. 'The Evolution of Fisheries
    Management Policy.' In Anthony Scott and Philip A. Neher, eds.,

The Public Regulation of Commercial Fisheries in Canada, Prepared for the Economic Council of Canada, Ottawa: Canadian Government Publishing Centre, 1981, 9–20.

Seguin, Margaret, ed. *The Tsimshian: Images of the Past, Views for the Present.* Vancouver: University of British Columbia Press, 1984.

Shaffer, Marvin. *An Economic Study of the Structure of the British Columbia Salmon Industry.* Ottawa: Salmonid Enhancement Program, Department of Fisheries and Oceans, Canada, and Minister of the Environment, British Columbia, 1979.

Shankel, George. 'The Development of Indian Policy in British Columbia.' PhD dissertation, University of Washington, Seattle, 1945.

Shetlings, Janice Colette. 'Death of a Community? Rebirth of a Homeland?' MA thesis, McGill University, 1989.

Shoop, Greg B. 'The Participation of Ohiaht Indians in the Commercial Fisheries of the Bamfield–Barkley Sound Area of British Columbia.' MA thesis, University of Victoria, 1972.

Sinclair, Sol. *Licence Limitation – British Columbia: A Method of Economic Fisheries Management.* Ottawa: Department of Fisheries, 1960.

Sinclair, W.F. *The Importance of the Commercial Fishing Industry to Selected Remote Coastal Communities in British Columbia.* Vancouver: Department of Fisheries, 1971.

Skogan, Joan. *Skeena, a River Remembered.* Vancouver: BC Packers, 1983.

Slattery, Brian. 'The Hidden Constitution: Aboriginal Rights in Canada.' In Menno Boldt and J. Anthony Long, eds., *The Quest for Justice: Aboriginal Peoples and Aboriginal Rights,* Toronto: University of Toronto Press, 1985, 114–38.

—   'Understanding Aboriginal Rights.' *Canadian Bar Review* 66 (1987) 727–83.

Smith, Courtland L. 'Fisheries as Subsistence Resources: Growth and Decline of the Columbia River Salmon Fishery.' In Estelle Smith, ed., *Those Who Live from the Sea,* American Ethnological Society, Monograph No. 62, St Paul, Minn.: West Publishing, 1977, 215–34.

Sparrow, Leona M. 'Work Histories of a Coast Salish Couple.' MA thesis, University of British Columbia, 1976.

Spradley, James P., with Sewid, James. *Guests Never Leave Hungry: The Autobiography of James Sewid, a Kwakiutl Indian.* New Haven, Conn., and London: Yale University Press, 1969.

Sproat, Gilbert M. *The Nootka: Scenes and Studies of Savage Life.* First published in 1868. Victoria: Sono Nis Press, 1987.

Spry, Irene M. 'The Tragedy of the Loss of the Commons in Western

Canada.' In A.L. Getty and Antoine S. Lussier, eds., *As Long as the Sun Shines and the Water Flows: A Reader in Canadian Native History*, Vancouver: University of British Columbia Press, 1983, 203–28.

Stacey, Duncan A. *Sockeye and Tinplate: Technological Change in the Fraser River Canning Industry 1871–1912*. Heritage Record No. 15. Victoria: B.C. Provincial Museum, 1982.

Stearns, Mary Lee. *Haida Culture in Custody: The Masset Band*. Seattle, Wash.: University of Washington Press, 1981.

Steele, John H. *The Structure of Marine Ecosystems*. Cambridge, Mass.: Harvard University Press, 1974.

Steltzer, Ulli, and Kerr, Catherine. *Coast of Many Faces*. Vancouver: Douglas & McIntyre, 1982.

Sterritt, Neil J. 'Gitksan and Wet'suwet'en: Unflinching Resistance to an Implacable Invader.' In Boyce Richardson, ed., *Drum Beat: Anger and Renewal in Indian Country*, Toronto: Summerhill Press for Assembly of First Nations, 1989, 265–94.

Stevens, Homer, and Knight, Rolf. *Homer Stevens: A Life in Fishing*. Madeira Park, BC: Harbour Publishing, 1992.

Stewart, Hilary. *Indian Fishing: Early Methods on the Northwest Coast*. Vancouver, BC, and Seattle, Wash.: Douglas & McIntyre and University of Washington Press, 1977.

Storrow, Marvin, QC, and Bryant, Michael J. 'Litigating Aboriginal Rights Cases.' In Cassidy, ed., *Aboriginal Title*, 178–92.

Suttles, Wayne. 'Affinal Ties, Subsistence, and Prestige among the Coast Salish.' In Suttles, *Coast Salish Essays*, 15–25.

— 'Central Coast Salish.' In Suttles, ed., *Northwest Coast*, 454–75.

— *Coast Salish Essays*. Vancouver, BC, Seattle, Wash., and London: Talonbooks and University of Washington Press, 1987.

— 'Coping with Abundance: Subsistence on the Northwest Coast.' In Suttles, *Coast Salish Essays*, 45–63.

— 'Environment.' In Suttles, ed., *Northwest Coast*, 16–29.

— 'Introduction.' In Suttles, ed., *Northwest Coast*, 1–15.

— ed. *Northwest Coast*. Vol. 7 of *Handbook of North American Indians*. Washington, DC: Smithsonian Institution Press, 1990.

Tennant, Paul. *Aboriginal Peoples and Politics: The Indian Land Question in British Columbia, 1849–1989*. Vancouver: University of British Columbia Press, 1990.

Thompson, Laurence C., and Kinkade, M. Dale. 'Languages.' In Suttles, ed., *Northwest Coast*, 30–51.

Thompson, William F., and Freeman, Norman L. *History of the Pacific Halibut*

Fishery. International Fisheries Commission, Report No. 5. Vancouver: Wrigley Printing, 1930.

Tough, Frank. 'Fisheries Economics and the Tragedy of the Commons: The Case of Manitoba's Inland Fisheries.' Discussion Paper No. 3. York University, Department of Geography, Toronto, 1987.

Trebilcock, Michael J. 'The Consumer Interest and Regulatory Reform.' In Doern, ed., *The Regulatory Process in Canada*, 94–127.

Trosper, Ronald L. 'That Other Discipline: Economics and American Indian History.' In Colin G. Galloway, ed., *New Directions in American Indian History*, Norman, Okla., and London: University of Oklahoma Press, 1988, 199–222.

Union of British Columbia Indian Chiefs. *The Lands We Have Lost: A History of Cut-off Lands and Land Losses from Indian Reserves in British Columbia.* Prepared by Reuben Ware. Vancouver: Union of BC Indian Chiefs, Land Claims Research Centre, 1974.

Usher, Peter J. 'Aboriginal Property Systems in Land and Resources.' In Cant, Overton, and Pawson, eds., *Indigenous Land Rights*, 43–50.

— 'Estimating Historical Sturgeon Harvests on the Nelson River, Manitoba.' Prepared for Cross Lake Band of Indians, Cross Lake, Man., and Savino & Co., Winnipeg, Man., March 1992.

— 'Property as the Basis of Inuit Hunting Rights.' In Terry L. Anderson, ed., *Property Rights and Indian Economies: The Political Economy Forum*, Boston: Rowman & Littlefield, 1992, 45–66.

— 'Some Implications of the *Sparrow* Judgment for Resource Conservation and Management.'*Alternatives* 18 no. 2 (1991) 20–1.

Usher, Peter J., and Banks, N.D. *Property, the Basis of Inuit Hunting Rights – a New Approach*. Ottawa: Inuit Committee on National Issues, 1986.

Van West, John J. 'Ojibwa Fisheries, Commercial Fisheries Development and Fisheries Administration, 1873–1915: An Examination of Conflicting Interest and the Collapse of the Sturgeon Fisheries of the Lake of the Woods.' *Native Studies Review* 6 no. 1 (1990) 31–66.

Vancouver Province.

Vancouver Sun.

Victoria *Colonist*.

Victoria *Daily Times*.

Wadley, James B. 'The Common Lands Concept: A "Commons" Solution to a Common Environmental Problem.' *Natural Resources Journal* 14 (1974) 361–81.

Ward, Peter. *White Canada Forever: Popular Attitudes and Public Policy toward*

Orientals in British Columbia. Montreal and Kingston: McGill-Queen's
    University Press, 1978.
Warriner, G. Keith, and Guppy, L. Neil. 'From Urban Centre to Isolated
    Village: Regional Effects of Limited Entry in the British Columbia
    Fishery.' *Journal of Canadian Studies* 19 no. 1 (1984) 138–55.
Waugh, Geoffrey. *Fisheries Management: Theoretical Developments and
    Contemporary Applications*. Boulder, Col.: Westview Press, 1984.
Weaver, Sally M. *Making Canadian Indian Policy: The Hidden Agenda, 1968–
    1969*. Toronto: University of Toronto Press, 1981.
Webster, Peter S. *As Far as I Know: Reminiscences of an Ahousat Elder*.
    Campbell River, BC: Campbell River Museum and Archives, 1983.
Wilen, James E. 'Modelling Fishermen and Regulatory Behaviour in
    Schooling and Search Fisheries.' In Scott, ed., *Progress*, 153–70.
Wilson, W.A. *The Socio-Economic Background of Commercial Fishing in British
    Columbia*. Vancouver: Department of the Environment, Fisheries
    Service, Pacific Region, 1971.

INDEX

hurt by licence regulations, 107,
118–20, 123, 141–2, 155, 158, 160–
3, 205; importance of village
fisheries, 64, 88–9, 109, 118–20,
131–2, 138, 143–5, 147, 155, 163,
166–9, 181, 204–5; no comprehensive fishery framework
agreement, 177; as owners of
fishing technologies, 41, 107;
poverty, 137, 143; salmon
enhancement schemes, 153, 162;
trade patterns, 30, 207; travelling
to fish, 32–3, 43–4, 54, 76, 95, 109,
111, 144, 206, 214; village processing plants, 200–1
Indian women: berry harvesting,
65; boat pullers, 76; displaced in
salmon canneries by Japanese
women, 85, by white women,
133; employment opportunities,
4, 86, 135, 139, 155, 157, 164, 203,
209; fishing, 76, 138, 141, 144, 157,
172, 178; gardening, 53, 182;
identified as 'Kloochmen,' 53;
making and repairing fish nets,
109; preserving fish, 39, 182–3,
189; replacing Japanese women
and white males in the canneries,
Second World War, 109, 116;
spawn-on-kelp harvesting and
trading, 191–2; striking in the
salmon-canning industry, 82;
supplying clams and crab to fish
plants, 141, 203; trading fish
nets, 30; valued more than Indian
fishers, 76, 86, 109, 134; working
in fish plants, 4, 47, 53–4, 76–82,
85–7, 108–11, 116, 120–2, 128, 131,
133–5, 141, 156–7, 207, 211; working in salmon hatcheries, 164

Indians: definition, 24; government
control of, 15, 21–3; hunters, 23,
29, 40, 44, 48, 56–7, 59, 88, 90;
knowledge of environment, 28,
38, 98, 142, 206; military service,
108, 115; participation in the
industrial economy, 22, 25, 123,
131–2, 139, 215; population size
relative to non-Indian population,
21, 52, 64, 67, 132; social goals,
210; social status in fishing
industry, 115, 132; taxation of,
116; on welfare, 85, 123, 128, 142–
3, 157, 173, 212, 214
industrial fisheries: aboriginal
rights, 4–5, 88, 113, 118–20, 145,
172–3, 175–9, 192; aquaculture as
alternative, 171; changes, 66, 83,
103–5, 127, 206–7, 214; competition, 70, 75, 84–5, 92, 114, 122,
131, 139, 155, 163–5, 195, 211;
definition of, 24; earnings in, 55,
81, 83, 89, 109, 111, 115, 128–9,
141; and future of Indians, 129–
31, 138–9, 142, 160, 180–1, 187–8,
205, 207, 210; as restricting food
fishery, 62, 89, 91–3, 97, 120, 146,
215; strikes in, 71, 82, 84, 115, 128,
137, 154, 166, 168; tax incentives,
155, 159
industrial fishing licences. See
fishing licences; licence-limiation
International Pacific Fisheries'
Commission, 146
International Pacific Halibut
Commission, 185–7

Jack v. The Queen, 175, 210
Jamieson, S.M. *See* Hawthorn,
Belshaw, and Jamieson

ILLUSTRATION CREDITS

Vancouver Public Library: Friendly Cove, Nootka Sound 1798 (9573); federal fisheries officers removing Kwakiutl salmon trap (photo by Benjamin W. Leeson, 13904); gillnetting for salmon c. 1905 (8496); the tug *Tyee* towing a scow (photo by C.S. Downing, 4891).

British Columbia Archives and Records Service: dip-net fishing on the Fraser River (HP16188); salmon weir on the Cowichan River (HP57607); salmon trap at Hagwilget Canyon (photo signed 'Mogensen,' HP15426); smoke-houses at Hagwilget (HP15489); Haida family fish camp 1901 (Department of Mines photo, HP88751); Haida woman dressing halibut meat c. 1901 (Department of Mines photo, HP071714); Ed Whonnock's mother drying salmon (HP83561): village at Bella Coola (photo by Richard Maynard, HP10402); Canada fisheries patrol vessel *Cloyah* (photo by J. McGregor, HP75516); Songish chiefs sister (HP94498); Indians on their way to work c. 1900 (HP71059); Anglo-BC Packing Co. receiving salmon (photo by Bailey Bros, HP18985); students of St Michaels Indian Residential School, Alert Bay (HP83567); Mrs Dorothy Gordon and Mrs Ruben Mason (HP27028); Maurice Barns weighing clams (HP27037); canned salmon label c. 1900 (HP85293).

National Archives of Canada: interior, salmon cannery, Skeena River, c. 1890 (photo by Robert Reford, PA118162); automatic cleaning and canning line, Namu cannery, 1945 (PA114826).

Vancouver Sun: Haida commercial fishboats in Sedgewick Bay 1986 (photo by Mark Van Manen); drying salmon on the Fraser River 1987 (photo by Jon Murray); protest fleet on the Fraser River 1992 (photo by Ian Lindsay).

Vancouver Province: old sign found on the Fraser River near Hell's Gate 1982; federal fisheries officer and Indian dip-net fishers 1978 (photo by Wayne Leidenfrost); fishers picket BC legislature 1993 (photo by Stotesbury).

The maps were prepared by Daniel Cartography (Starshell Maps), Victoria, BC.